IMPLEMENTING CONSTITUTIONAL GOALS

PROPOSALS FOR PAPUA NEW GUINEA

Vergil Narokobi

IMPLEMENTING CONSTITUTIONAL GOALS

PROPOSALS FOR PAPUA NEW GUINEA

New Guinea Communications

Volume 18

GALDA VERLAG 2024

ISBN 978-3-96203-312-5 (Print)
ISBN 978-3-96203-313-2 (Ebook)

Bibliografische Information der Deutschen Nationalbibliothek
Die Deutsche Nationalbibliothek verzeichnet diese Publikation in der Deutschen Nationalbibliografie; detaillierte bibliografische Daten sind im Internet über http://dnb.ddb.de abrufbar.

Originally presented as the author's dissertation (doctoral thesis), Victoria University of Wellington, Wellington, New Zealand, 2016.

NEW GUINEA COMMUNICATIONS
A SERIES

The aim is to provide a conduit for the publication of studies on the Island of New Guinea, with its two established political divisions, but will also include other associated patterns of islands.

It will enable contributions from new knowledge workers—with their dissertations—and from established scholars. As there are numerous scholars who would like better coverage of the areas in which they have explored—as a tribute to the people they have worked with—as well as local scholars who understand the importance of their unique areas. It is felt that the approaches being trialed in the visual anthropology part of the series as area studies will bring a wider attention to the remarkable nature of the island.

The first volumes will be on modes of communication: oral history and folklore, and the emergence of a local literature. While the representation of all disciplines is welcome, comparative and whole island studies would be of great interest as well. For this, collaborative works or edited volumes may be needed.

It will allow for academic publications of a more preliminary kind—rather than exhaustive monographs, which are becoming more and more impossible to produce.

Where is the knowledge we have lost?

John Evans
SERIES DEVELOPER
BOOK2BUK2PLES LTD.

CONTENTS

PREFACE

This book is based on my PhD thesis I did at the Victoria University of Wellington under a New Zealand Pacific PhD scholarship. I am grateful for the opportunity I was given by the New Zealand government.

The book identifies an issue in Papua New Guinea's Constitution with regard to the non-implementation of its National Goals and Directive Principles (NGDP) and Basic Social Obligations (BSO). I have described them as Papua New Guinea's Constitutional aims. Situated in the Preamble to the Constitution, the NGDP and BSO provide a guide for the future development of Papua New Guinea.

Upon a careful study of ss 25 and 63 of the Constitution, which enjoins governmental bodies in Papua New Guinea to implement the NGDP and BSO, the central argument presented in this study is that they are indirectly justiciable.

Characterising the NGDP and BSO as indirectly justiciable would facilitate their implementation within the present constitutional framework by considering the functions of each of the limbs of government and the Ombudsman Commission as interconnected. Using indirect justiciability and the interconnectedness approach, the book outlines several proposals for the legislature, the executive, the judiciary and the Ombudsman Commission.

The book contends these proposals can facilitate the effective and efficient implementation of the NGDP and BSO. I have decided to follow very closely my PhD thesis in this book for the simple reason that the thesis was written to provide practical legal proposals to implement the National Goals and Directive Principles and Basic Social Obligations of Papua New

Guinea's Constitution, situated in her quite extensive Preamble. Changing the focus of the book will take away the emphasis on the ideas presented in the book. For this simple reason the book has taken a similar format to my PhD thesis.

In my research for my PhD I travelled to Papua New Guinea, and visited the Law Collection and the New Guinean Collection of the Michael Somare Library; the National Parliament Library; the Supreme Court Registry; the Ombudsman Commission office; and the National Archive. The help of the librarians and the Ombudsman Commission staff was invaluable, especially to make available historical documents and reports.

I dedicate this book to my wife Grace Narokobi. Her love, prayers and sacrifice has enabled me to walk the journey I have travelled.

The law stated in this book is at 1 January 2023.

GLOSSARY

Basic Social Obligations	BSO
Constitutional Planning Committee	CPC
Constitutional Planning Committee Final Report 1974	CPC Final Report
Government Paper, Proposals on Constitutional Principles and Explanatory Notes	PCPEN
National Executive Council	NEC
National Goals and Directive Principles	NGDP
Organic Law on the Duties and Responsibilities of Leadership	OLDRL
Organic Law on the Ombudsman Commission	OLOC
Supreme Court Reference	SCR

CHAPTER ONE
INTRODUCTION

I. National Goals and Directive Principles and Basic Social Obligations

How can Papua New Guinea's Constitutional objectives or National Goals and Directive Principles (NGDP) and Basic Social Obligations (BSO) be implemented following the constitutional duty to do so under ss 25 and 63 of the Constitution? This is the central question addressed in this book. The NGDP and BSO are in the preamble of the Constitution. Since independence in 1975 there has been no meaningful effort made by governmental bodies to implement them. There are legal and constitutional avenues available to the legislature, the executive, the courts, and the Ombudsman Commission that have not previously been explored, which can ensure the effective and efficient implementation of the NGDP and BSO in compliance with Papua New Guinea's Constitution.

II. Methodology

The common law method of legal analysis is used to arrive at the findings offered here. In the first instance, predominantly the Papua New Guinea Constitution and court decisions from the National Court and the Supreme Court are studied. Organic Laws and ordinary legislation will also feature in the analysis, as will decisions from the Papua New Guinea Leadership Tribunal. The text of the Constitution and various interpretations of it by the courts are discussed throughout the book.

Where comparative materials are considered useful, they are referred to. For comparative inspiration, common law countries with a similar government and legal system to Papua New Guinea are studied. These have primarily been Australia, Canada, India, New Zealand, South Africa and the United States. Legislation and cases from these countries are analysed for their relevance to the issue of implementing the NGDP and BSO. Of particular interest in the foreign material are discussions on the constitutional enforcement of social rights.

In addition to primary legal materials, secondary sources are relied on to support the analysis presented in this book.

III. Findings

Very little has been written on how the Constitution of Papua New Guinea can implement the NGDP and BSO through governmental bodies. In the few texts that exist, the typical argument is that the NGDP and BSO should be made directly justiciable to ensure implementation.

No legal scholarship on how the present constitutional arrangement can efficiently and effectively implement the NGDP and BSO has been offered. This book addresses this gap in the literature.

This book asserts that the best means of ensuring implementation of the NGDP and BSO is to confer on them an indirectly justiciable status. For the indirect justiciable nature of the NGDP and BSO to work well, the legislature, the executive, the judiciary and the Ombudsman Commission must see that their functions are interconnected or, as the book describes, use an "interconnectedness approach". Using these two approaches—indirect justiciability and the interconnectedness approach—the legislature, the executive, the courts, and the Ombudsman Commission can implement the NGDP and BSO.

IV. Outline

This book is presented in 11 chapters. A summary of each chapter and what each chapter discusses is provided below. Chapter 1 is this short introduction and Chapter 11 concludes the book with a summary of the main points.

Chapter 2 sets out the political and legal context in Papua New Guinea. It presents an overview of the NGDP and BSO and of the type of political and constitutional institutions established by the Constitution. First, an overview of the NGDP and BSO is provided. Second, the various sources of laws in Papua New Guinea are identified. Third, different constitutional institutions are introduced. Fourth, the civil and political rights and freedoms are set out. Chapter 2 presents the main constitutional framework against which implementation of the NGDP and BSO will take place.

Chapter 3 discusses the historical background of the NGDP and BSO. The chapter first covers the historical forces that shaped the NGDP and BSO. Second, the process of developing the NGDP and BSO is considered;

and third, the role intended for the NGDP and BSO in the Constitution is identified and presented.

Chapter 4 outlines the legal nature of the constitutional duty to implement the NGDP and BSO under ss 25 and 63 of the Constitution. The judicial view has been that the NGDP and BSO are entirely non-justiciable. Consequently, the NGDP and BSO are seen by the courts as merely aids of interpretation, only to be used in situations of ambiguity, and thereby obscuring the constitutional duty to implement them in all cases where relevant or appropriate. This book asserts that the correct legal character of the NGDP and BSO, on a proper interpretation of ss 25 and 63, is one of indirect justiciability, enabling the fulfilment of the constitutional duty to implement. Indirect justiciability (as opposed to non-justiciability) places greater emphasis on the role of each arm of government to implement the NGDP and BSO.

Chapter 5 looks at two matters. First, the implementation record of the legislature, the executive, the courts, and the Ombudsman Commission, concluding that they have not meaningfully implemented the NGDP and BSO. The second part of the chapter presents some legal reasons that have contributed to the non-implementation of the NGDP and BSO: the Supreme Court's mischaracterisation of the NGDP and BSO as entirely non-justiciable; the lack of active engagement of the preamble in constitutional and statutory interpretation; and finally, the lack of implementation of s 24 of the Constitution.

Chapter 6 presents an argument for an "interconnectedness approach" to mediate the non-justiciable/justiciable divide in relation to the NGDP and BSO. It starts by considering the doctrine of separation of powers generally; and it then focuses on the interconnectedness approach as a modification of the doctrine for Papua New Guinea.

Against the background provided by chapters 1 to 6, chapters 7, 8, 9 and 10 address the theme of this book by proposing how each limb of government and the Ombudsman Commission implement the NGDP and BSO: the legislature in chapter 7; the executive in chapter 8; the courts in chapter 9; and the Ombudsman Commission in chapter 10.

Chapter 7 discusses the way the legislature can implement the NGDP and BSO in its law-making function. There are two possible methods of implementation—direct and indirect—neither of which should be confused with the application of indirect justiciability (discussed in chapter 4). Failure to observe the direct means of implementation by enacting laws that do not implement the NGDP and BSO can result in legislation being declared unconstitutional (on the basis of indirect justiciability).

In the indirect means there is no legal sanction (on the basis of non-justiciability). However, there are a number of ways in which Parliament can perform its duty to implement, for example: by making specific reference to a particular NGDP and BSO in legislation; through the use of the Budgets and Estimates Committee to ensure adequate resources are allocated to realise the NGDP and BSO in the annual budget; and finally in parliamentary debates by referring to the NGDP and BSO when discussing various government decisions. In addition, Chapter 7 further explores the application of direct and indirect implementation vis-à-vis indirect justiciability.

Chapter 8 deals with the role of the executive in implementing the NGDP and BSO. This study proposes that the National Executive Council adopts a Cabinet Manual that makes specific reference to the NGDP and BSO. This will help the executive to anchor its decisions to the NGDP and BSO.

Chapter 9 presents proposals for the judiciary. First, engaging the NGDP and BSO through the use of a contextual means of statutory interpretation. Second, development of the underlying law on the basis of the NGDP and BSO. Third, judicial review of administrative action on the basis of compliance with the NGDP and BSO. Fourth, the use of weak-form judicial review. And finally, the enforcement of human rights in harmony with the NGDP and BSO. Adoption of these proposals would ensure the judiciary implements the NGDP and BSO.

Chapter 10 considers the Ombudsman Commission. The first proposal made relates to this entity's administrative complaints function. Ways in which this function can be used to implement the NGDP and BSO are offered. The second proposal deals with the Ombudsman Commission's Leadership Code function. Here, this study looks at how leaders may be found guilty of misconduct in office for breaching the NGDP and BSO. The third proposal is for the Ombudsman Commission to initiate judicial review of Bills (proposed laws can be reviewed before they are enacted) or legislation that fail to implement the NGDP and BSO.

V. Conclusion

This book provides legal and constitutional avenues the legislature, the executive, the courts, and the Ombudsman Commission can use to ensure the effective and efficient implementation of the NGDP and BSO in accordance with the dictates of the Constitution.

CHAPTER TWO

POLITICAL AND LEGAL CONTEXT

I. Introduction

Papua New Guinea's Constitution has been described as a political road map.[1] Not only did it establish the country's political and legal system at independence, but equally it prescribed the type of society the people aspired to. This was part of the constitution-maker's apparatus for a home-grown Constitution.[2] This view of the type of society Papua New Guinea should evolve into is set out in the National Goals and Directive Principles (NGDP) and Basic Social Obligations (BSO) of the Constitution. The preamble of the Constitution establishes the NGDP and BSO.[3] Sections 25 and 63 place a constitutional duty on all governmental bodies to implement the NGDP and BSO.

There are five National Goals. Goal 1 is titled Integral Human Development, which touches on development of the person. Goal 2 is called National Sovereignty and Self-Reliance, which articulates the attributes of the system of government that should obtain in Papua New Guinea. Goal 3 is headed National Sovereignty and Self-Reliance, advocating for political and economic independence. Goal 4 is named Natural Resources and Environment, requiring sustainable use of resources. And Goal 5 is branded Papua New Guinea Ways, promoting of Papua New Guinea's cultural identity.[4] Each National Goal has a number of directive principles appended to them. Following the NGDP, the BSO places a number of obligations on all

---

1 John Goldring *The Constitution of Papua New Guinea* (The Law Book Company, Sydney, 1978) at 1.

2 Constitutional Planning Committee *Final Report of the Constitutional Planning Committee, Part One* (Government Printer, Port Moresby, 1974) at 1–2 [CPC Report].

3 Constitution, sch 1.2.3.

4 The five National Goals are listed in Appendix One.

persons, including obligations to respect the rights of others, to contribute to the country's economy, and to observe the NGDP.[5]

This chapter provides a brief political and legal context and has eight parts. Part I is this introduction. Part II introduces the main problem this work addresses. Part III provides a basic outline of Papua New Guinea's political and legal system. Part IV sets out the laws of Papua New Guinea as defined by the Constitution. Part V provides an overview of human rights and freedoms. Part VI describes the main features of Papua New Guinea's constitutional institutions, and Part VII is the conclusion. Each part provides an overview of the current system established by the Constitution in which implementation of the NGDP and BSO will take place.

II. Introducing the Problem

Governmental bodies have a constitutional duty, both justiciable and non-justiciable, to implement the NGDP and BSO.[6] Governmental bodies with a duty to implement the NGDP and BSO include the traditional three arms of government—legislature, executive and judiciary—and constitutional institutions such as the Ombudsman Commission.[7] While the Ombudsman Commission has been given specific responsibility for enforcement,[8] there is no official state policy on implementation.[9] Chapter 5 analyses the selected governmental bodies' record of implementation.

Approaches to implementation from each arm of government have been piecemeal, with no central coordination, and absent a systematic approach by government. This situation exists despite the fact the Constitutional Planning Committee (CPC) made it very clear the NGDP and BSO were the basis upon which the Constitution was written, and that the newly independent state of Papua New Guinea must take adequate measures to implement these aspirations.[10]

---

5 The Basic Social Obligations are listed in Appendix Two.

6 Constitution, ss 25 and 63. The duty to implement the NGDP and BSO will be elaborated in chapter 4.

7 At sch 1.3 and s 99(2).

8 At ss 25(4) s 63(4). Chapter 10 proposes how the Ombudsman Commission can implement the NGDP and BSO.

9 Sam Sirox Kari "The Origin and Setting of the National Goals and Directive Principles in the Setting and Writing of the Constitution" (PhD Thesis, Queensland University of Technology, 2005).

10 CPC Report, above n 2, at 2/1 [6].

Forty (40) years after independence and there is widespread discontent about government's failure to effectively deliver goods and services.[11] The NGDP and BSO directly address many of these concerns. But how can these principles and obligations be meaningfully implemented within the present constitutional arrangements? This is the main question this book addresses.

III. Basic Outline of the Political and Legal System

Papua New Guinea is a third world liberal democracy.[12] The Constitution created the independent state of Papua New Guinea. It is established as a constitutional monarchy with Queen Elizabeth II as the Head of State, and is governed through a Westminster-style parliamentary democracy. The Constitution established Papua New Guinea's political and legal system, including its state institutions and their functions, together with a complex system for the control of the exercise of public power through independent constitutional offices such as the Ombudsman Commission.

Members of Parliament are elected to a single chamber house through universal adult suffrage.[13] Election is based on limited preferential voting system. There are 111 electorates representing 22 provinces, which include the National Capital District and the Autonomous Region of Bougainville. The Prime Minister is elected from the legislature after a general election, and cannot face a vote of no confidence challenge until she or he has held office for 18 months or in the 12 months before a general election.[14] Elections are held every five years. Since independence, no single party has been able to form a government except by a loose coalition of political parties. People join political parties more out of perceived ability to distribute resources than a commitment to a particular political ideology.

The executive arm of the government is headed by the Queen, represented by the Governor-General, but the effective head of the executive is the National Executive Council chaired by the Prime Minister. The Constitution confers on the Prime Minister the prerogative to appoint a deputy prime

---

[11] National Strategic Plan Taskforce *Papua New Guinea Vision 2050* (Government Printer, Port Moresby, 2009) at 1.

[12] Yash Ghai "Establishing a Liberal Political Order through a Constitution: The Papua New Guinea Experience" (1997) 28 Dev & Change 303.

[13] Constitution, s 101(1).

[14] Constitution, s 145.

minister, and a number of ministers with special responsibility for various departments.[15] Each department is managed by a departmental secretary under specific enabling legislation.

Of the 111 members of Parliament, 22 represent each province as provincial members and the rest are elected from the open electorates. Since 1976, the country has had a three-tier system of government: national, provincial and local. The 22 provincial members assume the post of Governor of the province in the provincial government.[16] The other members of the provincial government are the national open electorate members of Parliament and the presidents of the various local constituencies. At the third level of government, the presidents assume leadership roles in the local governments, which are made up of ward councillors. At present the country has 3,131 local level governments and 6,131 wards.[17]

The judiciary is independent from the legislature and executive branch of government.[18] The Supreme Court is the apex of the court system as the final court of appeal, and with an exclusive jurisdiction on constitutional issues.[19] The National Court is the court of first instance in many civil and serious criminal matters. There is no jury system in Papua New Guinea. National Court judges are also judges of the Supreme Court. There are no separate Supreme Court justices. District Court magistrates, whose jurisdiction is limited to matters arising within their geographical mandate, hear many civil and less serious criminal matters.[20]

At the village level, customary disputes are settled through village courts established under the Village Court Act 1989. A village court magistrate is appointed from the village. He or she has power to hear disputes that arise in the village setting. Custom is applied to these disputes.[21]

Customary land disputes are resolved through a separate process that encourages mediation in the first instance. This process is established under

---

15 Constitution, s 144.

16 Provided for under the Organic Law on the Provincial and Local Level Government 1995.

17 The National Research Institute *Papua New Guinea District and Provincial Profiles* (National Research Institute, Port Moresby, 2010) at 1.

18 Constitution, s 157.

19 Sections 18 and 155(2).

20 District Court Act, s 20.

21 Village Court Act 1989, s 57(1).

the Land Dispute Settlement Act ch 45. Land mediators are appointed within each area.[22] Failing mediation, the matter goes to the Land Court.[23] An appeal is possible to the Provincial Land Court.[24] In both courts magistrates deliberate on the disputes. As the process is informal, lawyers do not appear, unless for some special reason the court requires legal assistance, especially on evidentiary matters.[25] Aggrieved parties can seek judicial review (administrative review as opposed to an appeal) in the National Court of the Provincial Land Court's decision. A final appeal is available to the Supreme Court.

IV. Laws of Papua New Guinea

The Constitution expressly provides for the different types of laws that apply in Papua New Guinea:[26]

- Constitution;
- Organic Laws;
- Acts of Parliament;
- Emergency Regulations;
- Provincial laws;
- Subordinate legislative enactments; and
- Underlying law.

They are listed in order of importance.[27] Any law that is inconsistent with the Constitution can be struck down by the Supreme Court as invalid and of no effect.[28]

Further legislation in the form of Organic Laws provides details of the composition, functions and powers of the institutions initially established

---

22 Land Dispute Settlement Act ch 45, s 11.

23 Section 26.

24 Section 54.

25 Section 72.

26 Constitution, s 9.

27 *Ombudsman Commission of PNG v Denis Donohoe* [1985] PGSC 14, [1985] PNGLR 348, 3 December 1985 at 356 per Amet J.

28 Constitution ss 11 and 19.

under the Constitution. Organic Laws and the Constitution together make up the constitutional laws of Papua New Guinea.[29] Organic Laws must be contemplated in the Constitution.[30] For example, s 217(7) of the Constitution states that an Organic Law shall make further provision for the Ombudsman Commission's powers and procedures. The Organic Law on the Ombudsman Commission was subsequently enacted. In other words, Parliament can only enact an Organic Law if it is expressly envisaged an Organic Law on a particular subject ought to be enacted. The Organic Law must therefore be consistent with the Constitution.

Ordinary legislation is subject to the Constitution and Organic Laws.[31] Unlike the Constitution and the Organic Laws, the majority required for the passage of ordinary legislation and the timeframes involved are not as onerous.[32] Ordinary legislation composes the majority of laws in Papua New Guinea. Upon independence many of the Acts operating prior to independence were repealed and re-enacted.[33]

The other important law in Papua New Guinea is the underlying law. It is made up of customary law, the common law of England prior to 16 September 1975, and case law developed by the courts in Papua New Guinea.[34] Before custom is applied it must be proved to exist as a matter of fact.[35] After the court establishes the existence of a custom, the custom must then be considered for its consistency with written law (including human rights provisions in the Constitution) and with the NGDP and the BSO.[36]

The courts observe common law principle of case precedent or stare decisis in resolving disputes.[37] Previous Supreme Court decisions are persuasive in the same court, but are binding on all lower courts, including the National

---

29 Constitution, sch 2.1.

30 Section 12.

31 Section 10.

32 Section 64.

33 Repealing pre-independence legislation and re-enacting it was to satisfy the stated aim of the Constitution to be home-grown or autochthonous. These re-enacted laws are given chapter numbers. Legislation enacted after independence does not have a chapter number allocated, only the year of enactment.

34 Underlying Law Act 2000, s 4.

35 Customs Recognition Act, ch 19, s 5.

36 Underlying Law Act, s 4(2).

37 Constitution, sch 2.5.8.

Court and the District Court.[38] A growing body of case law, especially on constitutional law and administrative law, has emerged since independence.

V. Civil and Political Rights and Freedoms

The Constitution protects a number of civil and political rights and freedoms. Together with the NGDP and BSO they form the basis upon which the Constitution was framed.[39] The rights and freedoms are directly enforceable.

Rights and freedoms are subdivided into two categories: fundamental rights and freedoms, and qualified rights and freedoms. The distinction between the two is that the former cannot be qualified, while the latter can be qualified by Organic Laws and ordinary legislation under certain circumstances as set out in ss 38 and 39 of the Constitution.

Fundamental rights and freedoms are covered under ss 32 to 36 and include the right to life, the right to freedom from inhuman treatment, and the right to protection of the law (such as presumption of innocence). Qualified rights and freedoms start from s 42 and end with s 56.[40] A number of "manner and form" requirements must be satisfied before a qualified right can be restricted.[41] This includes considering whether the law imposing the

---

38 Constitution, sch 2.5.9.

39 CPC Report, above no 2, at 2/1 [20].

40 The rights and freedoms are:

- Section 42 Liberty of the person.
- Section 43 Freedom from forced labour.
- Section 44 Freedom from arbitrary search and entry.
- Section 45 Freedom of conscience, thought and religion.
- Section 46 Freedom of expression.
- Section 47 Freedom of assembly and association.
- Section 48 Freedom of employment.
- Section 49 Right to privacy.
- Section 50 Right to vote and stand for public office.
- Section 51 Right to freedom of information.
- Section 52 Right to freedom of movement.
- Section 53 Protection from unjust deprivation of property.
- Section 54 Special provision in relation to certain lands.
- Section 55 Equality of citizens.
- Section 56 Other rights and privileges of citizens.

41 *The State v NTN Pty Ltd and NBN Ltd* [1992] PGSC 11, [1992] PNGLR 1, 7 April 1987.

qualifications can be justified in a democratic society.[42] The NGDP and BSO are taken into account in making that determination.[43]

Civil and political rights have had a significant impact not only in the legal arena but also on the political discourse of Papua New Guinea. The courts have upheld the supremacy of the Constitution in many instances by declaring legislation unconstitutional vis-à-vis human rights and freedoms.[44]

VI. Constitutional Institutions

Part IX of the Constitution defines constitutional office holders and constitutional institutions. The latter are defined as any office or institution established or provided for by the Constitution, other than the office of Head of State or Minister or National Executive Council.[45] The constitutional offices include that of judges, the public prosecutor and members of the Ombudsman Commission. This list is not exhaustive and further legislation can create additional constitutional offices.[46]

Constitutional offices are a mechanism of accountability. They are an extension of the idea of the three arms of government and the principle of separation of powers. Specific roles are conferred on these offices, which are given a level of independence to perform their functions.

Constitutional offices are established under a number of Organic Laws. The common characteristic of these institutions is that they are not subject to direction and control from a political head.[47] Appointment of the heads of these bodies is through a largely independent process, by an apolitical appointment body.[48] Particular details of the offices are then spelt out in

---

42 Constitution, ss 38 and 39.

43 Sections 38 and 39.

44 *SCR No 2 of 1982 (No 1); Re the Organic Law on National Elections (Amendment) Act 1981* [1982] PGSC 19, [1982] PNGLR 214, 5 April 1982 is an early example where provisions of an election law were found invalid for offending s 50 of the Constitution. *Special Reference by Fly River Provincial Executive Council; Re Organic Law on Integrity of Political Parties and Candidates* [2010] PGSC 3, SC1057, 7 July 2010 is a relatively recent case, where the court invalidated a number of provisions of the Organic Law on the Integrity of Political Parties and Candidates for offending a number of provisions of the Constitution including s 50.

45 Constitution, s 221(i).

46 Section 221.

47 Section 223(2).

48 Section 223(1).

Organic Laws. Because Organic Laws are constitutional laws, security of office is provided against sudden political changes.[49] Specific majorities and timeframes are required for amending these laws.[50]

Additional protection granted to these offices are the specific requirements for the removal of constitutional office holders. *Re Public Prosecutor's Power to Request the Chief Justice to Appoint a Leadership Tribunal* set out in some detail the procedures for removal.[51] Only after following this process can a constitutional office holder be removed.

In *SCR No 1 of 1978; Re Ombudsman Commission Investigations of the Public Solicitor* the Court held constitutional offices are different from statutory bodies established by ordinary legislation as they were established by the people directly through the Constitution and not by Parliament.[52]

When looking at a specific body to promote implementation of the NGDP and BSO, one constitutional institution: the Ombudsman Commission will be focused on. The reason being that the Constitution provides ample scope to the Ombudsman Commission for implementation as compared to other constitutional institutions.[53]

VII. Conclusion

The NGDP and BSO set out what Papua New Guinea aspires to as a nation. This aspiration reflects the social and cultural realities of Papua New Guinea, and the NGDP and BSO chart a new way forward. The Constitution establishes certain mechanisms to enable their implementation within the current constitutional arrangements. This chapter has set out in brief the political and legal system in which the NGDP and BSO are to be fulfilled. Later parts of this book will highlight some of the reasons for the non-implementation of the NGDP and BSO, and detail proposals for their effective and efficient implementation.

---

[49] For example, the Organic Law on the Ombudsman Commission sets up the Ombudsman Commission.

[50] Constitution ss 14, 15, 16 and 17.

[51] *Re Public Prosecutor's Power to Request the Chief Justice to Appoint a Leadership Tribunal* [2008] PGSC 48, SC1011, 29 August 2008.

[52] *SCR No 1 of 1978; Re Ombudsman Commission Investigations of the Public Solicitor* [1978] PGSC 7, [1978] PNGLR 345, 6 October 1978.

[53] The roles and function of the Ombudsman Commission and recommendations for the Ombudsman Commission to implement the NGDP and BSO will be discussed in chapter 10.

CHAPTER THREE

ROLE OF THE NATIONAL GOALS AND DIRECTIVE PRINCIPLES AND BASIC SOCIAL OBLIGATIONS

I. Introduction

This chapter will consider the historical background of the NGDP and BSO and their primary role. Much of the discussion will come from the Final Report of the Constitutional Planning Committee (CPC Report).[1] The CPC Report made recommendations on the form of the Constitution to the House of Assembly.[2] Part I of the chapter is the introduction. Part II discusses the historical influences underpinning the NGDP and BSO. Part III considers the process in which the NGDP and BSO were adopted. Part IV presents the role of the NGDP and BSO in the Constitution. Part V concludes the chapter. This chapter highlights the importance of the NGDP and BSO as part of the groundwork for their legal implementation.[3]

---

1 There are two parts of the Final Report of the Constitutional Planning Committee. The NGDP and BSO feature prominently in the first part and will be the basis of the discussion here in chapter 3 and throughout the book. Volume 1 will be mainly referred to. Section 24 of the Constitution states the CPC Report is an aid to constitutional interpretation. Principles of constitutional interpretation are covered in chapter 4.

2 Constitutional Planning Committee *Final Report of the Constitutional Planning Committee, Part One* (Government Printer, Port Moresby, 1974) [CPC Report]. The main parts of the CPC Report that relate to the NGDP and BSO are chapters 2 and 5 respectively.

3 Chapter 4 makes the case for the constitutional duty to implement, by considering the legal nature of the implementation framework.

II. Overview of Historical Forces Shaping the NGDP and BSO

A. Introduction

There has been little critical study on the historical formation of the NGDP and BSO. Perhaps the only work was a sociological doctoral dissertation by Sam Sirox Kari, who focused on the NGDP.[4] His thesis was to rebut the claim that the NGDP was a home-grown initiative.[5] According to Kari, the NGDP was a social construct of Papua New Guinean elites and Australians to inculcate a national ideology to support Papua New Guinea's independence.[6] In considering Kari's conclusions, one must be mindful of the fact they are based on sociological theoretical assumptions.[7] The response to Kari would therefore be confined to supporting the legal claim, that is, that the NGDP and BSO are the underlying aims of the Constitution. The Constitution identifies certain aids to constitutional interpretation, and it is these sources this legal dissertation considers first to support its conclusions. One authoritative source is the CPC Report (Constitution, s 24). Kari usefully observes the NGDP was the result of social and political tensions in Papua New Guinea.[8] Bernard Narokobi, one of the contemporary legal advisers to the CPC, makes the same point.[9] The CPC in fact stated one of the reasons for a constitution is to address existing tensions.[10] A general description of these tensions up to the time of independence in Papua New Guinea follows. The description provides an overview of the historical forces which shaped the NGDP and BSO.[11]

---

4 Sam Sirox Kari "The Origin and Setting of the National Goals and Directive Principles in the Setting and Writing of the Constitution" (PhD Thesis, Queensland University of Technology, 2005).

5 At 2.

6 At 39.

7 At 19–28.

8 Kari, above n 5, at 37.

9 Bernard Narokobi "The Constitutional Planning Committee, Nationalism and Vision" in Anthony J Regan, Owen Jessep, and Eric L Kwa, *Twenty Years of the Papua New Guinea Constitution* (The Lawbook Company, Sydney, 2001) 25.

10 CPC Report, above n 2, at 2/1 [1].

11 Curiously, Kari does say the NGDP should be made into law as they are still useful for Papua New Guinea: see Kari, above n 5, at 309.

B. Historical Overview

In the period between the conclusion of the Second World War in 1945 and independence in 1975, Papua New Guinea had separate but concurrent existence as Papua, a colony of Australia and as New Guinea (a Trust Territory of the United Nations, also administered by Australia). From its uneasy colonial experience with the Germans in the North, the British in the South, and until the early part of the 20th century with the Australians, a strong sense of identity and dislike of the colonial rulers emerged.[12]

Unlike many Polynesian and Micronesian states in the Pacific, Papua New Guinea is culturally diverse with over 800 different languages. Despite its unique cultures, Christianity has, since its difficult introduction over 200 years ago by Western missionaries, produced a new element to the country's identity as a "Christian country".[13]

Importantly, too, for Papua New Guinea was the concept of rights and freedoms. Experiences of racial discord saw anti-discrimination legislation enacted in 1963.[14] The Human Rights Ordinance was passed in 1971. The new Constitution would build on these past colonial laws by entrenching basic human rights and freedoms. In addition, the CPC was of the view that in order for rights and freedoms to flourish, people had to observe corresponding duties to each other.[15] This found expression in the BSO. Chapter five of the CPC Report on human rights contained the recommendations on the BSO to demonstrate this commitment to balancing rights and freedoms with duties. All this marked a unique consciousness of nationalism, national identity, and a free and just society.

---

12 For example, in the House of Assembly debates on the CPC Report, Tony Ila, a Member of the House of Assembly spoke about colonial exploitation, see House of Assembly Debates, Third House, Fifteenth Meeting of the First Session, 23 September to 27 September, Volume III, no 35 [House of Assembly Debates] at 4445.

13 The Preamble to the Papua New Guinea Constitution, states "[we] pledge ourselves to guard and pass on to those who come after us our noble traditions and the Christian principles that are ours now". This statement does not affect the freedom of conscience, thought and religion protected by s 45 of the Constitution. See Gary D Bouma, Rod Ling and Douglas Pratt, *Religious Diversity in Southeast Asia and the Pacific, National Case Studies* (Springer Dordrecht Heidelberg, London and New York, 2010) at 86.

14 See Papua New Guinea Discriminatory Practices Act 1963.

15 CPC Report, above n 2, at 5/1/15 [93].

Against this backdrop the Constitution had to make important statements about sovereignty and promotion of the indigenous way of life. The Constitution would not be an abstract legal document removed from the social, cultural and economic realities of Papua New Guinea. Examples of this are Goal 3 on national sovereignty and Goal 5 on Papua New Guinea ways. The former stipulates leaders must make decisions in the best interest of the country without being compromised by foreign influence. The latter requires the use of Papua New Guinean indigenous traditions to inform social, economic and political advancement.

As pointed out above, the Constitution was developed at a time of tension. Some authors describe these pressures as resulting from "micronationalist" movements.[16] Bougainville and Papua wanted to secede from the proposed new state.[17] The island of New Britain had very strong anti-colonial sentiments, organised around the Mataungan Association.[18] Certain sections of the Highlands provinces did not think it was time for independence.[19] So how does a Constitution accommodate all these various interests?

The NGDP and BSO provided an ideal to demonstrate to the people that the Constitution, the symbol of the new state, was not going to be interpreted and applied by a few elite citizens or only benefit certain regions of the country. Rather, the Constitution should be directed towards the realisation of the aspirations of all citizens. This comes out clearly in National Goal 2 on equality and participation. Everyone, including women, were to participate in the new country in all areas of life. This idea of a constitution realising the aspirations of the people is connected to the notion of a home-grown constitution, and is symbolised by the NGDP and BSO.[20] The Constitution was, therefore, an attempt to resolve these tensions and chart a new path for an inclusive society in Papua New Guinea.

---

16 Ron May (ed) *Micronationalist Movements in Papua New Guinea* (Department of Political and Social Change, Research School of Pacific Studies, The Australian National University, Canberra, 1982).

17 Bernard Narokobi "The Constitutional Planning Committee, Nationalism and Vision", above n 10, at 27.

18 At 27.

19 At 26.

20 CPC Report, above n 2, at 15/1 [2].

There was a strong awareness of the development challenges facing Papua New Guinea in the pre-independence era. The main policy initiative to enable development was the Eight Point Plan, which had a marked influence on the NGDP.[21] This Plan was announced by Michael Somare, the territory's chief minister, soon after self-government in 1972.[22] The correlation between the Plan and the NGDP was one of the main reasons the government supported the CPC's recommendations.[23] The Plan's main focus was on the economy: self-reliance, small scale business activities, and greater participation by Papua New Guineans in the economy.[24] The CPC thought the Plan is best summed up by the ideas of equality, self-reliance, and rural development.[25] The NGDP and BSO expanded the focus on economic development to a holistic conception of the person in a community within a specific cultural and environmental context.

The Plan was incorporated into the NGDP in a number of ways, for example, Goal 3 required the economy to be self-reliant.[26] According to the CPC, the NGDP are generally consistent with the Plan but are "more specifically targeted at achieving a free and just society ...".[27] The CPC went on to define its concept of development more broadly than economic progress, stating "the only authentic development is integral human development".[28]

---

21 The Eight Point Plan (the CPC refers to them as the Eight Aims) is reproduced in the CPC Report at 2/1 [7]–2/2 [7]. For a short history of the origins of the Eight Point Plan see Peter Fitzpatrick "The Making and the Unmaking of the Eight Aims" in Peter King, Wendy Lee and Vincent Warakai (eds) *From Rhetoric to Reality? Papua New Guinea's Eight Point Plan and National Goals After a Decade, Papers from the Fifteenth Waigani Seminar* (University of Papua New Guinea Press, Port Moresby, 1985) 22.

22 Central Planning Office, *Papua New Guinea's improvement plan for 1973-1974* (Cabinet Committee on Planning, Port Moresby, 1974).

23 House of Assembly Debates, above n 12, at 4562.

24 Ron May *From Promise to Crisis: A Political Economy of Papua New Guinea – State and Society in Papua New Guinea* (ANU Press, Canberra, 2004). For an earlier more detailed discussion of the connection between the implementation of the eight aims and the NGDP: see Peter King, Wendy Lee and Vincent Warakai *From Rhetoric to Reality, Papua New Guinea's Eight Point Plan and National Goals After a Decade* (University of Papua New Guinea Press, Port Moresby, 1985).

25 CPC Report, above n 2, at 2/2 [8].

26 May, above n 27.

27 CPC Report, above n 2, at 2/1 [9].

28 At 2/3 [14].

This idea is expressed in Goal 1. The CPC saw integral human development as the appropriate form of development for the people.

The CPC advocated harmony between social and economic progress.[29] A further element moderating economic progress was the concern for the natural environment.

Goal 4 on natural resources and the environment advocates sustainable use of resources and protection of Papua New Guinea's sacred and scenic sites. What emerged from the NGDP and BSO was, therefore, an integrated view of economic development fully cognisant and respectful of the human person in his or her social, cultural and natural environment.

III. Process of Developing and Adopting the NGDP and BSO

What was the process employed to develop and adopt the NGDP and BSO? In short, it went hand-in-hand with the creation of the Constitution. The first strategy was to ask the people what they themselves wanted for their system of government. A committee (the CPC) was established in June 1972 by the legislature (House of Assembly) of the self-governing territory—already called Papua New Guinea—which reported to Canberra from time to time. A Chief Minister headed the territory's executive. This was part of Australia's plan to prepare the territory for independence.

Generally, the CPC was to propose "a constitution for full internal self-government in a united Papua New Guinea with a view to eventual independence".[30] The caveat being the proposal had to be home-grown.[31] The CPC was composed of Members of the House of Assembly representing various regions.[32] The CPC was to consider how different organs of government and their functions could be incorporated into the Constitution. The organs of government include the role of the legislature, the executive, the judiciary, and an ombudsman.[33] A Bill of Rights was also included in the terms of reference.[34]

---

29 At 2/3–2/5.

30 At 1/1 [1].

31 At 15/1 [2].

32 Bernard Narokobi "The Constitutional Planning Committee, Nationalism and Vision", above n 9, at 25.

33 CPC Report, above n 2, at iv.

34 At iv.

It is not difficult to see liberal democratic principles reflected in the mandate. This was in all likelihood a result of the strong influence of the colonial system of government inherited from Australia. The central tenets of liberal democracy—separation of powers, human rights and an independent judiciary—are insisted upon. Could this be a home-grown Constitution if its central features had already been pre-determined? As discussed previously, Kari picks up on this point in his critique of the NGDP as being rooted in colonial influence and the work of elite Papua New Guineans.[35] However, a careful assessment of the CPC Report and the process used to adopt the NGDP and BSO identifies three ways in which this concern can be rebutted. First, the CPC was not restricted to the institutional mechanisms proposed by the House of Assembly.[36] The mandate allowed the CPC to consider whatever else it thought was relevant. Second, the CPC undertook a process of wide consultation.[37] This allowed the people to provide the specifics of the institutions. The next Part expands on this point. Third, even if the NGDP and BSO were elitist constructs, the fact remains they were adopted by the representatives of the people.[38]

Kari was right in that there was no mandate for broad ideals to underlie the Constitution, or what those ideals should be.[39] But the fact that the NGDP and BSO arose after wide consultation revealed the CPC's commitment to its mandate (which was also to consider anything else deemed relevant). According to the CPC, the NGDP resulted from a long process of discussion (over 100 public meetings) and consideration of written public submissions.[40] It would have been interesting to see whether Kari would have maintained his position if he had interviewed former CPC members.[41] Goldring was,

---

35 Kari, above n 5.

36 CPC Report, above n 2, at 1/1 [1].

37 At 1/1 [4]–1/3 [12] and 2/2 [10].

38 See the House of Assembly Debates from 23 September 1974 to 27 September 1974 and the National Constituent Assembly Debates, vol 1(1) from 23 May 1975 to 26 August 1975 [Constituent Assembly Debates], especially debates from 23 May 1975 to 5 June 1975 at 66–87.

39 The CPC's terms of reference are reproduced in the CPC Report, above n 2, at iv.

40 CPC Report, above n 2, at 2/2 [10].

41 Kari states his attempts to interview Somare, John Momis, the former Deputy Chairman of the CPC and Bernard Narokobi, the legal advisers to the CPC were unsuccessful due to their participation in the 2002 national elections: see Kari, above n 5, at 19.

however, impressed with the CPC's deliberations, describing them as "unparalleled in comparative constitutional history".[42]

The CPC began the consultation process by releasing discussion papers on six different topics, including citizenship and relations between the central government and other levels of government.[43] The papers were distributed in the three major languages—English, Pidgin and Hiri Motu—to as many parts of the country as possible. They were distributed by print material in the newspapers, on the radio and direct distribution. After receiving the people's contributions on these six topics, the CPC made direct contact with community centres throughout the country. Teams from the CPC conducted meetings throughout the country on the six discussion points, the outcomes of which were recorded and analysed. Further, the CPC received over 2000 written submissions.[44] The consultation confirmed the people more or less accepted liberal democratic institutions. But the people also made it clear they wanted the new system of government to reflect their way of life. The NGDP and BSO best encapsulates how that way of life would be contained in the Constitution. The CPC produced three reports following the consultations. The final report (CPC Report) was presented to the Chief Minister, instead of the Australian administration.[45]

The Chief Minister submitted the CPC Report (which had been preceded by two interim reports) to the House of Assembly for debate in August 1974.[46] At the same time, the Somare government also tabled a response to the CPC Report, entitled Proposals on Constitutional Principles and Explanatory Notes (PCPEN).[47] The latter report's main objective was to clarify some areas it thought were unclear, or to present an alternative view to that of the CPC.[48] The United Party, an opposition party, presented a second response. All these

---

42 John Goldring *The Constitution of Papua New Guinea* (The Law Book Company, Sydney, 1978) at 15.

43 CPC Report, above n 2, at 1/1 [4].

44 CPC Report, above n 2, at 1/2.

45 CPC Report, above n 2, at i.

46 At 1/1 [2].

47 Government Paper "Proposals on Constitutional Principles and Explanatory Notes" (Port Moresby, August 1974).

48 For example, the critique of the CPC Report by Dr John Guise, a Member of the House of Assembly was quite strong, stating the CPC Report confuses matters of detail with that of principle: see House of Assembly Debates, 24 September 1974, at 4438.

documents were placed before the House of Assembly for debate. The NGDP were contained in chapter two of the CPC Report and the BSO in chapter five. After the debate, the House of Assembly resolved for chapters two and five to form the drafting instructions for inclusion in the Constitution, with two major modifications (discussed below). Four drafts of the Constitution were produced as a result, with the fourth draft being considered for adoption by the Constituent Assembly.

In May 1975, the House of Assembly was dissolved by its own motion and reconstituted itself as the Constituent Assembly. This was to demonstrate the Constituent Assembly owed its existence to its own authority and not to colonial laws.[49] The Constituent Assembly's two main purposes were to debate and adopt the Constitution, and act as a break from Papua New Guinea's colonial past.[50] Members of the Constituent Assembly were designated as "representatives" rather than "members", and were to debate freely without commitment to their political party affiliations. The Constituent Assembly considered the draft Constitution from 23 May 1975 to 26 August 1975. The Constitution was adopted on 15 August 1975, with the preamble containing the NGDP and BSO which, in substance, was the form recommended by the CPC. There were two main changes. First, instead of adopting an investment code to implement Goal 3 on economic self-reliance, the Constituent Assembly preferred to rely on ordinary investment legislation. Second, in place of establishing an implementing entity (similar to a law reform commission) to review laws and policies for consistency with the NGDP and BSO, ss 25 and 63 were adopted.[51]

IV. Role of the NGDP and BSO

A. Introduction

It is quite clear the NGDP and BSO, being described as "goals" and "obligations", underlie the Constitution's aims. While other roles may be attributed to the NGDP and BSO, for example, that they provide the terms of a social contract, those other roles are not the current focus. Essentially, this Part sets out to establish the importance of the NGDP and BSO such that their implementation becomes a critical matter for the Constitution to undertake.

---

49 CPC Report, above n 2, at 15/1.

50 House of Assembly Debates, 23 May 1975, at 5811.

51 Further discussion on these two changes will be taken up in chapter 4.

B. NGDP and BSO: Underlying Aims/Objectives of the Constitution

1. Introduction

The role of the NGDP and BSO in forming the Constitution's underlying aims or objectives is evident from a number of sources. These include the CPC Report, the enactment of the NGDP and BSO as part of the preamble of the Constitution, and a number of provisions of the Constitution and legislation. These sources will be considered together.

A preliminary note on the interaction of the NGDP and BSO is important. Much will be said here on the NGDP, but the NGDP and BSO go hand in hand. The CPC recommended the implementing provisions for the NGDP should extend to the BSO.[52] The importance of everyone in Papua New Guinea observing fundamental obligations, as demonstrated by the BSO, was an integral part of achieving the NGDP.[53] One of the BSO states everyone in Papua New Guinea has an obligation to fulfil the NGDP.[54] It is in this context the BSO are considered with the NGDP on the question of implementation. Provisions on implementation of the NGDP (s 25) and BSO (s 63), which are expressed in almost identical terms, support this interaction.[55] The point is the fundamental, concurrent role envisaged for the NGDP and BSO.

2. Aims/Objectives of the Constitution

According to the CPC, the NGDP and BSO express the needs and aspirations of the people in meaningful terms.[56] They outline what the people and the government hope to achieve. The CPC Report compares the NGDP and BSO principles as a philosophy of life: "it gives us a chance to define for ourselves the philosophy of life by which we want to live".[57] In their interim report the CPC describes them as social goals of the nation.[58] The CPC goes on to state it is crucial that the country has long term objectives.[59] The CPC used

52 CPC Report, above n 2, at 5/1/34 [21].

53 At 5/1/15 [92] and at 5/1/34 [21].

54 BSO at [h].

55 Additional analysis of ss 25 and 63 of the Constitution is taken up in chapter 4.

56 CPC Report, above n 2, at 2/1 [11].

57 At 2/1 [2].

58 Constitutional Planning Committee, *Second Interim Report of the Constitutional Planning Committee* (Port Moresby, 1973) at 2/1.

59 CPC Report, above n 2, at 2/1 [3].

the metaphor of a traveller who had to know where she or he was going before starting their journey.[60] Society was discerned as having a common purpose. Naturally the NGDP and BSO were enacted as part of the preamble of the Constitution because of their role in underlying Constitution's objectives. For example, the introduction to the NGDP in the Constitution states, "we ... set before ourselves these National Goals and Directive Principles that underlie our Constitution". The introduction to the BSO has "all persons in our country have the following basic obligations to themselves and their descendants, to each other, and to the Nation".

Many constitutions capture their underlying objectives in the preamble.[61] An example is the Solomon Islands. Justice Kapi in *Minister for Provincial Government v Guadalcanal Provincial Assembly* stated the preamble in the Solomon Island's Constitution defines the principles within which the Constitution is construed and implemented.[62] In a comparative study of roles of preambles in constitutions, they were classified as having five categories, one of which is establishing supreme goals of the country.[63] The preamble of the United States Constitution has one of the most influential phrases, which has been adopted in many constitutions: "We the people ...". Papua New Guinea has a similar phrase in its preamble. It has been held in the United States that the preamble "indicates the general purpose for which the people ordained and established the Constitution".[64] Preambles in essence capture the basic ideals underlying a constitution.[65] This seems to be true for Papua New Guinea, too.

Another clear statement from the CPC on the NGDP as defining the underlying aims of the Constitution is where the NGDP is described as

---

60 At 2/1 [4].

61 Liav Orgad "The Preamble in Constitutional Interpretation" (2010) 8 Int'l J Const L 714; Kent Roach "The Uses and Audiences of Preambles in Constitution" (2001) 47(1) McGill LJ 129.

62 *Minister for Provincial Government v Guadalcanal Provincial Assembly* [1997] SBCA 1, CA-CAC 003 of 1997, 11 July 1997. Chapter 4 will discuss further the role of the preamble in constitutional interpretation.

63 Orgad, above n 33, at 717.

64 *Jacobsen v Massachusetts* 197 US 11 (1905) at 13-14, per Harlan J; cited in Orgad, above n 33, at 719.

65 Roach refers to Plato's view to include preambles in laws to encourage compliance: see Roach, above n 33, at 132.

the "fundamental charter of our society".[66] The Constitution should be "an instrument which helps achieve these goals".[67] The CPC further suggests that the Constitution's legitimacy depends on the realisation of the NGDP.[68] The people expect the Constitution to be an instrument to transform society, through the ideals it espouses. These ideals were the NGDP and BSO, largely because they had shaped the CPC's recommendations.[69] Sections 25 and 63 of the Constitution crystallise this by creating a constitutional duty to implement the NGDP and BSO. The Supreme Court has held the NGDP and BSO are statements of political visions and developmental aspiration upon which Papua New Guinea was founded.[70]

The NGDP, and the BSO to a lesser extent, feature regularly throughout the CPC Report. In chapter two, the CPC proposed establishing an implementing entity to review existing laws adopted at independence for consistency with the NGDP and BSO.[71] Chapter three on the Leadership Code asserts Papua New Guinea's leadership would have a critical role in ensuring implementation of the NGDP.[72] In chapter four, citizens are said to have certain obligations. Chapter five on human rights deals with the BSO, and requires the same implementing mechanism proposed for the NGDP.[73] Chapter eight requires the judiciary to take into account society's goals in performing their functions.[74] In chapter nine on finance, the NGDP are referred to as the guiding principles for raising and expenditure of public funds.[75] Chapter 10, in proposing the establishment of a provincial government system, refers to the concept of decentralisation of power from the central government to the local districts – something that Goal 2 on equality and participation expresses.

---

66 CPC Report, above n 2, at 2/1 [2].

67 At 2/1 [2].

68 At 2/1 [2].

69 At 15/1 [2].

70 *Reference by the Ombudsman Commission of Papua New Guinea* [2010] PGSC 40, SC1088, 17 December 2010 at [23]. Chapter 6 presents a critique of this case.

71 CPC Report, above n 2, at 2/25 [3].

72 At 3/2 [13].

73 At 5/1/34 [22].

74 At 8/1 [6].

75 At 9/1 [4].

Interestingly, when Papua New Guinea became independent, the CPC's recommendation to adopt a system of provincial government was ignored. As a result, Bougainville renewed its pre-independence secessionist demands. In 1976, the very first amendment to the Constitution introduced the provincial government system to quell Bougainville's attempt to break away from Papua New Guinea. These are examples of CPC recommendations for substantive provisions of the Constitution to implement the NGDP and BSO.

While the BSO have not featured as prominently, being discussed mainly in the context of human rights and freedoms, the CPC considered they complement the NGDP. Key sections on human rights and freedoms in the Constitution expressly refer to the NGDP and BSO. For example, s 32 requires consideration of the NGDP and BSO when interpreting and applying human rights and freedoms provisions in the Constitution. Further, Parliament may justify qualifying rights and freedoms on the basis it is necessary to advance the NGDP and BSO.[76] The NGDP and BSO determine the scope of human rights and freedoms in the Constitution.

If the NGDP and BSO were to underpin the Constitution, public awareness would be all important. The success or failure of the nation could be then be assessed against the standards set by the NGDP and BSO.[77] The CPC wanted the NGDP to be the yardstick against which the government performance was measured.[78] This is given effect by the Ombudsman Commission's functions. The Ombudsman Commission can take into account the NGDP and BSO when determining the propriety of government officials' conduct.[79] The Ombudsman Commission provides a constitutional alternative to the political process to hold leaders accountable for non-implementation.

A final example to support the claim the NGDP and BSO underlie the Constitution's aims and objectives relates to the underlying law, which

---

[76] See Constitution, ss 38–39, which are discussed further in chapter 9.

[77] Bernard Narokobi "Walking the Footpath of the Constitutional Planning Committee's Five National Goals and Directive Principles" in Ian Maddocks and Edward P Wolfers *Living History and Evolving Democracy Living* (University of Papua New Guinea Press, Port Moresby, 2010) 25 at 30.

[78] CPC Report, above n 2, at 2/1 [6].

[79] The function of the Ombudsman Commission in the implementation of the NGDP and BSO is considered in chapter 10. Sections 25(4), 63(4) and 219(1) of the Constitution gives effect to this view of the CPC.

requires the development of a Papua New Guinean indigenous jurisprudence. British common law was to be replaced by new case law emanating from Papua New Guinea's unique social and cultural circumstances. In this process, the Constitution requires the application of the NGDP and BSO to develop new laws and principles.[80] Consequently, the shape of the new laws of Papua New Guinea would assume the character of the NGDP and BSO.

The NGDP and BSO were therefore an attempt to promote the people's aspirations in a manner consistent with a typical liberal democracy and a Westminster system. It meant the Westminster system of government, with a number of modifications due for Papua New Guinea's circumstances, was going to be used to achieve the people's aspirations.

V. Conclusion

The NGDP and BSO arose out of the consultation process with the people. They reflect Papua New Guinea's socially complex nature. And while they are a product of specific historical circumstances, they also attempt to influence the future. The NGDP and BSO set out the Constitution's underlying aims and objectives. It is, therefore, the duty of all governmental bodies to implement the NGDP and BSO.

---

80 Constitution, sch 2.2; Chapter 10 considers the Underlying Law Act 2000, which implements the requirement s 20 of the Constitution for Parliament under to enact a law to declare the underlying law.

CHAPTER FOUR

THE CONSTITUTIONAL DUTY TO IMPLEMENT

I. Introduction

This chapter examines the legal nature of the constitutional duty to implement the NGDP and BSO, which is created under ss 25 and 63 of the Constitution respectively.[1] It is a constitutional duty imposed on all governmental bodies in Papua New Guinea. And under the principle of the supremacy of the Constitution, it is a duty that warrants compliance.[2]

The legal nature of this constitutional duty is best defined as "indirect justiciability." Indirect justiciability works well with the idea that in order for governmental bodies to fulfil their legal obligations to implement the NGDP and BSO effectively, they must view themselves as part of an interconnected system where each arm of government influences the other in implementation.[3] There are four parts to this chapter: Part I is the introduction; Part II looks at principles of constitutional interpretation; Part III analyses the terms of ss 25 and 63; and Part IV is the conclusion. The objective of this chapter is to establish the clear constitutional duty governmental bodies have to implement the NGDP and BSO.

II. Principles of Constitutional Interpretation

A. Introduction

The present judicial view as expressed in *Medaing v Ramu Nico Management (MCC) Ltd (Medaing on appeal)* is that ss 25 and 63 of the

---

1 Other provisions of the Constitution as they relate to the NGDP and BSO such as ss 32, 38, 39 and 69 will be discussed in other parts of the book, including chapter 9.

2 See for example Constitution, s 11.

3 The idea of interconnectedness amongst the limbs of government and the Ombudsman Commission is fully presented in chapter 6.

Constitution are non-justiciable.[4] As a result governmental bodies do not take this duty seriously. The alternative view of ss 25 and 63 proposed by this book enables a better implementation of the NGDP and BSO. Explicating ss 25 and 63 is a process of constitutional interpretation. Literature on comparative constitutional law discusses different methods of constitutional interpretation.[5] The methods of interpretation are not universal, and are contested. The Papua New Guinea Constitution lays down specific principles of constitutional interpretation. Other principles are found in a number of Supreme Court decisions such as *Reference by Ombudsman Commission of Papua New Guinea (Ref by OCPNG).*[6] They are applied in the aggregate, but depending on the issue(s) before the court, certain emphasis is placed on a particular rule (or rules). The relevant provisions of the Constitution detailing these rules of constitutional interpretation and the cases which applied and developed some of these rules are highlighted below.

B. Constitutional Supremacy

Written constitutions place specific limitations on the exercise of public power. This is done through the courts being given the power to review the acts of the other branches of government. This is the concept of constitutional supremacy or primacy of the constitution. Jurisdictions in the common law tradition often refer to the celebrated American case of *Marbury v Madison*, where the United States Supreme Court asserted its power to declare invalid ordinary legislation inconsistent with the Constitution.[7] *Marbury* has been cited in cases in Papua New Guinea.[8] One of the main reasons the Constitution is considered supreme law in Papua New Guinea is the fact it embodies the will of the people as enacted through their elected representatives in the

---

[4] In *Medaing v Ramu Nico Management (MCC) Ltd* [2011] PGSC 40, SC1144, 22 December 2011 [*Medaing on appeal*], the Supreme Court held the NGDP was non-justiciable, and by implication the BSO also. This chapter argues this interpretation shows a misunderstanding of ss 25 and 63 of the Constitution.

[5] See Jeffrey Goldsworthy (ed) *Interpreting Constitutions, A Comparative Study* (Oxford University Press, Oxford, 2007).

[6] For example see the decision of Injia CJ for a summary of these principles in *Reference by the Ombudsman Commission of Papua New Guinea* [2010] PGSC 10, SC1058, 4 June 2010 [*Ref by OCPNG*].

[7] *Marbury v Madison* 5 US 137 (1803), 1 Cr 137.

[8] *SC Reference No 3 of 1999; Re Calling of the Parliament* [1999] PGSC 55, [1999] PNGLR 285, 25 June 1999.

Constituent Assembly.[9] The power of the people by their freely given consent is vested in the National Government, and its three arms.[10] The arms of government exercise their powers in accordance with the Constitution under s 99(1). Perhaps the clearest expression of the principle of constitutional supremacy in Papua New Guinea is s 11 of the Constitution.[11] Section 11 highlights the operation of this principle by declaring the Constitution and the Organic Laws to be the supreme law of Papua New Guinea:

> 11. Constitution, etc, as Supreme Law.
>
> (1) This Constitution and the Organic Laws are the supreme law of Papua New Guinea, and, subject to Section 10 (construction of written laws) *all acts (whether legislative, executive or judicial) that are inconsistent with them are, to the extent of the inconsistency, invalid and ineffective* (emphasis added).

Section 10 of the Constitution elaborates on the principle of the supremacy of the Constitution by stating all written laws are to be read subject to it. This means that if the NGDP and BSO are considered constitutional law, then they ought to play a significant role in assessing the performance of "all acts … legislative, executive or judicial …".[12] Schedule 1.2.10 of the Constitution recognises the NGDP and BSO as constitutional law because of the duty to implement, which ss 25 and 63 create.

The courts, especially the Supreme Court, have the role of determining the constitutional validity of the government's decisions. This is given concrete expression in a number of ways, one of which is the Supreme Court's special jurisdiction under s 19 of the Constitution. Under s 19, a law or proposed law can be invalidated for offending the Constitution. Even an Organic Law (considered part of constitutional law) can be challenged on the basis it contravenes the Constitution.[13] Section 19 allows certain authorities to file Supreme Court references for the Court to decide on the constitutionality

---

9 Constitution, Preamble.

10 Section 99(3).

11 Vergil Narokobi "The Papua New Guinea 'Two Prime Minister's Saga': Parliament Testing the Supremacy of the Constitution" (2013) 24(2) PLR 92 at 93.

12 Constitution, s 11(1).

13 See for example *Ref by OCPNG*, above n 6.

of Bills, legislation, and decisions of Parliament such as the election of a Governor-General.[14]

C. Paramount Consideration to the Dispensation of Justice

The courts must give paramount consideration to the dispensation of justice.[15] Goldring suggests this may include the courts having recourse to abstract principles outside of the law.[16] Early post-independence cases such as *PLAR No 1 of 1980* relied on this constitutional provision amongst a host of others to reject the literal rule of statutory interpretation, and to adopt the purposive approach of interpretation where "the letter of the law should not prevail over the spirit of the law".[17] After reviewing several cases on this provision of the Constitution, Brunton and Colquhoun-Kerr concluded the requirement for justice was justice according to law, and not based on concepts for example natural law.[18]

D. The Constitution as a Living Document

The Constitution is considered a living document, dynamic in character, and speaking from time to time under sch 1.4 of the Constitution. Brunton and Colquhoun-Kerr propose a possible interpretation of sch 1.4. Constitutional laws are to be interpreted in their current meaning and not according to what the text may have meant at the time of its enactment.[19] Society changes and circumstances in existence at the time the Constitution was written may no longer exist. It is important for the law to develop as society evolves. This provision provides the legal basis to support this process. Balkin suggests the idea of a "living constitution" is not a rule of constitutional interpretation but one of constitutional construction.[20] That is, the courts do not interpret the

---

14 See *Special Reference by Morobe Provincial Executive; re Election of Governor General* (2010) SC 1085, 10 December 2010.

15 Constitution, s 158(2).

16 John Goldring *The Constitution of Papua New Guinea* (The Law Book Company, Sydney, 1978) at 124.

17 *PLAR No 1 of 1980; Request by Principal Legal Adviser on a Point of Law arising in a case where a Person tried upon Indictment has been Acquitted* [1980] PGSC 15, [1980] PNGLR 326, 10 October 1980 at 336.

18 Brian Brunton and Duncan Colquhoun-Kerr *The Annotated Constitution of Papua New Guinea* (University of Papua New Guinea Press, Port Moresby, 1984) at 362.

19 At 499.

20 Jack M Balkin "Framework Originalism and the Living Constitution" (2009) 103 Northwest U L Rev 549 at 550.

constitution to establish its meaning; rather, the courts ascribe a meaning that may not be envisaged from the text alone. There may be some merit in Balkin's claim as changing social conditions may see the courts develop new case law rather than relying on new interpretations of the Constitution's text and past precedents. For example, for the NGDP and BSO, the ascendancy of social rights discourse may require exploring different constructions consistent with international practice.[21]

E. Constitution Read as a Whole

Each constitutional law is intended to be read as a whole. In cases where the word or expression used in the Constitution is clear and capable of being accorded its plain or ordinary meaning, the court should accord that meaning and apply it to the circumstances of the case before it.[22] This does not preclude the court's reliance on the NGDP and BSO, which, by virtue of express provisions of the Constitution, must be considered in all cases where it is considered relevant.

F. Fair and Liberal Interpretation

The Constitution is required to be read as a whole, and interpreted liberally:

> Sch. 1.5. Fair meaning to be given to language used.
>
> (1) Each Constitutional Law is intended to be read as a whole.
>
> (2) All provisions of, and all words, expressions and propositions in, a Constitutional Law shall be given their fair and liberal meaning.

Injia CJ stated the court must ensure the legislature's intention, spirit and purpose are achieved.[23] The general thrust of interpreting the Constitution is to achieve, as far as possible, what the framers of the Constitution intended. This can be achieved by adopting a purposive approach and maintaining an awareness of changing social circumstances. In terms of the NGDP and BSO,

---

21 For a general treatment of emerging trends in enforcement of social rights international and comparative law see Malcolm Langford (ed) *Social Rights Jurisprudence, Emerging Trends in International and Comparative Law* (Cambridge University Press, Cambridge, 2009).

22 See Constitution, sch 1.5(1); and *Re Organic Law on National Elections; Kuberi Epi v Tony Farapo* (1983) (unreported) SC247 at 4.

23 *Ref by OCPNG*, above n 6, at [30].

however, the Supreme Court has considered them as aids to interpretation.[24] With respect, the better view on this point is that judges may of course use the NGDP and BSO as interpretive aids, but there is also a constitutional duty to implement. As will be seen later in this chapter, this view is consistent with ss 25(3) and 63(3) of the Constitution.

G. Self-executing Nature of the Constitution

Section 11(2) of the Constitution states the Constitution's provisions are self-executing to the fullest extent their respective nature and subject matter permits.[25] Constitutional provisions must be implemented, unless there are express provisions of the Constitution stating otherwise. Because ss 25 and 63 impose a constitutional duty, their status as constitutional provisions means they must be complied with.

H. Constitutional Directive to be Judicially Enlightened by the NGDP and BSO

The methodology the Supreme Court should take with regard to the NGDP and BSO was decisively set out in two Supreme Court cases: *Independent Leadership Tribunal; Ex Parte Sasakila (Sasakila)*;[26] and *SCR No 3 of 1986; Ref By Simbu Provincial Executive (Simbu)*.[27] In *Sasakila*, the Court (Kearney J) stated statutory interpretation was essentially an intuitive and subjective exercise. The Court must, therefore, observe the rule of statutory interpretation, which included ss 25(3) and 63(3) of the Constitution. This means considering the NGDP and BSO to guide the process of arriving at a settled meaning.[28] Developing this idea, Barnett J in *Simbu* said that in order to understand the Constitution, it was necessary to look at the Constitution as a whole including the NGDP set out in its Preamble.

---

24 Per Injia CJ at [31].

25 Peter Bayne "Judicial Method and the Interpretation of Papua New Guinea's Constitution" (1980) 11 FL Rev 121 at 129.

26 *The State v Independent Leadership Tribunal; Ex Parte Sasakila* [1976] PNGLR 491, 5 November 1976 [*Sasakila*].

27 *SCR No 3 of 1986; Ref By Simbu Provincial Executive* [1987] PGSC 17, [1987] PNGLR 151, 10 April 1987 [*Simbu*].

28 A different view is advocated by Wilson J in *Premdas v The State* [1979] PGSC 20, [1979] PNGLR 329, 1 September 1979 [*Premdas*].

The relevant parts of those two cases, which establish the constitutional directive to consider the NGDP and BSO in constitutional interpretation, is considered in some length in chapters 5 and 9.[29]

I. Use of Certain Materials as Aids to Interpretation

The Constitutional Planning Committee Final Report (CPC Report)[30] and a number of documents involved in the preparation of the Constitution are considered aids to constitutional interpretation and application.[31] Section 24 of the Constitution provides for the use of record of debates on the CPC Report from the pre-independence House of Assembly, the Constituent Assembly debates on the draft Constitution, the CPC Report, and other documents tabled in connection with the debates. Section 24 was intended to support the interpretation scheme in the Constitution, which rejected a literal approach and instead opted for a broad purposive method.[32] In *Haiveta, Leader of the Opposition v Wingti, Prime Minister; and Attorney-General; and National Parliament (Haiveta)*, the Supreme Court held the spirit and aspirations of the Constitution were to be given prominence.[33]

The CPC Report is an important documentary source the courts were to use to realise the ideals of the Constitution. Apart from the documents stipulated in s 24, it was unlikely other foreign sources could be relied on.[34] The Constitution was a home-grown document, formulated in Papua New Guinea by Papua New Guineans.[35] For this reason the CPC Report is used heavily to guide the interpretation process. In an assessment of the cases up to 1986, the CPC Report was identified as the main document the courts used from the list of documents identified in s 24.[36] That trend has continued,[37]

---

29 Case law exemplifying this method of constitutional interpretation will be discussed in chapters 5 and 9.

30 Constitutional Planning Committee *Final Report of the Constitutional Planning Committee, Part One* (Government Printer, Port Moresby, 1974) [CPC Report].

31 Constitution, s 24; see also *Sasakila*, above n 26, at 506 per Kearney J.

32 AJ Regan and EP Wolfers "Aids to Interpretation of the Constitution – Some Preliminary Thoughts" (1986) 14 Melanesian LJ 153 at 156–157.

33 *Haiveta, Leader of the Opposition v Wingti, Prime Minister; and Attorney-General; and National Parliament* [1994] PGSC 6, [1994] PNGLR 197, 25 August 1994 [Haiveta]– see especially the decision of Kapi DCJ.

34 CPC Report, above n 30, at ch 1 [2].

35 Goldring, above 16, at 15.

36 Regan and Wolfers, above n 32, at 166.

37 An assessment of the implementation record of the court is provided in chapter 5.

perhaps because the CPC Report is more accessible than the other documents listed in s 24.[38]

The Constitutional Documents (Manner of Proof) Act 1976 was enacted to facilitate the implementation of s 24 of the Constitution. It sets out the manner in which the courts can accept for use the documents enumerated in s 24. For the CPC Report, all that is necessary is the production of a copy that bears the signature of all fourteen members of the CPC.

Other documents identified in s 24 include the House of Assembly and Constituent Assembly debates. This book does not propose to consider any of them in any detail as the Constituent Assembly accepted almost entirely the proposals on the content of the NGDP and BSO. This means the CPC Report adequately reflects the importance of the NGDP and BSO.[39]

J. Home-Grown Constitution

Another principle of constitutional interpretation that has emerged over time is the courts' assertion the Constitution is home-grown, which is reflected in a wariness to rely on constitutional cases and doctrines from other jurisdictions. This was established in the case of *Special Reference by Fly River Provincial Executive Council; Re Organic Law on Integrity of Political Parties and Candidates (Fly River)*.[40] In *Fly River*, the Court refused to accept the Basic Structure doctrine enunciated in *Keshavanada Bharati v State of Kerala*.[41] The Court instead relied on the provisions of the Constitution to decide the case.

In addition to the Constitution, sources of the underlying law in Papua New Guinea include English common law and equity cases decided prior

---

38 The CPC Report is electronically available free (and perhaps relatively more easily accessible) compared to the other documents provided for in s 24 of the Constitution. A copy of the CPC Report is available at the Pacific Islands Legal Institute website: <www.paclii.org>. See also Edward P Wolfers "Finding the Law in the Pacific Islands: Observations with Special Reference to Papua New Guinea and Solomon Islands" (1982) 10 Int'l J Legal Info 93 at 94.

39 Regan and Wolfers caution against exclusive use of the CPC Report in constitutional interpretation and application as the Constitution differs to some extent from the CPC Report: see Regan and Wolfers, above n 32, at 161. One noted difference in terms of the NGDP and BSO is on implementation: see CPC Report, above n 30, at 2/25.

40 *Special Reference by Fly River Provincial Executive Council; Re Organic Law on Integrity of Political Parties and Candidates* [2010] PGSC 3, SC1057, 7 July 2010 at [100]–[112].

41 *Kesavananda v State of Kerala* (1973) 4 SCC 255, (1973) AIR 146.

to 16 September 1975.[42] Cases after that period are only of persuasive value. This book takes the view the Constitution does not prevent the use of foreign cases because the Constitution itself states it is a living document. Cases from other countries help develop Papua New Guinea jurisprudence by providing instructive experience. For example, s 39 of the Constitution provides factors for the court to consider when deciding whether a law is reasonably justifiable in a democratic society, which requires resort to international human rights instruments. Many cases in Papua New Guinea dealing with constitutional issues draw useful analogies with cases from other countries, and consider how similar provisions in their jurisdiction have been interpreted.

III. Sections 25 and 63 of the Constitution

Sections 25 and 63 of the Constitution provide for the implementation of the NGDP and BSO. There is no case law that has attempted to reconcile the non-justiciable and justiciable aspects of the NGDP and BSO.[43] A careful reading of ss 25 and 63, taking into account the principles of constitutional interpretation, indicates the most legally sound view is that the NGDP and BSO have a measure of justiciability dependant on the nature of a public authority's function, moderated by whether the governmental body's action is reasonable or not.

The specific principles of constitutional interpretation discussed above, which have influenced the proposed interpretation of ss 25 and 63 of the Constitution as indirectly justiciable are:

- The CPC Report;
- The supremacy of the Constitution;
- Reading the Constitution as a whole;
- Fair and liberal interpretation of the Constitution;
- Self-executing nature of the Constitution; and
- Constitutional directive to be judicially enlightened by the NGDP and BSO.

---

[42] Underlying Law Act 2000, s 3; see also Constitution, sch 2.2.

[43] Although *Sasakila*, above n 26, and *Premdas*, above n 36, considered s 25(3) and s 63(3), they did not look at the issue of justiciability. Other cases after that such as *Medaing on appeal*, above n 4, focused on the issue of justiciability.

Other principles of constitutional interpretation of the Constitution play a role, too, and may be referred to in the discussion below.

A. The CPC on Implementation

It is important to point out what the Constitutional Planning Committee (CPC) recommended in terms of implementation of the NGDP and BSO. Arguably, what the CPC had in mind was a form of "indirect justiciability", which is best expressed in ss 25 and 63 of the Constitution. The term indirect justiciability was first used by Brunton and Colquoun-Kerr although they appear to have limited it to the development of the underlying law, and not to the general duty of all governmental bodies to implement the NGDP and BSO.[44] The concept underpinning the general duty is that where a NGDP and/or BSO can be applied, it should be implemented, unless Parliament expressly states otherwise, or it is unreasonable to do so. This idea is further developed below.

The CPC devoted some attention to dealing with Goal 3 on "National Sovereignty and Self Reliance" separately, proposing an Investment Code.[45] A code would provide a detailed guide to implement Goal 3 of the NGDP. The code was to be enacted as part of the Constitution. It is unclear whether this code was intended to be justiciable, but the fact the CPC wanted it to be given "the force which provisions of Constitution should have" suggests it may have been intended to be legally enforceable.[46] The Constituent Assembly did not take up this proposal. It opted to have the investment code established in ordinary legislation to give the government greater freedom to develop its investment policies.

As to the NGDP generally, the CPC wanted all government activities and institutions to be based on the NGDP and be directed towards achieving them.[47] The NGDP were to guide judicial interpretation.[48] The CPC elaborated that in the event of an ambiguity of a law, including constitutional law, the interpretation consistent with the NGDP should be preferred.[49] Importantly,

---

44 Brunton and Colquhoun-Kerr, above n 18 at 69.

45 CPC Report, above n 30, at 2/16 [134].

46 At 2/16 [130]–[152].

47 At 2/1 [6].

48 At 2/25.

49 At 2/25.

the NGDP would not be directly justiciable, but should not be "regarded by any court, other adjudicatory tribunal or institution as being of less weight than other directly justiciable provisions".[50] To strengthen the implementation process, the CPC proposed a body that would review laws and policies to ensure consistency with the NGDP and BSO (as well as with human rights and freedoms).[51] The CPC did not clarify whether the body would do that before or after enactment of laws and policies. But it is possible to infer that as much pre-independence legislation was simply adopted at independence, the work would relate to both existing and new laws and policies.

It should be noted ss 25(3) and s 63(3) of the Constitution use more direct language than that of the CPC on enforcement, but with the same intention of giving prominence to the NGDP and BSO in decision-making by governmental bodies.

In addition, the Constitution makes the NGDP and BSO directly enforceable when it comes to the Leadership Code in ss 25(4) and 63(4). The reasons for this difference was discussed in the previous chapter.

B. NGDP and BSO as Part of the Preamble of the Constitution

The Interpretation Act 1975 defines the preamble of the Constitution under s 3(1), which includes the NGDP and BSO. The NGDP and BSO appear before Part 1 of the Constitution, so they are considered part of the preamble, something the Constitution itself reinforces under Schedule 13(1):

> Sch. 1.3(1). Form of the Constitutional Laws.
>
> (1) The Preamble to this Constitution (being the provisions that end immediately before the heading to Part I.) forms part of this Constitution, but expresses general principles and therefore must be read *subject to any other provision of this Constitution*, though it may be used as an aid to interpretation in cases of doubt (emphasis added).

If the NGDP and BSO were to remain as a part of the preamble only, they would be used only as an aid to interpretation in cases of doubt. But this position is subject to any other provision of the Constitution, and the

---

[50] At 2/25.

[51] At 2/25.

Constitution is required to be read as a whole. As a result, ss 25 and 63 confer a different status on the NGDP and BSO when compared to the other parts of the preamble.[52]

C. The Concept of Justiciability

Where a question is non-justiciable, it cannot be heard by the court.[53] On the other hand, a justiciable dispute is one the court can determine.[54] A provision of the law that is justiciable entitles a person who is aggrieved to come to court when that provision is breached. There are a number of provisions in the Constitution that are stated to be non-justiciable.[55] Sections 25 and 63 are two provisions that refer to the interaction between justiciability and non-justiciability in the context of the NGDP and BSO.

As an example of justiciability, s 14 of the Constitution establishes constitutional procedures to amend the Constitution. If this procedure is not complied with when parliament amends the Constitution, the constitutionality of the amendment can be challenged for non-compliance with s 14 of the Constitution.[56] This is because this provision is justiciable.

At the opposite end of the spectrum, an example of non-justiciability would be s 153(2) of the Constitution which states the procedures of the National Executive Council (NEC) are non-justiciable. If the NEC made a decision that did not comply with its internal procedures, the decision could not be challenged in court because s 153(2) makes the NEC procedures non-

---

52 Brunton and Colquhoun-Kerr, above n 18, at 69.

53 Constitution, sch 1.7. "Non-justiciable" states:

> Where a Constitutional Law declares a question to be non-justiciable, the question may not be heard or determined by any court or tribunal, but nothing in this section limits the jurisdiction of the Ombudsman Commission or of any other tribunal established for the purposes of Division III.2 (leadership code).

54 Ernest A Jelf "Justiciable Disputes" *Transactions of the Grotius Society Vol 7, Problems of Peace and War, Papers Read before the Society in the Year 1921* (1921) 59–71 (published by Cambridge University Press on behalf of the British Institute of International and Comparative Law) <http.labs.jstor.org>.

55 Constitution, ss 25(1), 63(1), 86(4), 87(2), 99(4), 134, 153(2), 153(3), 170(4), 187C(7) and 187D(3).

56 The procedures set out in s 14 of the Constitution are mandatory. Non-compliance with them would render a constitutional amendment unconstitutional and invalid. See *In the Matter of Constitutional Validity of Constitutional Amendment (Provincial Governments and Local-Level Governments)* [1995] PGSC 12; [1995] PNGLR 481 (20 September 1995).

justiciable.[57] To reiterate, "justiciablity" determines whether an issue can be resolved in court. It creates a right or cause of action determinable in the court.

The concept of justiciability is often used in international law.[58] The American Constitution was probably the first to apply it in a domestic setting. The question of a dispute's justiciability has also entered into the debate on the enforcement of social rights. This is useful when speaking about the NGDP and BSO because constitutions often give social rights the status of non-justiciable state policy.[59] In considering whether a social right can be enforced there are a number of "normative preconditions" that must exist: the claim, the setting, and the consequences of the claim.[60] The claim relates to the identification of the particular right from a legal instrument.[61] The setting is the judicial or quasi-judicial body that has jurisdiction to hear the claim.[62] The consequences of the claim entails the remedy the body hearing the claim can order for a breach.[63] Seen in this way, a legal dispute would be articulated with specificity. These three features that ensure the justiciability of a social right can be applied to appreciate the extent to which the NGDP and BSO can be made justiciable following the provisions of ss 25 and 63. Avenues for enforcement of the NGDP and BSO as a legal claim, and the available remedies on the basis of ss 25 and 63 of the Constitution can be explored under such a framework.

Another important factor to be considered about the extent of the justiciability of the NGDP and BSO is the appropriateness of the court to

---

57 See Lenalia J's decision in the National Court in *Tiensten v Koim* [2011] PGNC 127; N4420, 14 October 2011. A National Executive Council (NEC) decision can however be challenged for illegality, in that the NEC made the decision contrary to law. See also *Marat v Hanjung Power Ltd* [2014] PGSC 33; SC1357, 4 July 2014.

58 Jelf, above n 5.

59 See generally Langford, above n 21.

60 Takele Soboka Bulto "The Indirect Approach to Promote Justiciability of Socio-Economic Rights of the African Charter on Human and Peoples' Rights" in RH Murray (ed) *Human Rights Litigation and the Domestication of International Human Rights Standards in Sub-Saharan Africa* (jointly published by The Kenyan Section of the International Commission of Jurists, Nairobi and The Swedish Section of the International Commission of Jurists, Stockholm, 2009) 136 at 136.

61 At 136.

62 At 136.

63 At 136.

determine the dispute.[64] The importance of the question or the parties involved does not determine justiciability. Justiciability is a status conferred by law. One of the main reasons behind not conferring such a status is that there may be other, more appropriate avenues to effectively resolve disputes around a particular law. The idea that certain constitutional provisions are non-justiciable was taken up in the CPC Report, and found its way into the Constitution. Conferring a non-justiciable status on a constitutional provision highlights the importance of the provision, but refers any dispute arising from such provision to another body (other than the courts) to resolve.

D. Duty to Implement Under ss 25 and 63

1. *Introduction*

Sections 25 and 63 make the duty to implement the NGDP and BSO a substantive provision of the Constitution:

> 25. Implementation of the National Goals and Directive Principles
>
> (1) *Except to the extent provided in Subsections (3) and (4)*, the National Goals and Directive Principles are non-justiciable [emphasis added].
>
> (2) Nevertheless, it is the duty of all governmental bodies to apply and give effect to them as far as lies within their respective powers.
>
> (3) Where any law, or any power conferred by any law (whether the power be of a legislative, judicial, executive or administrative or other kind), can reasonably be understood, applied, exercised or enforced, without failing to give effect to the intention of the Parliament or to this Constitution, in such a way as to *give effect to the National Goals and Directive Principles*, or at least not to derogate them, it is to be understood, applied or exercised, and *shall be enforced that way* (emphasis added).

64 For instance the analysis of justiciability in the context of judicial review on the exercise of the power of mercy has not been clear cut. See BV Harris "Judicial Review, Justiciability and the Prerogative of Mercy" (2003) 62 The Cambridge Law Journal 631 at 631.

(4) Subsection (1) does not apply to the jurisdiction of the Ombudsman Commission or any other body prescribed for the purposes of Division III. 2 (leadership code), which shall take the National Goals and Directive Principles fully into account in all cases as appropriate.

In similar terms to s 25, s 63 of the Constitution states:

63. Enforcement of the Basic Social Obligations

(1) *Except to the extent provided in Subsections (3) and (4),* the Basic Social Obligations are non-justiciable [emphasis added].

(2) Nevertheless, it is the duty of all governmental bodies to encourage compliance with them as far as lies within their respective powers.

(3) Where any law, or any power conferred by any law (whether the power be of a legislative, judicial, executive or administrative or other kind), can reasonably be understood, applied, exercised or enforced, without failing to give effect to the intention of the Parliament or to this Constitution, in such a way as to *give effect to the Basic Social Obligations*, or at least not to derogate them, it is to be understood, applied or exercised, and *shall be enforced that way* (emphasis added).

(4) Subsection (1) does not apply to the jurisdiction of the Ombudsman Commission or any other body prescribed for the purposes of Division III. 2 (leadership code), which shall take the Basic Social Obligations fully into account in all cases as appropriate.

Clearly, ss 25 and 63 create a constitutional duty. However, the more pressing issue following from the duty to implement the NGDP and BSO is the question of its legal nature.

There are two possible competing approaches for the proper legal characterisation of ss 25(3) and 63(3) of the Constitution. The first is the "interpretive aid" approach, and the second, presented here, is "indirect justiciability". It is contended that the interpretive aid approach, while a legally sound exercise of "judicial power" under ss 25(3) and 63(3), is not the only legal avenue available. The other more compelling role of ss 25(3) and 63(3) would be that they confer an indirectly justiciable duty on governmental bodies to implement the NGDP and BSO. These two approaches will be discussed now beginning with the current judicially sanctioned position, the interpretive aid approach.

2. *Current jurisprudence on the use of ss 25(3) and 63(3) of the Constitution: The interpretive aid approach*

In the courts' view, ss 25(3) and 63(3) are provisions outlining rules of statutory interpretation. For example, in *Reference by the Ombudsman Commission of Papua New Guinea (ROCPNG)*, the Supreme Court held the NGDP and BSO could only be used to interpret the law and could not determine the constitutionality of laws.[65] Interestingly, the reasoning in *ROCPNG* does not preclude indirect justiciability. *ROCPNG* was followed a year later by *Medaing on appeal* which ruled on a 2–1 majority that ss 25(3) and 63(3) are rules of statutory interpretation. An analysis of both cases is presented below as well as in chapters 5, 7 and 9.

(a) Judicial definition of NGDP and BSO as interpretive aids

Sections 25 and 63 of the Constitution have been judicially determined as providing for the NGDP and BSO to be used as an interpretive aid. This reading of ss 25 and 63 of the Constitution stems from Kearney J's decision in *Sasakila*:[66]

> The process of statutory interpretation is essentially intuitive and subjective, in the absence of rules consistently applied. The Act is a Constitutional Law and thus subject to the general principles of interpretation set out in Constitution ss 10, 25 (3), 63 (3) and Basic Social Obligation (a) …

An interpretive aid, is essentially a tool for the courts to use to understand the meaning of a law or perhaps to confer a meaning on the law when two or more options are available. An example of how the NGDP and BSO are used as interpretive aids can be found in *Haiveta*. In

---

65 *Reference by the Ombudsman Commission of Papua New Guinea* [2010] PGSC 40, SC1088, 17 December 2010 [*ROCPNG*].

66 *Sasakila*, above n 26, at 507.

Haiveta, s 142(5) of the Constitution was the subject of the appeal. There were two different meanings of s 142(5) argued for by the appellant and the respondents respectively. Kapi DCJ preferred the meaning which accorded with the NGDP and BSO. In this instance the NGDP and BSO were used as interpretive aids.

Of itself, the interpretive aid approach is sound. But Supreme Court decisions such as *Medaing on appeal* have held the interpretive aid approach is the only legally and constitutionally acceptable means of using s 25(3) (and by implication s 63(3)) of the Constitution. This is where the difficulty arises especially with the implementation of the NGDP and BSO. This issue will be discussed further in the next chapter on impediments to implementation.

3. *The new approach: Indirect justiciability and its justification*

(a) Background

As it is clear there are exceptions to non-justiciability, the idea of indirect justiciability may best express how far the NGDP and BSO can be judicially enforced through a statement of claim to a court.

Constitutions from countries that have entrenched directive principles have not used the type of provision Papua New Guinea has adopted. For example, in the Constitution of Ireland (perhaps the first country to have directive principles in its Constitution) state policy is non-justiciable.[67] India takes a similar approach, having been inspired by the Irish Constitution, and its state policy and directive principles are designated as non-justiciable.[68] However, courts in India have circumvented non-justiciability by interpreting justiciable rights in a way that results in the implementation of directive principles.[69] In Uganda, the directive principles are non-justiciable, but the President must provide an annual report to Parliament on the extent of implementation.[70]

---

[67] Constitution of Ireland, art 45.

[68] Constitution of India, art 37.

[69] *Bandhua Mukti Morcha v India* [1981] 2 SCR 516. Justice Bhagwati stated the right to life "derives its life breath from the Directive Principles" (at 103).

[70] Constitution of Uganda, art 1(1).

Directive principles are often treated as social rights.[71] In South Africa, the Constitution has no directive principles but makes social rights justiciable along with civil and political rights and freedoms.[72] Therefore for Papua New Guinea the starting point for interpreting ss 25 and 63 must be the text of the Constitution, and its own developed principles of constitutional interpretation.

In other countries directive principles are treated as non-justiciable, but what may be instructive are the mechanisms other countries use to address the question of how the law mediates the idea of separation of powers when it comes to implementing directive principles and/or social rights. An example from South Africa that helpfully illustrates the point is discussed below and also in chapter 9.

The idea of indirect justiciability appears in the CPC Report. The CPC Report must be considered in interpreting the Constitution.[73] The relevant part of the CPC Report states:[74]

> (2) Except to the extent provided for in this recommendation, the National Goals and Directive Principles shall not be directly justiciable. However, these goals and principles should not be regarded by any court, other adjudicatory tribunal or institution of government as being of less weight than other directly justiciable provisions.

Support for the indirect justiciability of the NGDP and BSO is found in the pre-independence Papua New Guinea self-government comment on the CPC Report, although they did not use the term "indirect justiciability":[75]

> The CPC recommendation on the application of the National Goals seem to be aimed at ensuring that government bases policies and actions upon them as far as is practicable and that court decisions should be made following the spirit of the goals

[71] Patrick Macklem and Craig Scott "Constitutional Ropes of Sand or Justiciable Guarantees? Social Rights in a New South African Constitution" (1992) 141 U Pa L Rev 1 at 116.

[72] See, for example, s 26, the right to housing, under the South African Constitution.

[73] Constitution, s 24.

[74] CPC Report, above n 30, at 2/25 [3].

[75] Government Paper "Proposals on Constitutional Principles and Explanatory Notes" (Port Moresby, August 1974) at 4.

> as far as this is consistent with the law they must apply. Courts are not however to apply the goals as law but must administer the law as it stands ... the government agrees with this approach.

The government believed their proposal for s 25 best expressed the CPC's intention while avoiding confusion and ambiguity.[76] Because similar wording to s 25 is used for s 63, the same can be said for the BSO. The CPC did not say the NGDP and BSO were non-justiciable; but that they were not to be directly justiciable. The interpretation of the CPC position noted above is therefore reinforced.

As noted earlier, Brunton and Colquhoun-Kerr picked up the idea of indirect justiciability, but only in the context of the development of the underlying law.[77] They did not elaborate on whether the idea of indirect justiciability could be applied to other sources of law. Brunton's and Colquhoun-Kerr's view, as far as can be ascertained, is that where the source (for example customary law and common law) of an underlying law is inconsistent with the NGDP, it would not be adopted; but it would be indirectly justiciable.

There is no provision in the Constitution expressly requiring consistency with the NGDP and BSO, but courts should nevertheless consider them in the development of the underlying law.[78] Taylor briefly alluded to this idea in her article on the justiciability of the NGDP and BSO, but she did not use the term indirect justiciability.[79] In Taylor's view, the consistency of executive and administrative decisions with the NGDP and BSO must also be considered (and not just the underlying law).[80] Such a position entitles an aggrieved person to come to court for non-compliance with the NGDP and/or BSO, but in an indirect manner.

---

[76] At 3.

[77] Brunton and Colquhoun-Kerr, above n 18, at 69. The Underlying Law Act 2000 was passed subsequently, and supersedes sch 2.3.3 of the Constitution, which Brunton and Colquhoun-Kerr rely on; see Jennifer Corrin Care and Jean G Zorn "Legislating Pluralism, Statutory Developments in Melanesian Customary Law" (2001) 33 J Legal Pluralism 49. The Underlying Law Act will be discussed in chapter 9.

[78] Constitution, sch 2.3.

[79] Meg Taylor "The Constitution and the Environment" in Anthony J Regan, Owen Jessep and Eric L Kwa (eds) *Twenty Years of the Papua New Guinea Constitution* (Lawbook Co, Sydney, 2001) 333.

[80] At 340.

(b) Definition of indirect justiciability

Reading s 25 of the Constitution as a whole, and likewise for s 63, ss 25(2) and 63(2) requires governmental bodies to implement the NGDP and BSO "as far as lies within their respective powers". Consequently, ss 25(3) and 63(3), which are an exception to non-justiciability (provided for in ss 25(1) and 63(1)) require the exercise of "legislative power", "executive power", "judicial power", and "administrative power" to be exercised in a way that enforces the NGDP and BSO; or at least in a way that does not derogate from them. The legal justification for this interpretation (for indirect justiciability) is discussed below.

The indirect justiciability of the NGDP and BSO, as set out in ss 25 and 63 of the Constitution, differs from justiciability as understood in litigation arising from a breach of statutory provisions. It is not constitutionally permissible to directly compare statutory provisions with the NGDP and/or BSO and argue inconsistency. However, inconsistency can be inferred as follows: a governmental body (which includes the legislature, the executive, and the courts) must carry out its statutory (and constitutional) functions in a way that either implements the NGDP and BSO, or at least does not derogate from them. Failure to do so is a justiciable matter. Justiciability is dependent on the extent to which the governmental body has fulfilled its lawful functions in a way compatible with the NGDP and BSO.

Indirect justiciability is, therefore, a legal process where substantive legal claims (that is justiciable claims) or cause(s) of action are influenced or directed by underlying principles or higher norms. In and of themselves these principles and norms do not entitle a person to claim redress from an alleged offender, but they work in tandem, perhaps in a symbiotic relationship, to achieve society's higher goals. Where an opportunity exists for a governmental body to exercise its functions to implement the NGDP and/or BSO and it fails to do so, an aggrieved person can make a claim against that governmental body for failure to implement. The different types of claim that can be made under indirect justiciability, its scope and limitations, and type of remedies available, are discussed below and in chapters 7 and 9.

(c) Judicial attempts to consider indirect justiciability

Although the terminology of "indirect justiciability" has not used by Papua New Guinea courts, a survey of cases reveals at least two attempts to consider indirect justiciability in a way similar to that presented in this study. The first case, decided in 2010, was *Ref by OCPNG* (not to be confused with *ROCPNG* discussed above), which will be discussed later in the chapter. The second case, *Medaing v Ramu Nico Management (MCC) Ltd (Medaing)*, decided in 2011, is considered here.[81]

Medaing tested Taylor's view on the justiciability of the NGDP and BSO. The main difference between the interpretive aid approach and indirect justiciability in *Medaing* was the plaintiff actually relied on the NGDP and BSO as the basis of his claim against the defendants. In a case where the NGDP and BSO are used as an interpretive aid, the courts would have recourse to the NGDP and BSO proprio motu.

The three prominent issues in *Medaing* were whether the discharge of mine waste (Deep Sea Tailings Placement (DSTP)) into Astrolobe Bay in Madang Province of Papua New Guinea: (a) amounted to the tort of nuisance; (b) was contrary to the Environment Act 2000; and (c) conflicted with National Goal 4 on natural resources and the environment as it would be destructive to the marine ecology. The Court (Cannings J) denied the plaintiff's claim to public nuisance and breach of the Environmental Act but on the third issue held it was within the Court's province to express an opinion on whether DSTP would be contrary to the NGDP.

Justice Cannings was of the view the DSTP was contrary to Goal 4 on the environment.[82] Section 25(3) of the Constitution relates to the exercise of judicial power in a way that promotes the NGDP. A liberal definition of judicial power which the Constitution enjoins the Court to undertake (discussed above) would enable Cannings J to do what he did. But Cannings J did not go so far as to express the idea of indirect justiciability.

The better approach would have been for Cannings J to examine whether a governmental body had exercised its power to fulfil the NGDP and/or BSO. If it had not, then an appropriate order would be made to remedy the non-implementation of the NGDP and/or BSO. In this case could have been an injunction to stop the discharge of environmentally deleterious waste or for the government to carefully consider any competing interests (as promoted by the NGDP and/or BSO) before it issued a permit.

---

81 *Medaing v Ramu Nico Management (MCC) Ltd* [2011] PGNC 95, N4340, 26 July 2011[*Medaing*].

82 At [121].

If the court took an interpretive approach in *Medaing*, it is submitted it would have been limited in examining the implications of the waste discharge on the environment to the NGDP and/or BSO. The court would only have considered the NGDP and BSO if a question of interpretation arose. Since no question of interpretation arose, the scope for applying the NGDP and/or BSO would be limited. The majority in *Medaing on appeal* relied solely on the common law of public nuisance, and denied the appellant's claim to prevent environmental degradation. Indirect justiciability would have produced a different result as it would have raised a cause of action (with an attached substantive right) for the courts to consider and decide on.

Another interesting aspect of the *Medaing* case was the Court's declaration of inconsistency with the NGDP, although it was not binding. The non-binding declaration the National Court issued in *Medaing* may be another useful way to approach the idea of interconnectedness between the different arms of government (interconnectedness is discussed in chapter 6). As chapter 10 notes, a non-binding declaration is sanctioned by ss 25(2) and 63(2) of the Constitution, which supports implementation of the NGDP and/or BSO, but it does not align with the idea of indirect justiciability premised on ss 25(3) and 63(3). This is because indirect justiciability would, in an appropriate case, result in a substantive remedy requiring the governmental body to rectify its non-attendance to the NGDP and/or BSO.

(d) Justification from current jurisprudence for differentiating NGDP and BSO as not merely aids to interpretation

There are four reasons justifying the application of indirect justiciability. Each one of these reasons will be developed further to support the case for indirect justiciability.

(i) The duty to implement

The CPC did consider the NGDP and BSO to be an aid to interpretation, but it was to be more than an aid to interpretation. The CPC envisaged active reference to the NGDP and BSO. Reliance on the CPC's intention reinforces the view that ss 25 and 63 create a specific constitutional duty and a role beyond merely interpretation.

The Preamble to the Constitution establishes the duty to implement the NGDP and BSO. For the NGDP it states:

> WE HEREBY PROCLAIM the following aims as our National Goals, and direct all persons and bodies, corporate and unincorporate, to be guided by these our declared Directives in pursuing and achieving our aims:– …

The BSO is prefaced:

> WE HEREBY DECLARE that all persons in our country have the following basic obligations to themselves and their descendants, to each other, and to the Nation:– …

Sections 25 and 63 provide the implementation mechanism for the Preamble. Sections 25(2) and 63(2) state all governmental bodies have a duty to implement the NGDP and BSO respectively. They are constitutional provisions that confer a duty on governmental bodies to implement the NGDP and BSO. This is a clear signal to the courts they must look at legal mechanisms to give effect to the NGDP and BSO. The question is whether designating the NGDP and BSO as interpretive aids will achieve this requirement. But it is a question *ROCPNG* and the majority in *Medaing on appeal* did not confront. This shows a lack of appreciation of the duty to implement, which is more than a rule of statutory interpretation.

If ss 25 and 63 were to be defined as aids to constitutional interpretation, the Constituent Assembly might have used similar text in the provision immediately before s 25 of the Constitution: "s 24. Use of Certain Materials as Aids to Interpretation." Section 24 provides for the courts to have recourse to certain materials as aids to interpretation. This is not the same with s 25, which is titled "Implementation of the National Goals and Directive Principles"; or s 63 "Enforcement of the Basic Social Obligations". Sections 25(2) and 63(2) both impose a specific duty on governmental bodies to implement the NGDP and BSO as "far as lies within their respective powers". There is, therefore, an obvious distinction between a duty to implement, and an approach that treats the NGDP and BSO as an aid to interpretation.

To strengthen the position advanced by this study, it is helpful to consider texts of legislation from comparable jurisdictions which provide for certain norms to be used as aids to interpretation. The United Kingdom Human Rights Act 1998 states:

> 3. Interpretation of legislation.
>
> (1) So far as it is possible to do so, primary legislation and subordinate legislation must be read and given effect in a way which is compatible with the Convention rights.

A comparable provision can be found in section 6 of the New Zealand Bill of Rights Act 1990:

> 6. Interpretation consistent with Bill of Rights to be preferred
>
> Wherever an enactment can be given a meaning that is consistent with the rights and freedoms contained in this Bill of Rights, that meaning shall be preferred to any other meaning.

Both these provisions are considered as aids to interpretation. But in the case of Papua New Guinea, the Constitution specifically places a duty on all governmental bodies to implement the NGDP and BSO. It is, therefore, an error on the courts' part to consign the NGDP and BSO to the role of being merely interpretive aids. The phrase "can reasonably be understood, applied, exercised or enforced …" in s 25(3) and 63(3) does not have "can reasonably be interpreted" limit on its function as an interpretive aid.

Another compelling reason why the United Kingdom and New Zealand provisions cited above may not provide an appropriate comparison is that they relate mainly to norms arising from negative rights or civil and political rights and freedoms. They do not address social, economic and cultural goals in the way ss 25 and 63 of the Papua New Guinea Constitution do. Treating the NGDP and BSO as a mere interpretive aid would not sufficiently account for positive rights relating to social, cultural and economic advancement. NGDP and BSO have a much more important role than that given the Constitution states the NGDP and BSO must be complied with. Further, the Constitution states its provisions are self-executing to the fullest extent possible.[83]

(ii) Limitation of non-justiciability in ss 25(1) and 63(1)

A plain reading of ss 25(1) and 63(1) of the Constitution reveals non-justiciability applies to s 25(2) and s 63(2) only; but not to s 25(3) and s 25(4) (NGDP), and s 63(3) and s 63(4) (BSO). The courts have not given serious judicial attention to the extent of non-justiciability stated in ss 25(1) and

[83] Constitution, s 11(2). Discussed above in principles of constitutional interpretation.

63(1). This was the error the Supreme Court majority in *Medaing on appeal* made when it made a blanket application of non-justiciability of the NGDP (and BSO by implication).

The majority in *Medaing on appeal* consisting of Sawong and Hartshorn JJ approached the issue by first outlining the definition of non-justiciability in sch 1.7 of the Constitution. This was an indication non-justiciability would influence their reasoning. Consequently, Sawong and Hartshorn JJ went on to state:[84]

> The extent provided in s 25(3) for the National Goals and Directive Principles to be heard or determined is in relation to whether a law can be reasonably enforced to give effect to or not derogate from the National Goals and Directive Principles. It is not provided in s 25(3) that the National Court can give an opinion or make a declaration as to whether a law or power conferred by a law is contrary to the National Goal. By giving an opinion or making a declaration, the trial judge heard and made a determination as to a National Goal to an extent not provided for under s 25(3) of the Constitution.

In *Medaing*, the plaintiff had specifically pleaded the application of the NGDP in their cause of action. As a result, the court (Cannings J) made a ruling in the plaintiff's favour. The majority in *Medaing on appeal* appear to be saying this is not a proper use of the NGDP; rather it is for the court to apply the NGDP when an issue of interpretation arises. Such an approach does not adequately explain the limitations of non-justiciability established by ss 25(1) and 63(1).

(iii) Non-application of principles of constitutional interpretation

A careful reading of *ROCPNG* shows the Supreme Court took a cursory approach to interpreting s 25, and did not carefully construct that provision. The Supreme Court provides its reasoning in four short paragraphs. The most detailed was para 23 where the Court merely asserted its position with no substantive justification:

> Except where the Constitution itself provides the NGDP and BSO [are] to be used as an aid to the interpretation of specific

[84] *Medaing on appeal*, above n 4 at [163].

> statutes, they cannot be used as a ground to strike down legislation: see s 38 of the Constitution. The provisions of s 25(3) and 63(3) provide guide to exercise of power conferred by statute and of themselves do not provide a ground to invalidate an offending legislation.

The Court did not explain how s 38 of the Constitution supported its position that the NGDP and BSO are only interpretive aids.

Medaing on appeal maintained the position established by *ROCPNG*, although the Court did not expressly refer to *ROCPNG* in its decision. But a 2–1 majority ruled in favour of the NGDP and BSO being interpretive aids only under ss 25(3) and 63(3) of the Constitution. Davani J, in upholding Cannings J's decision in the National Court (discussed below), relied on sch 1.5 of the Constitution, which enjoins courts to interpret the Constitution liberally, to influence her interpretation of s 25(3):

> 123. Section 25(3) of the Constitution cannot be any clearer. If given its fair and liberal interpretation, states in no uncertain terms that a Judicial power, which includes the power to issue any declaration by a Court and which is also a judicial power to issue administrative relief being a Declaration, is issued to give effect to the National Goals and Directive Principles because it must be enforced in that way (s 25(3) of the Constitution).

The minority (Davani J) in *Medaing on appeal* attempted to apply principles of constitutional interpretation before arriving at her position. The majority (Sawong and Hartshorn JJ), as the *ROCPNG* Court did, merely asserted their position with no reference to principles of constitutional interpretation or case authorities.

Another important constitutional principle of interpretation is for each constitutional law to be read as a whole (Constitution, sch 1.5(1)). This would mean ss 25(1) and 63(1) alone should not dominate the interpretation of ss 25 and 63. Sections 25(1) and 63(1) first state there is an exception to the non-justiciability of the NGDP and BSO. This is in ss 25(3), 63(3), 25(4) and 63(4). Immediately following ss 25(1) and 63(1), ss 25(2) and 63(2) use the word "Nevertheless …" it is the duty of all governmental bodies to implement the NGDP and BSO. A synonym for nevertheless is "notwithstanding". So, despite ss 25(1) and 63(1), the NGDP and BSO are required to be implemented. The question that arises is how ss 25(1), 63(1), and ss 25(2) and 63(2) can be reconciled.

Sections 25(3) and 63(3) provide for this reconciliation. There is no specific provision stating ss 25(3) and 63(3) are directed towards the courts exclusively as a tool for interpretive aid. One can infer that the subject of ss 25(3) and 63(3) is not the courts, but governmental bodies. Why? Immediately before ss 25(3) and 63(3), in ss 25(2) and 63(2), the subject of the latter two provisions is to confer on governmental bodies a duty to implement the NGDP and BSO. The use of the terms "legislative power," "executive power", "judicial power", and "administrative power" supports this assertion as these powers are exercised by governmental bodies. Sections 25(3) and 63(3) reconcile the two preceding provisions, and provide the scope and limits of governmental bodies' duty to implement the NGDP and BSO. As will be argued later in the chapter, the legal nature of this duty is best described as "indirectly-justiciable".

As a result of the *Medaing on appeal* Court not carefully reading ss 25 and 63, and failing to apply relevant principles of constitutional interpretation, it has erred by treating the constitutional duty to implement the NGDP and BSO under ss 25 and 63 as entirely non-justiciable. This will be dealt with further on the section below on indirect justiciability.

(iv) Current jurisprudence does not preclude indirect justiciability

It is submitted *ROCPNG*, which is perhaps the most authoritative judicial pronouncement on ss 25(3) and 63(3), does not preclude the indirectly justiciable approach. *ROCPNG* was decided by a bench of five justices of the Supreme Court (as opposed to three justices in *Medaing on appeal*). Furthermore, *Medaing on appeal* was not unanimous. *ROCPNG* would therefore be the leading authority on the issue.

The *ROCPNG* Court said legislation could not be struck down on account of the NGDP. This is not disputed because that would involve direct justiciability. It is an open question whether the Supreme Court would consider favourably a claim made using the NGDP and/or BSO indirectly. There is no constitutional impediment to this view.

Arguably, *Ref by OCPNG* was a case that applied indirect justiciability without expressly referring to it in those terms. The Court was asked to deliberate on the constitutionality of an amendment to an Organic law taking into account the NGDP. The litigant's question (cause of action) expressly asked the Court to declare the amendment to be invalid for offending s 187C(2)(a) of the Constitution, taking into account the NGDP. The Court found the amendment was unconstitutional; the NGDP influenced this outcome. *Ref by OCPNG* is further analysed below, and in chapter 9.

4. *Practical application of indirect justiciability and its difference from the interpretive aid approach*

The main difference between indirect justiciability and the interpretative aid approach, as noted above, is that indirect justiciability shapes the cause of action of an aggrieved person, whereas an interpretive aid is a tool available to the court to use at its discretion as appropriate. It must also be stressed that an interpretive aid can become a useful tool to support indirect justiciability as *Ref by OCPNG* suggests.

The form indirect justiciability takes would depend on the type of power being exercised. In the case of legislative power, the question the court can be asked to determine is whether a particular law has provided the opportunity to implement the NGDP and BSO. If it does not, then it will be a ground to invalidate the legislation.

An example of indirect justiciability, as it applies to the exercise of legislative power, is proposed in chapter 7 when *ROCPNG* is discussed. The question in that case that would meet the requirements of indirect justiciability would be: "Is the repeal of s 59 of the Forest Act 1991 a derogation by parliament of its duty to implement the NGDP through its legislative power under s 25(3) of the Constitution?" To answer this question, the court would obviously have to consider whether Parliament considered the NGDP and/or BSO in the process of repealing the NGDP and/or BSO. As discussed in chapter 7, the court's supervision of parliamentary compliance would be through a procedural lens. If parliament did not consider the NGDP and/or BSO, the Supreme Court would declare the repeal of s 59 of the Forest Act 1991 unconstitutional and as a result invalid.

The NGDP and BSO then become an interpretive aid when the claim is before the court. In order for indirect justiciability to function effectively the courts would necessarily have to use the NGDP and BSO as an interpretive aid. This is an appropriate exercise of judicial power to complement legislative power to supervise the implementation of the NGDP and BSO.

Another example relates to the exercise of executive power. When the government makes a decision, an aggrieved person could challenge the decision on the grounds that it was unreasonable as the government had the opportunity to implement the NGDP and/or BSO, but it did not. *R v Minister of Agriculture ex parte Padfield (Padfiled)* provides an apt illustration.[85] The court ruled that the decision was unreasonable as it did not fulfil the objectives of the legislation. In a situation where the law makes specific reference to a NGDP and/or BSO, an aggrieved person could argue that the government's decision was unreasonable, as it did not take a course of action that would implement the NGDP and/or BSO. As discussed in chapter 9, this process can be pursued under existing administrative judicial review procedures and remedies.

As can be seen in *ROCPNG* and *Padfield*, the courts' role in supervising governmental bodies' compliance with the NGDP and BSO is mainly through a "procedural" lens as opposed to a "substantive" one. The court is looking for opportunities a governmental body had to implement the NGDP and BSO, but did not. If a court was to make a direct finding of incompatibility with the NGDP and/or BSO, it would not be necessary to consider other provisions of the law. The NGDP and BSO would operate as other provisions of the law and such an approach is not permitted in the scheme of ss 25 and 63 (as it would make the NGDP and BSO directly justiciable).[86]

When the NGDP and BSO are used as an interpretive aid, we confront a situation where the court, on its own motion, relies on the NGDP and BSO to interpret a law. Examples of the courts using the NGDP and BSO as an interpretive aid include the *Public Curator of Papua New Guinea v Public Trustee of New Zealand (Public Curator);*[87] *Sasakila; Peter v South Pacific Brewery Ltd;*[88] *Simbu; and Haiveta*. The aggrieved in each of these cases did not come to court questioning whether a governmental body failed to interpret the NGDP and BSO as its cause of action, but the court took the NGDP and BSO into account on its own motion to interpret the issues before the court.

---

85 *R v Minister of Agriculture ex parte Padfield* [1968] AC 997 (HL).

86 *ROCPNG*, above n 65.

87 *Public Curator of Papua New Guinea v Public Trustee of New Zealand* [1976] PGNC 48, [1976] PNGLR 427, 28 September 1976.

88 *Peter v South Pacific Brewery Ltd* [1976] PGSC 28, SC 109, [1976] PNGLR 345, 29 November 1976.

The ideal situation in which we can see the indirect justiciability approach in practice is when a cause of action is premised on the NGDP and/or BSO, and the court would have to determine the outcome of the matter based on the NGDP and/or BSO raised in the claim. Such a situation presented itself in *Ref by OCPNG* where the constitutional question to determine the validity of an amendment to the Organic Law on Provincial and Local-Level Government 1995 was put before the Supreme Court in the following manner:[89]

> Whether Sections 1 and 2 of the Organic Law on Provincial Governments and Local-Level Government (Amendment No 10) Laws 2006, in removing:
>
> (1) Heads of the rural Local-Level Government as Members of the Provincial Assembly; and
>
> (2) One representative to represent the heads of both urban authorities and urban council members of the Provincial Assembly; and
>
> (3) Either the heads of the rural Local-level Government or the representative of the heads of both urban authorities and urban councils from contesting the post of Deputy Governor
>
> Is contrary to the requirements of Section 187C(2)(a) of the Constitution to have "an elective or mainly elective legislature", as understood, applied and enforced within the meaning of the Second National Goal (Equality and Participation) of the National Goals and Directive Principles and therefore unconstitutional?

The NGDP was used to formulate the cause of action, but the substantive justiciable provision relied on was s 187C(2)(a) of the Constitution. The NGDP would then be used to determine the outcome of the case. In this instance the Supreme Court ruled that the amendment to the OLPLLG was unconstitutional and therefore invalid. More will be said of this case as regards the contextual approach to interpretation and its relationship to indirect justiciability in chapter 9.

---

[89] *Ref by OCPNG*, above n 4.

5. *The limits and scope of indirect justiciability*

On their own, the NGDP and BSO are not justiciable. They become justiciable in the context of a governmental body's specific statutory functions. There are, however, three exceptions or limitations on their application: first, where it would be contrary to Parliament's expressed intention; second, where it would be inconsistent with the Constitution; and third, where to do so would be unreasonable. Each of these exceptions follows on from the other.

(a) Contrary to Parliament's intentions

This exception arises from the phrase, "without failing to give effect to the intention of Parliament ..." in ss 25(3) and 63(3) of the Constitution. The effect of this phrase on implementation depends on whether Parliament considers there are overriding reasons why the NGDP and BSO are not an appropriate consideration in the specific context of the subject matter addressed by the law. But ss 25 and 63 require implementation in the first instance, so Parliament has a positive duty to make clear its intention to derogate from this obligation. This responsibility falls to Parliament – not the other arms of government.

The best way for Parliament to make its intentions clear (and to avoid future questions about its intentions) would be for Parliament to include a statement in legislation. Parliament can enact laws that have specific provisions stating Parliament did not wish the NGDP and/or BSO to be considered for implementation in the particular law. However, a survey of Papua New Guinea legislation that refers to the NGDP and BSO reveals Parliament has never expressed an intention against the implementation of the NGDP and BSO. On the contrary, laws have expressly required the implementation of the NGDP and BSO, but the practice should be consistent.

An interesting example where parliament has expressed its intentions on the NGDP and BSO is in the Underlying Law Act 2000. Under s 4 of the Underlying Law Act, customary law and common law would not apply if they are inconsistent with the NGDP and BSO (amongst other requirements). As an exception to both non-justiciability and indirect justiciability, this appears to be a case of direct justiciability; but parliament has made its intention express. Alternatively, parliament can equally express its intention that it is inappropriate to implement the NGDP and/or BSO in certain circumstances. The development of the underlying law is discussed further in chapter 9.

(b) Inconsistent with the Constitution

This exception follows straight after the first exception. Again, it arises from the phrase, "without failing to give effect to ... this Constitution ..." in ss 25(3) and 63(3) of the Constitution. The exception could be triggered when interpreting and/or applying a law to give effect to the NGDP and BSO, but in a way that is contrary to the Constitution, especially the provisions on human rights and freedoms. This situation has not arisen in Papua New Guinea, but it has in India in relation to its State Policies and Directive Principles, for example, *State of Madras v Champakam Dorairajan.*[90] In that case, a policy which was supposed to implement the directive principles was found to be inconsistent with justiciable fundamental rights and therefore unconstitutional. If such a scenario were to arise in Papua New Guinea, there is little doubt the Constitution would prevail.

Indirect justiciability would also be limited where another provision of the Constitution addresses expressly addresses the NGDP and BSO. Three examples are provided. The first obvious example is ss 25(4) and 63(4) of the Constitution on the Ombudsman Commission. The idea of indirect justiciability as premised on ss 25(3) and 63(3) would not apply to the Ombudsman Commission's Leadership Code function (discussed in chapter 10). Second, s 219(1)(a) of the Constitution talks expressly about the Ombudsman Commission's jurisdiction in administrative complaints taking into account the NGDP and BSO (also discussed in chapter 10). The third example relates to questions of whether a law is reasonably justifiable in a democratic society. Under ss 38 and 39 of the Constitution, the NGDP and BSO is one of the grounds that may allow parliament to restrict a right or freedom (discussed in chapter 9). These provisions would override the application of ss 25(3) and 63(3).

(c) Where it would be unreasonable

If implementation is not contrary to Parliament's express intention and not inconsistent with the Constitution, the question arises whether it would be unreasonable to expect governmental bodies to implement the NGDP and BSO within their statutory or constitutional functions. The question of what is reasonable will depend on the facts of each case. There can be no universal standards. However, the South African case of *Government of the Republic*

---

90 *State of Madras v Champakam Dorairajan* [1951] AIR 226 (SC).

of South Africa & Ors v Grootboom & Ors is a useful illustration of relevant considerations.[91]

Although South Africa does not have directive principles, it has social rights that are directly enforceable in its Constitution. Issues of implementation of social rights are similar in countries with directive principles alone.[92] In Grootboom, the plaintiffs claimed the right to housing, a social right under s 26 of the South African Constitution. This right is justiciable. The plaintiffs were squatters in a place called Wallacedene. Their shelter was rudimentary consisting of plastic, and they lacked basic sanitation and electricity. In assessing the plaintiffs' argument that their right to housing had been breached, the Court considered the government's duty in three areas:

1. the obligation to take reasonable legislative and other measures—
2. to achieve the progressive realisation of the right—
3. within available resources.

A Papua New Guinea court would do well to ask similar questions when determining whether a governmental body has fulfilled its obligation to implement the NGDP and BSO under ss 25 and 63 of the Constitution. The court would be asking if adequate steps have been taken to realise the NGDP and BSO and, if so, whether the government had done all it reasonably could in balancing competing demands for its available resources. This judicial scrutiny of other government bodies would be undertaken by the court applying a procedural lens. The question of reasonableness will be taken up further in chapters 7, 8, and 9 to see how it may work in practice.

6. *Indirect justiciability and remedies*

The availability of a remedy does not determine whether a question is justiciable. Each case is treated on its merits. For example, a claim may be justiciable, but the court may decline to award a remedy; or a person may come to court claiming a justiciable right or rights, but the court may not find

---

91 *Government of the Republic of South Africa v Grootboom* (CCT11/00) [2000] ZACC 19, [2001] 1 SA 46 (CC), [2000] 11 BCLR 1169, 4 October 2000 [*Grootboom*].

92 The experience of India was considered when deciding on the enforcement of social rights in South Africa's Constitution: see Bertus De Villiers "Directive Principles of State Policy and Fundamental Rights: The Indian Experience" (1992) 8 S Afr J Hum Rts 29.

it appropriate to award a remedy.[93] However, the remedy is significant to the idea of interconnectedness. The remedy that courts award can demonstrate to other limbs of government that each one of them have a duty to implement. A procedural lens enhances this approach of each arm seeing its functions as connected.

The type of remedy available when the question of implementation of the NGDP and/or BSO is at issue (by means of indirect justiciability) would be no different to the existing remedies. For example, in constitutional references it would be a declaration of unconstitutionality (or not). In administrative judicial review, these would be certiorari, prohibition, mandamus and a declaration. Chapters 7 and 9 expand on the discussion of available remedies, especially in relation to court scrutiny of parliament and other government bodies, including through the development of the underlying law, administrative judicial review and the protection and enforcement of human rights and freedoms. What can be said now, is indirect justiciability would not require the courts to develop a special remedy.

The court can reasonably be expected to undertake a careful analysis of the appropriate remedy depending on the nature of the claim. But there can be no universal rule, and the court must proceed on a case by case basis. The court must also respect the function of each arm of government, and the fact that there may be limited resources.

The court's primary role would be to consider whether the governmental body has considered the NGDP and/or BSO in the decision making process and decide whether the non-implementation was reasonable or not. In this regard the court would be assessing the other arms of government through a procedural lens.

In borderline cases, where appropriate, greater deference will be accorded to each arm of government because of the separate functions each performs. This is not to diminish the case for indirect justiciability, but to enhance it, by recognising the role each arm of government plays, and the challenges it faces, such as limited resources.

93 See, for example, in *Grootboom*, above n 91, the Court did not directly order the government to provide housing, which was a social right in the South African Constitution, but instead ordered the government to put in place policies and processes to support the provision of this right.

It is not for the court to assume the role of another branch of government, but to ensure each body performs its role fairly and in an accountable and transparent manner in accordance with the Constitution. What is important, however, is for the NGDP and/or BSO to be actively engaged in ways that each governmental body can implement.

E. A Note on Similarities and Differences between ss 25 and 63 of the Constitution

Sections 25 and 63 are similar, but there are some differences. Importantly, however, ss 25 and 63 demonstrate that when considering the implementation of the NGDP, the BSO is to be considered concurrently. One does not have priority over the other. While much of the discussion in the literature has been on the NGDP, the constitutional mandate is for the NGDP and BSO to be implemented without distinction.[94]

The first difference between ss 25 and 63 relates to the location of the provisions. Both the NGDP and BSO appear under Part III, "Basic Principles of Government". Part III of the Constitution has five divisions:

- Division 1 – National Goals and Directive Principles;
- Division 2 – Leadership Code;
- Division 3 – Basic Rights;
- Division 4 – Principles of Natural Justice; and
- Division 5 – Basic Social Obligations.

Division 3 on "Basic Rights," has three further sub-divisions:

- Sub-division A – Introductory;
- Sub-division B – Fundamental Rights; and
- Sub-division C – Qualified Rights.

The implementation framework for the NGDP, Basic Rights and BSO appears in Part III (the NGDP fall under Division 1; Basic Rights in Division 3 and the BSO is the last section of Division 5). However, despite their co-location in Part III, a different approach to enforcement of the Basic

---

94 Constitution ss 25 and 63. See also CPC Report, above n 8, at 5/1/34 [21].

Rights is provided for. Basic Rights are detailed from ss 32 to 58. Sections 57 and 58 enable a person to seek redress for breach of their rights and freedoms. The NGDP and BSO are implemented by ss 25 and 63 of the Constitution by way of non-justiciability and indirect justiciability. This is a legal distinction. A policy reason for this implementation difference could be the NGDP and BSO are considered as underlying aims of the Constitution and not as substantive rights and freedoms per se.

The fact that rights and freedoms are situated alongside the NGDP and BSO is not without significance. The state is to carry out its functions within certain legal and political boundaries. Accordingly, the Constitution has been described as programmatic.[95] To say it another way, a constitutional agenda is set for the country. Government laws and policies must conform to the constitutional mandate granted to them in the way they discharge their functions.

The second difference arises from the CPC's view on the interdependence of rights and obligations. In order for rights to be recognised, they must be accompanied by obligations.[96] In the CPC Report, human rights are considered concurrently with obligations. Chapter 5 is entitled "Human Rights and Obligations and Emergency Powers", and Part 1 is "Human Rights and Obligations". The CPC Report states:[97]

> As well as entrenching in our Constitution the fundamental rights and freedoms which we recommend should be protected, we believe that certain basic obligations should also be incorporated in the Constitution as duties which all people in this country should accept if our goals are to be achieved.

For this reason, s 63 is placed immediately after the provisions on rights and freedoms in the Constitution. The title of s 63 opens with the word "Enforcement". Section 25 commences with "Implementation". Both these terms place a positive duty on those to whom they apply to carry out what is stated in these provisions.

---

95 Anthony J Regan "Introduction" in Anthony J Regan, Owen Jessep and Eric L Kwa (eds) *Twenty Years of the Papua New Guinea Constitution* (Lawbook Co, Sydney, 2001) 1 at 3.

96 CPC Report, above no 30, see generally ch 5.

97 At 5/1/15 [92].

The other difference relates to s 25(2) and s 63(2). Different words are used to provide for implementation. In terms of the NGDP it is stated that the duty of all governmental bodies are to "apply and give effect to them ..." while for the BSO, all governmental bodies are conferred the duty to "encourage compliance with them".

The variance probably indicates a slight shift in urgency towards the NGDP over the BSO. The latter uses words depicting persuasion while the former has more direct language. Apart from that, the overall import is characteristic of implementation.

IV. Conclusion

Sections 25 and 63 of the Constitution impose duties on governmental bodies to implement the NGDP and BSO. What is the legal nature of this duty? Applying the various principles of constitutional interpretation and a plain reading of ss 25 and 63, suggests that there is an exception to the general non-justiciable nature of the NGDP and BSO. The NGDP and BSO are indirectly justiciable by virtue of ss 25(3) and 63(3). Proposals will be made to fulfil this duty to implement the NGDP and BSO within the constitutional functions of the courts, the legislature, the executive and the Ombudsman Commission in chapters 7, 8, 9 and 10 respectively.

CHAPTER FIVE

IMPLEMENTATION RECORD OF GOVERNMENTAL BODIES AND IMPEDIMENTS

I. Introduction

This chapter presents the current state of affairs of governmental bodies' performance record with regards to the implementation of the NGDP and BSO. The governmental bodies focused on include the three traditional arms of government and the Ombudsman Commission. After discussing governmental bodies' performance, the main legal impediments to implementation of the constitutional duty under ss 25 and 63 of the Constitution are identified. Essentially, the impediments have prevented governmental bodies from appreciating that their functions are interconnected, since interconnectedness supports (or would support) efficient implementation. This conclusion is established from assessing the performance record of the legislature, the executive, the courts, and the Ombudsman Commission.

This chapter has four parts. Part I is the introduction. Part II discusses the performance record of the legislature, the executive, the courts and the Ombudsman Commission on the implementation of the NGDP and BSO.[1] Part III presents the legal impediments which have stifled the contributions of the NGDP and BSO to Papua New Guinea's development. Part IV concludes the chapter.

---

[1] The three arms of government and the Ombudsman Commission have been selected to make proposals for the implementation of the NGDP and BSO, hence the review of their performance record.

II. Governmental Bodies' Record of Implementing the NGDP and BSO

A. Introduction

The first attempt to consider ways in which the NGDP can be implemented as well as the implementation record was in 1982 where an entire seminar was devoted to the government pre-independence economic policy, the Eight Point Plan or Aims, and the NGDP.[2] There was no discussion on legal avenues for implementation of the NGDP. The seminar did not consider the BSO.

B. The Legislature

Currently, legislative references to the NGDP and BSO occur haphazardly. Appendix Three, which identifies how legislation refers to the NGDP and BSO confirms this finding. Only 44 pieces of legislation (of the estimated total of 734) refer to the NGDP and BSO. Of the 44, a good number do so because of the constitutional requirement under s 38 of the Constitution. Under this provision, any legislation that restricts a qualified right and/or freedom, must expressly state in its preliminary provisions the particular right and/or freedom restricted, and advance a public reason for it. A public reason that entitles the Parliament to restrict a right and/or freedom would be implementation of the NGDP and BSO. But Parliament cannot simply enact a provision to state the law is for the advancement of the NGDP and BSO; there must exist factual basis for such a claim, which the courts can examine.[3]

Four main methods of reference to the NGDP and BSO can be identified from an analysis of the legislation studied:

- In the preamble;
- In the objective section;
- As part of the requirement for constitutional compliance under ss 38 and 39 of the Constitution; and
- In the substantive text of the legislation.

---

2 Peter King, Wendy Lee and Vincent Warakai (eds) *From Rhetoric to Reality? Papua New Guinea's Eight Point Plan and National Goals After a Decade, Papers from the Fifteenth Waigani Seminar* (University of Papua New Guinea Press, Port Moresby, 1985).

3 See *The State v NTN Pty Ltd and NBN Ltd* [1992] PGSC 11, [1992] PNGLR 1, 7 April 1987.

Only two Acts provide any mechanism to aid the implementing authority engage the NGDP and/or BSO in the decision-making process.[4] These two laws, the Salaries and Remuneration Commission Act 1983, and Underlying Law Act 2000, do not apply to the role of the executive. These Acts have an express requirement for the NGDP and/or BSO to be considered by Parliament and the courts, respectively. Such a device may be useful in drawing the attention of the executive to the NGDP and BSO. Regardless of express legislative reference, the executive has a constitutional duty to take into account the NGDP and BSO in its decisions. But it may be helpful to have express reference in the legislation. So, while different laws vest powers in various authorities to make decisions, there is little guidance on how to implement the NGDP and/or BSO in legislation that defines the functions of a governmental body.

The Standing Orders of Parliament provide a key guide for Parliament in the enactment of legislation. However, the Standing Orders lack a specific provision on how to engage the NGDP and BSO in Bills brought before Parliament. Part XIX on "Bills" sets out the different stages a Bill has to follow before enactment, but it does not refer to the duty to implement under ss 25 and 63. Part XIXA of the Standing Orders provides for separate treatment of amendments to constitutional laws. This, too, does not cater for the constitutional requirement to implement the NGDP and BSO. Even the Manual of Practice and Procedure prepared by the Clerk of the Parliament to help members of Parliament to understand their roles and functions under the Constitution and the Standing Orders lacks any reference to the NGDP and BSO.[5]

C. The Executive

There are many laws (Constitution, Organic Laws, and legislation) that confer power on the executive to make decisions over many different subject areas. Some of these laws apply directly to a minister or ministry, while others confer powers exclusively on the National Executive Council as a collective entity. It is in the application of these laws the NGDP and BSO are required to be implemented. Chapter 7 recommends that Parliament passes

---

[4] Appendix Three summarises how the NGDP and BSO are engaged by legislation. Salaries and Remuneration Commission Act 1983, s 14; and Underlying Law Act 2000, s 7.

[5] *National Parliament of Papua New Guinea Manual of Practice and Procedure* (1st ed, prepared by the Clerk of Parliament, Port Moresby, 2009).

legislation with specific reference to a particular NGDP and/or BSO, to guide the executive in the implementation process. This is one way the legislature and the executive can interact with each other in the implementation process. At present there is little scope for such interaction.

The Papua New Guinea government's most recent policy on development does try in some ways to address the NGDP and BSO. This is Vision 2050, the strategies to which decisions for national development are tied.[6] However, Vision 2050 did not consider how the Constitution, either in its present state or through reforms, could effectively respond to developmental challenges using the NGDP and BSO. Nor did it take up the CPC's proposal to create a permanent parliamentary committee to review laws and policies to determine their alignment with the NGDP and BSO.

D. The Courts

An early case setting out the courts' attitude to the importance of the NGDP and BSO was *Public Curator of Papua New Guinea v Public Trustee of New Zealand (Public Curator).*[7] The decision in *Public Curator* interpreted legislation (interpretive aid approach) to give effect to the NGDP. This case showed immediately after independence the CPC's enthusiasm and idealism was reflected in judicial creativity. This interest has waned to such an extent that in 1992, Anthony Regan observed that the Papua New Guinea judiciary had made little use of the NGDP.[8] His article did not refer to the BSO. According to Regan, the blame did not lie solely with the judiciary; the other arms of government were also responsible – an example being the re-distribution of wealth.[9] Many parts of the country did not have access to basic services, which was a responsibility of the government. Be that as it may, the courts still have an important role as the "guardian of the Constitution" to ensure that these various arms of government interact well in regards to the

---

6 National Strategic Plan Taskforce *Papua New Guinea Vision 2050* (Government Printer, Port Moresby, 2009).

7 *Public Curator of Papua New Guinea v Public Trustee of New Zealand* [1976] PGNC 48, [1976] PNGLR 427, 28 September 1976 [*Public Curator*].

8 Anthony Regan "Constitutionalism, Legitimacy and the Judiciary" in RW James and I Fraser (eds) *Legal Issues in a Developing Society* (Faculty of Law, University of Papua New Guinea, Port Moresby, 1992) 12 at 32.

9 At 32.

NGDP and BSO.[10] The Constitution aids this process by allowing the courts to be liberal in their interpretative functions.[11] Even the CPC anticipates the courts being called upon to deliberate on politically sensitive matters.[12] Laws have an important role in directing the evolution of human societies, and the courts are inextricably linked to this process of applying the law so as to fulfil the Constitution's vision.[13]

There are two cases which are perhaps emblematic of the courts' performance. The first is *In Re Reference by the Ombudsman Commission of Papua New Guinea (ROCPNG)*.[14] In that case, the Court was asked to determine the validity of legislation in relation to the NGDP. What is relevant with regard to the implementation of the NGDP and BSO is that the Court said they were non-justiciable, and valuable only as an aid to interpretation:[15]

> Except where the Constitution itself provides the NGDP and BSO are to be used as an aid to the interpretation of specific statutes, they cannot be used as a ground to strike down legislation: see s 38 of the *Constitution*.

There may have been scope for creativity such as to make non-binding declarations against the legislature (which the court of first instance did in the second series of cases discussed below).[16] However, the Court took the position that it should not interfere with the role of the legislature and the executive.

A greater role in the implementation of the NGDP and BSO may have been possible in the second case of *Medaing v Ramu Nico Management (MCC) Ltd (Medaing on appeal)*.[17] This case was an appeal from *Medaing*

---

10 See Amet CJ's decision in *Haiveta, Leader of the Opposition v Wingti, Prime Minister, Attorney-General, and National Parliament* [1994] PGSC 6, [1994] PNGLR 197, 25 August 1994.

11 Constitution, sch. 1.2.5.

12 Constitutional Planning Committee *Final Report of the Constitutional Planning Committee, Part One* (Government Printer, Port Moresby, 1974) at 8/1 [5] [CPC Report].

13 At 8/1 [6].

14 *Reference by the Ombudsman Commission of Papua New Guinea* [2010] PGSC 40, SC1088, 17 December 2010 [*ROCPNG*].

15 At [23].

16 Chapter 9 will elaborate on this proposition.

17 *Medaing v Ramu Nico Management (MCC) Ltd* [2011] PGSC 40, SC1144, 22 December 2011 [*Medaing on appeal*].

v Ramu Nickel (Medaing). In *Medaing*, the Court made a non-binding declaration that a government decision to issue an environmental permit to discharge waste into the waters of Basamuk Bay was inconsistent with the NGDP.[18] This decision was subsequently overturned in *Medaing on appeal*. Indigenous landowners from an area where a nickel mining project was to take place took the mining company and the state to court for possible future environmental damage from mining waste. The waste was to be piped to Basamuk Bay and discharged 400 metres from the sea-shore. Overwhelming scientific evidence indicated the ecology would be fundamentally disturbed. The Court said such an activity was contrary to Goal 4 on natural resources and the environment. On appeal the Supreme Court overruled the court of first instance, holding the NGDP were non-justiciable.[19] Chapter 4 discussed the reasons for the Court's position. This was despite the fact this aspect of the decision had no legal effect on the parties' rights.

ROCPNG was decided in 2010 and *Medaing on appeal* followed a year later. Together, these decisions have relegated the NGDP and BSO to a position where there is no direction from the judiciary to the other arms of government on how and whether to engage the NGDP and BSO.

E. The Ombudsman Commission

The two main functions of the Ombudsman Commission are, first, to investigate administrative complaints against governmental bodies, and second, supervision and enforcement of the Leadership Code. These two functions will be discussed in detail in chapter 10. What can be said now is while the Ombudsman Commission has maintained a strong reputation for independence, its work has not seriously taken on board the requirement to implement the NGDP and BSO under s 219 of the Constitution on administrative complaints, and under ss 25(4) and 63(4) of the Constitution with regard to the Leadership Code function.

Under the administrative complaints function, the Ombudsman Commission has issued a number of reports, many of which have been tabled in Parliament, after which they become public documents. A review of the reports from 2008 to date reveals the Ombudsman Commission, while

---

[18] *Medaing v Ramu Nico Management (MCC) Ltd* [2011] PGNC 95 N4340, 26 July 2011 [*Medaing*].

[19] *Medaing on appeal*, above n 17, at [163].

effective in its function as an independent oversight body of government actions, has not effectively grasped the opportunity to implement the NGDP and BSO. If the Commission did so, it would ensure other government agencies take due account of the NGDP and BSO. The conclusion is the Ombudsman Commission has not implemented the NGDP and BSO under its own mandate. If it did, it would similarly ensure other arms of government also implement the NGDP and BSO. Proposals to help the Ombudsman Commission are detailed in chapter 10.

The same observation about the Ombudsman Commission on the lack of engagement with the NGDP and BSO in its administrative complaints function applies to how it accounts for the NGDP and BSO in its Leadership Code function. Since its establishment, the Ombudsman Commission has referred a large number of leaders for prosecution for misconduct. The type of leaders captured under the leadership code function covers persons occupying office in all three arms of government.[20] There is scope for the Ombudsman Commission to oversee the conduct of other arms of government, ensuring greater engagement with the NGDP and BSO. An assessment of the cases brought before the leadership tribunal since independence reveals the Ombudsman Commission has typically focused on the actual breach of provisions of the Constitution and the Organic Law on the Duties and Responsibilities of Leadership when framing misconduct allegations. But the Commission, which has a narrow view of its functions, has not incorporated the NGDP and BSO in the allegations.[21]

III. Impediments to Implementation of the National Goals and Directive Principles and Basic Social Obligations

A. Introduction

The reasons for non-implementation have been identified from primary and secondary legal materials. It is beyond the scope of this work to conduct an empirical study of the social/political reasons behind the non-implementation of the NGDP and BSO as the approach is normative rather than sociological. Such a distinction between legal, philosophical and sociological analysis

---

[20] Section 26 of the Constitution defines the type of leaders subject to the Leadership Code.

[21] Proposals for how the Ombudsman Commission can overcome this will be taken up in chapter 10.

has been made, for example, by Joel Colon-Rios.[22] Nevertheless, it is also important to have a general overview of some of the possible non-legal reasons behind non-implementation as relevant background information.

B. Reasons for Non-Implementation of the NGDP and BSO

1. *Brief over-view of non-legal reasons for non-implementation*

(a) Liberal democratic system of government

The CPC identified leadership in the country as central to implementing the NGDP and BSO.[23] Perhaps the point Colquhoun-Kerr raises is an impediment to implementation.[24] In Colquhoun-Kerr's view, liberal democratic regimes such as Papua New Guinea have shifting policy orientations. Each political party that controls the executive is at liberty to formulate government policy. The NGDP and BSO are premised on social democratic ideals.[25] But what if a new government is elected on a neo-liberal policy platform? Implementing the NGDP and BSO would create a potential conflict: the government may implement an agenda that had popular support but which is at odds with the Constitution. This is a potential if not actual barrier to implementation, although no political party has publicly disavowed the NGDP and BSO.

(b) Lack of political will

Much of the secondary literature indicates little effort to implement the NGDP and BSO.[26] This resulted in the first concerted review of

---

22 Joel Colon-Rios *Weak constitutionalism: democratic legitimacy and the question of constituent power* (Routledge, New York, 2012) at 103. Colon-Rios relies on works of Beetham, Kelsen and Rawls to distinguish the different approaches to legitimacy from sociological to legal and philosophical respectively.

23 CPC Report, above n 12, at 3/2 [14].

24 DJ Colquhoun-Kerr "Sources of Political Legitimacy in Conflict and Naturalised Foreigners: Some Comments on the General Constitutional Commission's Final Report, 1983" in De Vere, Colquhoun-Kerr and Kaburise (eds) *Essays on the Constitution of Papua New Guinea* (Government Printer, Port Moresby, 1985) at 116.

25 The CPC Report states the NGDP are designed to achieve a free and just society: see CPC Report, above n 12, at 2/2 [8].

26 See for example Meg Taylor "The Constitution and the Environment" in Anthony J Regan, Owen Jessep and Eric L Kwa (eds) *Twenty Years of the Papua New Guinea Constitution* (Lawbook Co, Sydney, 2001) at 333; and Bernard Narokobi "Walking the Footpath of the Constitutional Planning Committee's Five National Goals and Directive Principles" in Ian Maddocks and Edward P Wolfers *Living History and Evolving Democracy Living* (University of Papua New Guinea Press, Port Moresby, 2010) at 24.

the Constitution to suggest that of the NGDP and BSO, at least the NGDP should be made enforceable.[27] Parliament did not take up the recommendations. The reason why Parliament did not adopt the review's findings is unclear, but a lack of political will was a probability.[28] Bernard Narokobi agrees with the General Constitutional Commission that lack of political will was a key factor behind non-implementation.[29] What is however addressed in this work is the legal impediments within the present constitutional arrangement from a constitutional and legal perspective.

(c) Level of literacy

The country's adult (15 and over) literacy rate is at 60 per cent of the population.[30] Literacy does not necessarily equate to awareness of legal and political institutions.[31] The NGDP's and BSO's continuous inclusion in the Constitution demonstrates their supposed acceptance but does not necessarily indicate the level of citizens' awareness. The consultative model the CPC used to engage the people in constitution-making has not been followed in other major legal/constitutional changes in Papua New Guinea.[32] The momentum for change that captured the imagination of the people during the independence era has waned. People's awareness can be enhanced through active participation in the system of government, but the engagement must be continuous to remind the people of the government's requirement to implement the NGDP and BSO.[33]

27 Cited in Colquhoun-Kerr, above n 24, at 118.

28 This is the position as at 20 January 2015.

29 Bernard Narokobi *Life and Leadership in Melanesia* (Institute of Pacific Studies, University of the South Pacific, Suva and University of Papua New Guinea, Port Moresby, 1983) at 108.

30 UNESCO *Adult and Youth Literacy, 1990-2015, Analysis of data of 41 Countries* (Unesco Institute for Statistics, Montreal, 2012) at 13 <www.uis.unesco.org>.

31 Andrew Heywood *Politics* (Macmillan Press Ltd, London, 1997) 186.

32 For example, Parliament amended the Constitution in 2014. The amendment makes it difficult for Parliament to move votes of no-confidence in the Prime Minister in the first 30 months of the five year life of the Parliament. This did not arise from consultation with the people: see Tobias Kulang "We need complete review of Constitution" *The National* (online ed, PNG, 16 July 2013).

33 See for example King, Lee and Warakai, above n 2, who document a conference which took place in 1982 to assess how far the NGDP and the pre-independence eight aims have been implemented. Nothing similar has been done since then.

(d) Present relevance of the NGDP and BSO

The relevance of the NGDP and BSO to the present social circumstances in Papua New Guinea is also important. The NGDP and BSO were developed out of the experiences of the period leading up to independence in 1975. Against this, one can ask whether the NGDP and BSO remain relevant to help Papua New Guinea meet its contemporary challenges. This is a question of legislative reform that could arise from political and social empirical studies.

2. *Legal reasons for non-implementation*

The NGDP and BSO have been impeded by the courts in three ways. First, by incorrectly characterising the NGDP and BSO as entirely-non-justiciable; second, by adopting a restrictive role of preambles in statutory interpretation; and third, by using them as an aid to constitutional interpretation. The first concerns a constitutional duty and the second and third relate to the courts' function in statutory interpretation. These impediments have had a flow-on effect on the other arms of government, affecting the way they view the NGDP and BSO and incorporate them (or not) into the exercise of their functions.

(a) Lack of recognition of indirect justiciability

Sections 25(1) and 63(1) characterise the NGDP and BSO as both non-justiciable and justiciable. This perhaps was a result of the CPC's request that although the NGDP and BSO are non-justiciable, they should nevertheless be treated as no less justiciable than other provisions of the Constitution.[34] In analysing the CPC's position, chapter 4 concluded the most appropriate legal status of the NGDP and BSO was indirect justiciability, and explained what this could mean. The most recent authoritative decisions from *ROCPNG* and *Medaing on appeal* suggest the idea of non-justiciability alone should determine the application of the NGDP and BSO. This was despite the active use of the NGDP in early cases such as *Public Curator and Peter v South Pacific Brewery Ltd.*[35] As a result, the correct legal nature of the NGDP and BSO remains unsettled. *Medaing on appeal* was not a unanimous decision. Davani J's minority decision upheld the lower Court finding on its power to express an opinion on the consistency of government decisions in light of the NGDP. However, commentators on the NGDP and BSO have taken the view

[34] CPC Report, above n 12, at 2/25.

[35] *Peter v South Pacific Brewery Ltd* [1976] PGSC 28; SC109, [1976] PNGLR 345, 29 November 1976.

the NGDP and BSO are non-justiciable, and have not gone on to examine the nature of justiciability.[36]

The effect of not making the NGDP and BSO indirectly justiciable is evident in the legislature and the executive, neither of which have been keen implementers. Consequently, there is no effective legal means to enforce the NGDP and BSO against the other arms of government. In fact, the very idea of non-justiciability is to see compliance left to public authorities outside of the court. The CPC Report, as chapter 6 will show, encourages each arm of government to work with the other to implement the NGDP and BSO. In such a scenario, presently promoted by the court (such as in *Medaing on appeal*), the separation of powers affects how each arm of government views their relations with each other. Each limb of government is left to implement of its own volition; interconnectedness and interaction suffer.

(b) The role of preambles

(i) Introduction

One of the reasons why the courts have insisted on the non-justiciable aspects of the NGDP and BSO is the fact the NGDP and BSO are placed in the preamble. This should not, however, lessen the legal impact of the NGDP and BSO. As will be shown below, courts have generally adopted a narrow view of preambles in statutory interpretation rather than a more expansive approach in line with the liberal and purposive approach required in constitutional interpretation in Papua New Guinea. In this way, preambles are emphasised more as moral postulates, rather than as having substantive legal effect.

(ii) An overview of the nature of preambles

Chapter 3 briefly addressed the role of preambles as setting out a constitution's underlying aims. Preambles play an important role in legislation generally, being placed after the long title and before the enacting words and the substantive sections.[37] The objectives of the law and the process leading up to enactment are often recited in the preamble.[38] Preambles have an effect of

---

36 Anthony Regan "Constitutionalism, Legitimacy and the Judiciary" in RW James and I Fraser (eds) *Legal Issues in a Developing Society* (Faculty of Law, University of Papua New Guinea, Port Moresby, 1992) 12.

37 Constitution, sch 1.2.3; Interpretation Act, s 3.

38 Kent Roach "The Uses and Audiences of Preamble in Legislation" (2001) 47(1) McGill LJ 129. See also Anne Twomey "The Preamble and Indigenous Recognition" (2011) 15(2) AILR 4 at 7.

motivating compliance with the law, by pointing out the aspirations leading up to the enactment of the law.[39] In a way, constitutional preambles point citizens and the government to the state's founding principles and beyond a narrow consideration of the demarcated boundaries of the various entities constituting the state. This is true for Papua New Guinea; the NGDP and BSO are contained in the preamble of the Constitution and direct all persons to observe them.[40] Many constitutional preambles have an aspirational role rather than a legal one.[41] They set out states' historical realities, and are not intended to have a legal status. Something more than this is expected of the NGDP and BSO.

The preamble contains express statements about the Constitution's purpose, setting out very broadly the reasons why the Constitution was established, before it details the NGDP and BSO. Similar to the American Constitution, it uses the phrase "We the people …". Fundamental principles declared to be self-evident in Papua New Guinea society are expressed in the preamble: for example, cultural heritage, adopted Christian values, and community interdependence. In a way, the preamble outlines what was in existence prior to the Constitution, such that the Constitution was to "formally" recognise this prior social order. Certainly, the NGDP and BSO build on that theme.

(iii) Common law comparative experience

The Solomon Islands case of *Guadalcanal Provincial Assembly v Speaker of National Parliament* (High Court) determined the constitutionality of legislation that created a provincial government system.[42] The law in question, the Provincial Government Act 1996, was found to be inconsistent with the underlying principle of responsible and representative government expressed in the preamble of the Solomon Islands Constitution. The decision was overturned on appeal to the Court of Appeal. Justice Kapi's decision is instructive:[43]

---

39 Roach, above n 38.

40 Preamble of the Constitution, reproduced in Appendix One.

41 Sanford Levinson "Do Constitutions Have a point? 'Reflections on Parchment Barriers' and Preambles" 28(1) Soc Phil & Pol'y 150.

42 *Guadalcanal Provincial Assembly v Speaker of National Parliament* [1997] SBHC 5, HC-CC 309 of 1996, 26 February 1997; see also *Folotalu v Attorney-General* [2001] SBHC 149, HC-CC 234 of 2001, 19 October 2001.

43 *Minister for Provincial Government v Guadalcanal Provincial Assembly* [1997] SBCA 1, CA-CAC 003 of 1997, 11 July 1997 at 8.

> I would conclude from this that it was clearly intended by the framers of the Constitution that the purposes stated in the Preamble are to be defined and clearly set out in the enacting provisions of the Constitution. It would follow from this conclusion that one has to go to the enacting provisions to define the principle and the extent to which such a Preamble may apply. The extent to which a preamble may be used as aid to construction will be determined from reading the preamble with the whole of the enacting provisions of the Constitution.

The Canadian case of *In Re Provincial Judges Reference* placed heavy reliance on the preamble of the constitution in developing legal principles having the force of law.[44] This was a case about the constitutionality of legislation reducing the salaries of judges in federal and provincial courts on the basis of the common law principle of judicial independence. The relevant part of the Canadian Constitution Act 1867 preamble states:

> Whereas the Provinces of Canada, Nova Scotia, and New Brunswick have expressed their Desire to be federally united into One Dominion under the Crown of the United Kingdom of Great Britain and Ireland, with a Constitution similar in Principle to that of the United Kingdom … .

The Court relied on the provision "with a Constitution similar in Principle to that of the United Kingdom" to declare this involved adopting legal principles from the United Kingdom. Judicial independence was one such principle adopted from the United Kingdom and, as a result, it achieved the status of a constitutional norm in Canada. The court stated, "It is the means by which the underlying logic of the Act can be given the force of law".[45] On that basis the Canadian Supreme Court found the legislation unconstitutional as it offended the principle of judicial independence. It is suggested here that the CPC's view, and indeed the Constitution's clear position under ss 25 and 63, has always been that the substantive provisions of the Constitution were to give expression to the ideals contained in the NGDP and BSO. In Canada, the "gaps" were left to be filled by the court as there was no express statement in the preamble of the adoption of principles such as judicial independence. But

---

44 *Re Provincial Judges Reference* [1997] SCR 3.

45 Per Lamer CJ at [95].

for Papua New Guinea, its founding principles are expressed in its preamble via the NGDP and BSO.

Sections 25 and 63 of the Constitution direct the Papua New Guinea Constitution toward the Indian experience. It was the preamble to the Indian Constitution in *Kesavananda Bharati v State of Kerala* that resulted in the much publicised basic structure doctrine.[46] Under this doctrine, where certain values are enshrined in the Indian Constitution (Preamble, "Equality of status and of opportunity") substantive provisions of the Constitution promoting these values cannot be repealed or amended by Parliament (notwithstanding an established amendment process). It was argued in *Special Reference by Fly River Provincial Executive Council; Re Organic Law on Integrity of Political Parties and Candidates* that the Papua New Guinea Constitution has a basic structure which Parliament cannot amend, but the Supreme Court rejected this doctrine.[47] Underlying the Supreme Court's rejection was its view that the Papua New Guinea Constitution was home-grown or autochthonous and "foreign doctrines" had no application.[48] The Papua New Guinea Constitution was detailed and provided its own mechanisms to deal with issues of constitutionality.

It is true the Papua New Guinea Constitution is home-grown, and the Court did not need to rely on foreign precedents to support its conclusion. But the methodology in *Kesavanananda* is appropriate – using relevant principles in the preamble to elevate substantive provisions that realise these principles. It seems the *Fly River* Court was not properly guided on how the basic structure operated. The Court was not referred to the fundamental importance of the NGDP and BSO, supporting a common vision of a new society in Papua New Guinea that was home-grown, and not based on foreign ideology.[49] In that way the home-grown nature of the Papua New Guinea Constitution would have been kept intact, relying on the NGDP and BSO, to support a "basic structure doctrine".

---

46 *Kesavananda v State of Kerala* (1973) 4 SCC 255, (1973) AIR 146.

47 *Special Reference by Fly River Provincial Executive Council; Re Organic Law on Integrity of Political Parties and Candidates* [2010] PGSC 3, SC1057, 7 July 2010.

48 At [100].

49 Interestingly at [182] the Supreme Court referred to integral human development as the basis upon which political culture was to develop and not to be legislating through prohibiting political freedoms.

(iv) Constructive versus contextual role of preambles

There appears to be two common law positions on the role of preambles in statutory interpretation: constructive and contextual.[50] The first approach is to refer to the preamble only when there is an ambiguity in the provision of a statute.[51] In all issues that go before the court, the court will in the first instance refer to the substantive provisions of the law to determine the case. Only when it cannot do that, are preambles called upon for guidance to settle the ambiguity. This position was articulated by Griffith CJ in *Bowell v Goldsbrough, Mort & Co Ltd*:[52]

> ... where the words of a Statute are plain and clear, their meaning cannot be cut down by reference to the preamble. But, if the words are uncertain as applied to the subject matter, and bear more than one meaning, then you may, in a proper case, refer to the preamble to ascertain what was the occasion for the alteration of the law.

Gibbs CJ in a much later case, *Wacando v Commonwealth*, also adopted the constructive approach.[53]

In the second (contextual) approach, the preamble is referred to as part of the whole process of determining the ordinary meaning of enactments.[54] This approach calls for the whole legislation to be read, including the preamble, to arrive at a suitable interpretation. The preamble is read together with the rest of the legislation to provide the background to ascertain the correct meaning.

---

50 Anne Winckel "The Contextual Role of a Preamble in Statutory Interpretation" (1999) 23 (1) MULR 184.

51 *R v Pierce* (1814) 3 M & S 62, [1814] 105 ER 534 at 536; *Attorney-General v Prince Ernest Augustus of Hanover* [1957] AC 436 (HL) at 474.

52 *Bowtell v Goldsbrough, Mort & Co Ltd* (1906) 3 CLR 444 at 451; see also Gibbs CJ's decision in *Wacando v Commonwealth* [1981] HCA 60; (1981) 148 CLR 1 at 14–16.

53 *Wacando v Commonwealth* [1981] HCA 60; (1981) 148 CLR 1 at 15–16; see also DC Pearce and RS Geddes *Statutory Interpretation in Australia* (7th ed, LexisNexis Butterworths Australia, Chatswood, 2011) at 155 to 156.

54 Winckel, above n 50, at 188.

Interestingly, the contextual approach was also used in *Wacando v Commonwealth*, but by Mason J (Gibbs CJ's opposing view is noted above):[55]

> It has been said that where the enacting part of a statute is clear and unambiguous it cannot be cut down by the preamble. But this does not mean that the court cannot obtain assistance from the preamble in ascertaining the meaning of an operative provision. The particular section must be seen in its context; the statute must be read as a whole and recourse to the preamble may throw light on the statutory purpose and object … .

The contextual approach works well with the idea the NGDP and BSO are indirectly justiciable. It calls for the exercise of public power in a way that promotes the NGDP and BSO by looking at the background reasons for a law or decision.

A third, more direct approach, is to treat the preamble as directly justiciable. This approach is not normally used in common law jurisdictions but a 1971 decision of the French Constitutional Council is an example of this use of the preamble.[56] While this is an attractive option for effective implementation, the manner in which ss 25 and 63 are worded suggests the NGDP and BSO are indirectly justiciable. As such, the French approach would not be applicable.[57]

(v) The legal status of the use of preamble in Papua New Guinea

The Constitution has generally adopted the first (constructive) approach by stating that in the event of doubt the preamble may be referred to under sch 1.3(1) of the Constitution:

> Sch. 1.3(1). Form of the Constitutional Laws.
>
> (1) The Preamble to this Constitution (being the provisions that end immediately before the heading to Part I.) forms

---

[55] *Wacando v Commonwealth*, above n 53, at 333. See also the Solomon Islands cases of *Minister for Provincial Government v Guadalcanal Provincial Assembly*, above n 46, where the contextual approach was applied.

[56] *French Constitutional Council, decision no 71-44DC*, 16 July 1971, JO 7114, 18 July 1971, Recueil 29.

[57] Brian Brunton and Duncan Colquhoun-Kerr *The Annotated Constitution of Papua New Guinea* (University of Papua New Guinea Press, Port Moresby, 1984) at 69; also as discussed in chapter 4.

> part of this Constitution, but expresses general principles and therefore must be read subject to any other provision of this Constitution, though it may be used as an aid to interpretation in cases of doubt.

Two important matters come out of this provision. First, the preamble is to be read subject to other provisions of the Constitution, and second, it is to be used as an aid to interpretation in cases of doubt. The view that the preamble is only to be referred to in cases of doubt appears to have dominated judicial interpretation in Papua New Guinea.[58] This approach is not entirely correct because the NGDP and BSO have been conferred a different status by other provisions of the Constitution including ss 25 and 63.[59]

Sections 25 and 63 of the Constitution privilege the NGDP and BSO over other provisions of the preamble. It says that where a power can be exercised in a way that realises the NGDP and BSO, then it *should* be exercised that way. Failure to fulfil this duty is indirectly justiciable. The extent to which it is directly justiciable was seen in chapter 4. The contextual role of the preamble provides a more accurate account of the role of the NGDP and BSO in statutory interpretation under ss 25 and 63. The courts ought to assign a contextual role to the NGDP and BSO to fulfil the ss 25 and 63 mandate: when the NGDP and BSO are used to provide context, it will influence the manner in which the Constitution is interpreted and applied. The contextual approach shows the circumstances in which the provisions were enacted and the purpose they must achieve. The natural result of the contextual approach is, therefore, indirect justiciability.

In constitutional and statutory interpretation, the meaning which implements the NGDP and BSO is to be preferred. The use of the NGDP and BSO should not be limited to cases of doubt. The role ss 25 and 63 play in this regard was discussed in chapter 4.

Case law confirms the debate over whether the proper role of the preamble is only constructive or sets out the context of the whole legislative scheme is very much alive in Papua New Guinea. The two leading cases on the opposing views are *Independent Leadership Tribunal; Ex Parte Sasakila v The State*

[58] *Medaing on appeal,* above n 17.

[59] Other provisions of the Constitution include ss 23, 32, 38, 39, and sch 1.2.

(*Sasakila*)[60] for the contextual approach and *Premdas v Independent State of Papua New Guinea* (*Premdas*)[61] for the constructive approach.

Sasakila concerned a Member of Parliament, Moses Sasakila, who was referred by the Ombudsman Commission to the Public Prosecutor for prosecution before a Leadership Tribunal for misconduct in office. The referral centred on the Constitution and the Organic Law on the Duties and Responsibilities of Leadership (OLDRL). Mr Sasakila challenged the constitutionality of a particular provision of the OLDRL, and sought orders for his prosecution to be quashed. The Supreme Court comprising of Frost CJ, Saldanha and Kearney JJ upheld his challenge. Kearney J's approach to interpreting the constitutional issue was important for the way ss 25(3) and 63(3) of the Constitution were utilised:[62]

> The process of statutory interpretation is essentially intuitive and subjective, in the absence of rules consistently applied. The Act is a Constitutional Law and thus subject to the general principles of interpretation set out in Constitution ss. 10, 25 (3), 63 (3) and Basic Social Obligation (a), and 158 (2); and to the more specific canons in Constitution ss. 24, 109 (4) when read with 12, and Sch. 1.5. In my opinion these provisions amount to a direction to the Court that in carrying out its functions under Constitution s 18 (1) the words actually used in the Act do not have to be strictly adhered to but are to be construed with the assistance of the materials referred to in Constitution s. 24, so as best to attain what Parliament intended.

Kearney's J statement, while coming from a single judge, has been highlighted in legal commentary for its authority. Brian Brunton and Duncan Colquhoun-Kerr in their work,

The Annotated Constitution of Papua New Guinea, described this as the "judicial ingenuity approach", which can also be equated to the contextual approach.[63] They referred to the competing approach as the "case of doubt

---

60 *The State v Independent Leadership Tribunal; Ex Parte Sasakila* [1976] PNGLR 491, 5 November 1976 [*Sasakila*].

61 *Premdas v The State* [1979] PGSC 20, [1979] PNGLR 329, 1 September 1979 [*Premdas*].

62 *Sasakila*, above n 60, at 506.

63 Brunton and Colquhoun-Kerr, above n 57, at 5.

approach," or referred to here as the constructive approach.[64] In *Premdas* Wilson J said:[65]

> As there can be no doubt as to the interpretation of the provisions to which reference will be made, (i.e. this is not a "case of doubt"), I find it unnecessary (indeed I think it inappropriate) to use the preamble to the Constitution and, in particular, the national goals and directive principles "as an aid to interpretation" and, in any event, the preamble, although forming part of the Constitution, "must be read subject to any other provision" of the Constitution (see Sch. 1.3(1) of the Constitution).

According to this approach if the provisions of the Constitution itself are clear, it would be unnecessary to refer to the NGDP and BSO in the interpretation and application of the Constitution. But a careful reading of s 25(1) and s 25(3) and s 63(1) and s 63(3) suggests Kearney J's approach in *Sasakila* squares with the constitutional duty to implement the NGDP and BSO. Those provisions make the NGDP and BSO mandatory considerations in constitutional interpretation and application.

Brunton and Colquhoun-Kerr's 1984 work noted that the Supreme Court had not provided a definitive statement on the correct approach.[66] *SCR No 1 of 1990; Reference by the Executive Council of the Enga Provincial Government* (*Enga*) attempted to reconcile *Premdas* and *Sasakila*.[67] The difference remained because the Court ended up discussing s 24 only, and did not discuss the use of ss 25 and 63 and their role in elevating the NGDP and BSO beyond a restrictive constructive role. *Enga* held there was no discrepancy between these two different views:[68]

> We do not consider that there is any conflict between Wilson J on the one hand and Kearney J or Barnett J on the other. What Wilson J said is clear from his judgment and that is that

64 At 5.

65 *Premdas*, above n 61, at 375 per Wilson J.

66 Brunton and Colquhoun-Kerr, above n 57, at 5.

67 *Reference by the Executive Council of the Enga Provincial Government* [1990] PGSC 10, [1990] PNGLR 532, 28 December 1990 [*Enga*].

68 *Enga*, at 537 per Kidu CJ, Amet, Los and Brown JJ.

> some provisions do not require to be interpreted by referring to the Constitutional Planning Committee Report or any other material put before the Constituent Assembly. For instance, s 187a of the Constitution says "There shall be a system of Provincial Government for Papua New Guinea in accordance with this Part"; s 169(1) of the Constitution says "An office of Chief Justice of Papua New Guinea is hereby established" and s 103(1) says: "A member of the Parliament must not be less than 25 years of age." There is absolutely no reason to resort to the Constitutional Planning Committee Report, the Debates of the Constituent Assembly and other relevant documents to ascertain what these provisions means — they are clear and require no interpretation.

The difficulty with this statement is that if a provision of the Constitution is clear, such as the ones the Court refers to, s 169(1) and s 103(1), the matter would not be litigated. The question of whether the NGDP and BSO should be applied to the interpretation of these provisions would not arise, because it would not be a matter before the court. And even if it did come before the court, it would not be the central issue. For example, if a losing candidate was to dispute an election result on the basis that the winning candidate did not meet the required age to contest the election, the issue would be an evidentiary matter, and would not rely on the interpretation of s 103(1).[69]

The fact that many subsequent Supreme Court decisions do not refer to the NGDP and BSO suggests the Court's approach is only to refer to them in the case of doubt rather than to actively promote them. It is difficult to implement the NGDP and BSO if they are going to be referred to only in the case of an ambiguity. A proactive role is suggested as this is consistent with ss 25 and 63, despite the fact the NGDP and BSO are part of the preamble.

(c) Non-implementation of s 24 of the Constitution

Much of the justification establishing the necessity for the NGDP and BSO is found in the CPC Report and in the records of the House of Assembly

---

[69] See for example *Aimo v Anisi* [2012] PGNC 182, N4870, 28 November 2012 where a losing candidate questioned the results on the basis the winning candidate was not 25 years old at the time of his election.

debates. These documents would help promote the implementation of the NGDP and BSO by providing supporting historical information on them.

Reference to parliamentary material helps the court understand the challenges the Parliament faced when enacting the law. Courts must decide the correct legal position after hearing opposing views. Referring to parliamentary materials does not determine the outcome of a case, but it would assist the court to arrive at its decision.

At the time the Constitution was adopted in 1975, the general rule in the United Kingdom was that references to parliamentary material as an aid to statutory construction was not permissible – this was the exclusionary rule.[70] The House of Lords did not depart from this position until 1993, in *Pepper (Inspector of Taxes) v Hart.*[71] Lord Wilkinson-Brown outlined three steps before parliamentary materials are referred to. First, if the legislation is ambiguous; second, if there is a series of statement by the Bill's promoter and they need to be referred to; and third, only if the statement relied on is clear.[72] But it is significant to note that there is some literature on the different approach to interpretation by the courts of a constitution as compared to an ordinary statute.[73]

In terms of statutes, Australia's position only changed in 1984[74] and in New Zealand, s 5(1) of the Interpretation Act 1999 allows reference to parliamentary material and other relevant external sources.[75] In Australia and in the United States, there is an interesting debate over the relative merits of focusing on the original intention of the framers of the Constitution versus textual intention (or referring to the text alone).[76] In both countries, the use of historical documents is not expressly provided for in the Constitution and has

---

70 *Davis v Johnson* [1978] UKHL 1, [1979] AC 264.

71 *Pepper (Inspector of Taxes) v Hart* [1992] UKHL 3, [1993] AC 59.

72 At 28.

73 Ahron Barak *Purposive Interpretation in Law* (transl S Bashi, Princeton University Press, 2005), relevant excerpts reprinted in Tony Blackshield and George William Australian Constitutional Law and Theory (5th ed, The Federation Press, Sydney, 2010) at 304.

74 Acts Interpretation Amendment Act 1984 (Australia, Cth) s 7.

75 *Awatere Huata v Prebble* [2005] 1 NZLR 289 (SC) at [51], per Elias CJ. See also Cathy Nijman "Ascertaining the Meaning of Legislation – A Question of Context" (2011) 38(3) VUWLR 629 at 643.

76 Anthony Mason "The Role of a Constitutional Court in a Federation: A Comparison of the Australian and the United States Experience" (1986) 16 FL Rev 1.

evolved from judicial activity. In Papua New Guinea, s 24 of the Constitution permits reference to parliamentary material:

> 24. Use of Certain Materials as Aids to Interpretation.
>
> (1) The official records of debates and of votes and proceedings—
>
> (a) in the pre-Independence House of Assembly on the report of the Constitutional Planning Committee; and
>
> (b) in the Constituent Assembly on the draft of this Constitution, together with that report and any other documents or papers tabled for the purposes of or in connection with those debates, may be used, so far as they are relevant, as aids to interpretation where any question relating to the interpretation or application of any provision of a Constitutional Law arises.

It was necessary for legislation and administrative processes to be put in place to implement s 24 of the Constitution. An Act of Parliament, the Constitutional Documents (Manner of Proof) Act 1976 was enacted to provide for the manner of proof of the official records of debates, and of votes and proceedings. This Act sets out the following documents as forming the documents referred to in s 24 of the Constitution:

- Draft (revised and renumbered) Constitution of the Independent State of Papua New Guinea presented to the Constituent Assembly on 29 May 1975;[77]
- Record of the debates of the pre-Independence House of Assembly on the report of the CPC;[78]
- Record of the debates of the Constituent Assembly on the draft Constitution;[79]
- Minutes of proceedings of the pre-independence House of Assembly bearing proceedings concerning the adoption of the CPC Report;[80]

---

77 Constitutional Documents (Manner of Proof) Act 1976, s 2.

78 Section 3(a).

79 Section 3(b).

80 Section 4(a).

- Minutes of Proceedings of the Constituent Assembly relating to the proceedings of the Constituent Assembly on the draft Constitution;[81]
- Final Report of the Constitutional Planning Committee 1974 Part 1;[82]
- Final Report of the Constitutional Planning Committee 1974 Part 2;[83]
- Government Paper Proposals on Constitutional Principles and Explanatory Notes;[84] and
- United Party Proposals for the Constitution Port Moresby 1974.[85]

It is apparent that apart from the CPC Report, there is no official record of the documents referred to in s 24 of the Constitution and the Constitutional Documents (Manner of Proof) Act. No particular government agency is responsible for securing these documents on account of their need in constitutional construction. Brunton and Colquhoun-Kerr observe that no official published record of the debates exist.[86] A review of the cases, especially Supreme Court decisions after independence, and major government policy initiatives, does not reveal much use of these historical documents, with the exception of the CPC Report. The lack of attention to these historical documents and parliamentary materials contributes to a lack of appreciation of the nature of the NGDP and BSO, and of the reasons why they were included in the Constitution.

Regan and Wolfers have suggested that even if these documents were available they would not be helpful because the Constitution is an amalgamation of different proposals and therefore no clear intention can be discerned from all these documents.[87] The practicality of the use of these documents should not, however, obviate the need to have them available.

---

81 Section 4(b).

82 Section 5(a).

83 Section 5(b).

84 Section 6.

85 Section 7.

86 Brunton and Colquhoun-Kerr, above no 57, at vi.

87 AJ Regan and EP Wolfers "Aids to Interpretation of the Constitution – Some Preliminary Thoughts" (1986) 14 Melanesian LJ 153 at 161.

Even the CPC Report, which is a little more accessible than the House of Assembly debates, is contested. The sharp divide was considered together with ss 25 and 63 of the Constitution in *Sasakila*[88] and *Premdas*[89] discussed above. What is important about Kearny J's statement in *Sasakila* is that when s 24 is considered together with ss 10, 25, 63, 109(4), 158(2) and sch 1.5 of the Constitution, it amounts to a direction to the Court to always search for Parliament's intention. But in *Premdas* Wilson J focused on s 24 only:[90]

> As, on the authorities and having regard to the Constitution itself, there can be no doubt as to the interpretation or application of any of the provisions of the Constitution to which reference will be made, I find it unnecessary (indeed I think it inappropriate) to use the final report of the pre-Independence Constitutional Planning Committee dated 13th August 1974, and presented to the pre-Independence House of Assembly on 16th August 1974, as 'aid to interpretation'.

Obviously Wilson J favoured a more restricted and literal approach to interpreting the Constitution but he seemed to be referring only to the provisions at issue in that case, not to the general interpretation of the Constitution. Using his approach, implementation of the NGDP and BSO would not be engaged in the same way it would if Kearney J's approach was followed.

In *Enga Provincial Government*, reference to the CPC Report was considered appropriate only in cases of doubt.[91] In contrast to *Enga*, which envisaged a less prominent role for the CPC Report as an aid to interpretation, the Court in *Sasakila* required reference to the CPC Report to consider its relevance.[92]

It is accepted that parliamentary materials are used on a case by case basis. The "in case of doubt" approach for the role of the preamble in some common law jurisdictions would be very useful for allowing the CPC Report to be used to facilitate the implementation of the NGDP and BSO. But that is a different proposition altogether from not having these materials available.

---

88 *Sasakila*, above n 60.

89 The CPC Report is available electronically at <www.paclii.org>.

90 *Premdas*, above n 61, at 376; also cited in Brunton and Colquhoun-Kerr, above no 57, at 67.

91 *Enga*, above n 67.

92 Sasakila, above n 60, at 506.

3. *Cumulative effect of legal impediments*

The cumulative effect of the various legal reasons for non-implementation has resulted in an ad hoc approach to addressing the duty to implement the NGDP and BSO. The point underlying ss 25 and 63 of the Constitution, which governmental bodies have misunderstood, is that each arm of government has authority to implement the NGDP and BSO. Failure on the part of one arm has an effect on the other. Significantly, because the courts and the Ombudsman Commission have not held the other arms to account for the non-implementation, the legislature and the executive are left to largely ignore the NGDP and BSO.

Indirect justiciability under ss 25 and 63 of the Constitution mediates the non-justiciable/justiciable divide. Such an approach would help each arm of government to see themselves as being interconnected with each other. It is the failure of governmental bodies to undertake this dual role of indirect justiciability and the interconnectedness approach that has resulted in the non-implementation of the NGDP and BSO. The nature of the latter view (the "interconnectedness approach") is outlined in chapter 6. Adopting this approach to the implementation of the NGDP and BSO under the duties in ss 25 and 63 will support greater coordination between the legislature, the executive, the judiciary and the Ombudsman Commission. The proposal is outlined in more detail in chapters 7, 8, 9 and 10 respectively. Again, the best legal means of ensuring an "interconnected approach" is "indirect justiciability".[93]

IV. Conclusion

The main focus in this chapter was to highlight the issue of non-implementation of the NGDP and BSO, and the legal impediments to implementation of the NGDP and BSO. Non-implementation was identified through the performance of the legislature, the courts, the executive, and the Ombudsman Commission. There are three principal legal impediments to implementation of the NGDP and BSO. First, the lack of recognition of the indirect justiciability of the NGDP and BSO. Second, the difference in opinion on the role of preambles in statutes generally and in the Constitution more specifically.

---

[93] Brunton and Colquhoun-Kerr, above n 57, at 69.

The courts appear to favour a constructive role for the preamble over a contextual one. However, the provisions of the Constitution on implementation of the NGDP and BSO respectively, particularly ss 25(3) and 63(3), require a contextual role for the preambles. Third is the non-implementation of s 24 of the Constitution. Non-accessibility of the official records of the House of Assembly debates (apart from the CPC Report) has resulted in a gap in the historical record of the role of the NGDP and BSO in Papua New Guinea's legal, political and social development. This has led to the absence of a coordinated approach by the various arms of government to the implementation of the NGDP and BSO.

CHAPTER SIX

IMPLEMENTATION FRAMEWORK AND THE INTERCONNECTEDNESS APPROACH

I. Introduction

The main objective of this chapter is to present a framework for the implementation of the NGDP and BSO, within the doctrine of separation of powers, which ensures the proposals for the legislature, the executive, the courts, and the Ombudsman Commission (to be presented in chapters 7, 8, 9 and 10 respectively) does not see the different arms of government encroaching on one another's functions. The separation of powers, as a stand-alone principle of government in most Western liberal democracies, often assumes a neutral position to the executive's policy objectives, which are likely to be influenced by where a government sits on the left-right political spectrum. In Papua New Guinea, all arms of government have a constitutional duty to implement the NGDP and BSO (which have social-democratic aims), which may require some adjustment of the principle of separation of powers.

The organising principle in which implementation is to take place is the "interconnectedness approach". The interconnectedness approach is an application of the separation of powers to Papua New Guinea's constitutional context to ensure effective and efficient implementation of the NGDP and BSO by the government. According to ss 25 and 63, the legislative, executive, judicial and administrative powers of government are required to be exercised in a manner that fulfils the NGDP and BSO.

The interconnectedness approach is not a constitutional norm as such, but it is a means of ensuring the practical and effective application of the separation of powers in the Papua New Guinea constitutional scheme to achieve the constitutional objectives of fulfilling the NGDP and BSO. The interconnectedness approach helps the different arms of government mediate both the non-justiciable and justiciable aspects of the NGDP and BSO. This approach therefore attempts to promote a more comprehensive methodology of implementation. It works well with the indirectly justiciable nature of the NGDP and BSO.

This chapter has four parts. Part I is this introduction. Part II outlines the principle of separation of powers. Part III presents the separation of powers as it applies in Papua New Guinea, detailing the interconnectedness approach. Part IV concludes the chapter.

II. Separation of Powers

A. Introduction

The separation of powers is one of the main principles underlying the constitution of many countries in the world today. Power is conferred on three separate arms of government: the legislature, the executive and the judiciary. The main objective of the principle of separation of powers is to prevent the abuse of power, which can occur when power is lodged in only one person or arm of government. This part of the chapter briefly looks at the origins of this principle and its application in some countries today. It will set the basis for assessing what form of separation of powers Papua New Guinea applies in its constitutional system.

B. Origins of Separation of Powers

The separation of powers as a theory of politics and government gained influence through the French political theorist Montesquieu.[1] Before him, other commentators of note who espoused similar ideas included Aristotle and Locke.[2] Montesquieu held the view that there must be a check on power to ensure political liberty. This would come about by recognising and keeping separate three types of government power: legislative, executive and judicial. Montesquieu stated:[3]

---

1 Baron de Montesquieu *The Spirit of the Laws* (transl Thomas Nugent, Hafner Press, 1949) at 150.

2 Blackshield and Williams, Australian Constitutional Law and Theory (5th ed, The Federation Press, Sydney, 2010) at 8.

3 Baron de Montesquieu, above n 1, at 150.

> There would be an end of everything, were the same man or body, whether of the nobles or of the people, to exercise those three powers, that of enacting laws, that of executing the public resolutions, and of trying the causes of the individuals.

Montesquieu's work led to the modern classification of powers. Montesquieu formulated his theory based on his observation of the English political system. A common criticism of Montesquieu is that there was no actual separation of powers in England in the sense of each arm of government being completely independent from each other.[4] In England, the executive was drawn from the legislature and was accountable to the legislature. Members of the executive, the Prime Minister and ministers, were also members of the House of Commons. Members of the English upper house, the House of Lords, acted as both law makers and sat in court as judges in the final court of appeal.[5] Nevertheless the idea has taken root and influenced democratic government systems the world over.

C. Separation of Powers

In the scheme of separation of powers, the legislature has the power to make, alter, or repeal laws;[6] the executive function is the carrying out of laws;[7] and the judicial function consists of the interpretation of laws and their application by rule or discretion to the facts of a particular case.[8] One arm of government should not assume the role of another arm of government.

The separation of powers has operated in practice by following four assertions.[9] First, the existence of three agencies: the legislature, the

---

[4] Laurence Claus "Montesquieu's Mistakes and the True Meaning of Separation" (2005) 25(3) OJLS 419.

[5] The Supreme Court reforms have since separated the judicial function of the House of Lords under the Constitutional Reform Act 2005 (UK), creating the Supreme Court as the highest court of appeal.

[6] Owen Hood Philips and Paul Jackson *Constitutional and Administrative Law* (7th ed, Sweet and Maxwell, London, 1987) at 11.

[7] At 12.

[8] Philips and Jackson, above n 6, at 12.

[9] Michael A Ntumy *Administrative Law of Papua New Guinea* (2nd ed, CBS Publishers & Distributors, New Delhi, 2002) 46.

executive and the judiciary.[10] Second, the membership of each branch of government would be composed separately.[11] Third, there would be no overlapping membership from one branch with another. Fourth, if each arm of government was to operate in its own sphere of influence, it would act as a check on the other arm of government.[12] Systems of government have tried in varying degrees to follow these four principles of the separation of powers in their constitutional arrangements.

Notwithstanding the above classification, a complete separation of powers is not possible in practice, since it would bring government to a standstill.[13] For example, in many countries, the executive has been delegated law-making power.[14] This is because the legislature does not have the time or the expertise to deal with detailed technical issues. Even courts when interpreting the law, are often accused of usurping Parliament's power to make laws. Therefore the actual distinction of powers, when applied to various national constitutions, becomes blurred.[15] What is important is the prevention of tyranny by the government.[16]

D. Comparative Experiences of Application of Separation of Powers

Two countries that have incorporated the separation of powers are the United States and Australia. Like Papua New Guinea, both countries have a written constitution. Australia's government system has historical links to the Westminster system as does Papua New Guinea.

What is witnessed in Australia and the United States are certain core functions granted to each arm of government and cooperation in certain areas to enable the smooth functioning of government operations. For example, in the United States Supreme Court Justices are appointed by the President, but appointments must be ratified by the legislature in the form of the Senate. Another observation made about government in the United States

---

10 At 46.

11 At 46.

12 At 46.

13 Blackshield and Williams, above n 2, at 10.

14 *Victorian Stevedoring and General Contracting Co Pty Ltd v Dignan* (1931) 46 CLR 73 [*Dignan's Case*].

15 Blackshield and Williams, above n 2, at 9.

16 Blackshield and Williams, above n 2, at 10.

is the development of an additional limb of government, since classified as the administrative branch. The extraordinary growth of government regulation, such as the Commerce Commission, which has quasi-judicial and law-making powers, has attracted this further classification of a fourth branch.[17]

In Australia, ministers are appointed by the Crown with the support of the lower house; the minister must be a Member of Parliament. An important control over Parliament in Australia is the courts' ability to invalidate laws on constitutional grounds in the context of federal and state relations. There is no strict separation. Some American states and the French Constitution 1891 have tried to follow strict separation of powers but failed.[18] Separation of powers is a theory and must give way to the realities of government.[19]

III. Separation of Powers in Papua New Guinea and the Interconnectedness Approach

A. Introduction

The separation of powers has been adopted in Papua New Guinea with many modifications, and even a judicial pronouncement in *SCR No 1 of 1978; Re Ombudsman Commission Investigations of the Public Solicitor* (*Public Solicitor*) going so far as to suggest it has no application in Papua New Guinea.[20] The Constitutional Planning Committee (CPC) addressed the principle of separation of powers by devoting one chapter for the legislature,[21]

---

17 President's Committee on Administrative Management *Administrative Management in the Government of the United States* (United States Government Printing Office, 1937) at 36.

18 For example the Massachusetts Constitution of 1780, Part the First, art XXX: "In the government of this Commonwealth, the legislative department shall never exercise the executive and judicial powers or either of them: The executive shall never exercise the legislative and judicial powers or either of them: The judicial shall never exercise the legislative and executive powers, or either of them: to the end it may be a government of laws and not of men.": cited from The University of Chicago Press <http://press-pubs.uchicago.edu>.

19 Gerard Carney, "Separation of Powers in the Westminster System" (1994) 8(2) Legis Stud 59 at 60.

20 See Pritchard J's decision in *SCR No 1 of 1978; Re Ombudsman Commission Investigations of the Public Solicitor* [1978] PGSC 7, [1978] PNGLR 345, 6 October 1978 [*Public Solicitor*].

21 Constitutional Planning Committee *Final Report of the Constitutional Planning Committee, Part One* (Government Printer, Port Moresby, 1974) [CPC Report] at 6/1 "chapter 6 'The Legislature'".

the judiciary[22] and the executive.[23] It did not discuss the doctrine as a separate concept.

The CPC assumed the general Western liberal description of the separation of powers,[24] and went on to recommend additional independent constitutional institutions, providing for a very complex power sharing scheme. It is interesting to see how the Constitution reflects the CPC recommendations, and also how the CPC wanted the NGDP and BSO to be implemented by the national government, within certain parameters. What is evident is the supremacy of the Constitution, rather than three arms of government having separate and equal powers.

In Papua New Guinea, two main concerns influenced the CPC's version of the separation of powers. First, the prevention of abuse of power; and second, developing a national agenda for development. Unlike the United States, which was primarily concerned with preventing the abuse of government power (following the Lockean political philosophy of limited government), Papua New Guinea added a further task of fulfilling a national philosophy. The first concern—control of public power—is evident in the establishment of constitutional institutions such as the Ombudsman Commission, which provides an additional mechanism to protect the people from abuse of power.

The Ombudsman Commission is an independent institution, not subject to the direction and control of the other arms of government. Its roles and functions will be discussed in chapter 10, especially as it pertains to the implementation of the NGDP and BSO.

The CPC's second concern related to the implementation of a national philosophy. This is the requirement to implement the NGDP and BSO. The NGDP and BSO are the fulcrum upon which public power is exercised and therefore require close attention to how the separation of powers becomes a means to this end. The cooperation of all arms of government and constitutional offices such as the Ombudsman Commission is necessary to address the CPC's concerns, and ensure implementation of the NGDP and BSO.

---

22 CPC Report, at 7/1 "chapter 7 'The Executive'".

23 CPC Report, at 8/1 "chapter 8, 'The Administration of Justice'".

24 See for example the CPC's statement on the courts as constituting the third pillar of the government of a country: see CPC Report at 8/1 [2].

B. Constitutional Recognition of Separation of Powers

The separation of powers is expressly recognised under Part VI of the Constitution:

> 99. Structure of Government.
>
> (1) *Subject to and in accordance with this Constitution, the power, authority and jurisdiction of the People shall be exercised by the National Government* [emphasis added].
>
> (2) The National Government consists of three principal arms, namely:–
>
> (a) the National Parliament, which is an elective legislature with, subject to the Constitutional Laws, unlimited powers of law-making; and
>
> (b) the National Executive; and
>
> (c) the National Judicial System, consisting of a Supreme Court of Justice and a National Court of Justice, of unlimited jurisdiction, and other courts.
>
> (3) *In principle, the respective powers and functions of the three arms shall be kept separate from each other* [emphasis added].
>
> (4) Subsection (2) is descriptive only and is non-justiciable.

Section 99(1) makes a clear connection between the people (identified in the preamble as the source of all government power) and who is to exercise their power – the National Government. The National Government is composed of the traditional three arms of government (Constitution, s 99(2)). Importantly, these three arms of government must exercise their powers "Subject to and in accordance with ..." the Constitution. In *Public Solicitor* Prentice CJ observed:[25]

> ... one refers to s 99 of the Constitution which asserts the 'power, authority and jurisdiction' of the people is to be exercised by the National Government.' But this is 'subject to and in accordance with the Constitution'.

---

[25] *Public Solicitor*, above n 20, at 350 per Prentice CJ.

This immediately brings to attention ss 25 and 63 of the Constitution. When the National Government exercises the people's power, it is required to comply with ss 25 and 63. There is express reference to the three arms of government in ss 25(3) and 63(3). In addition, "administrative power" is identified. In fact, ss 25(3) and 63(3) place a duty that requires legislative, judicial, executive and administrative power to be exercised in a manner that fulfils the NGDP and BSO. There is, therefore, a strong link between s 99 and ss 25 and 63 of the Constitution.

Section 99(3) of the Constitution then states that the legislature, the executive and the judiciary must exercise their powers and functions separately from each other. However, the separateness operates only "in principle". "In principle ..." has a specific legal meaning:

> Sch. 1.6. Statements of general principle.
>
> Where a provision of a Constitutional Law is expressed to state a proposition "in principle", then—
>
> (a) an act (including a legislative, executive or judicial act) that is inconsistent with the proposition is not, by reason of that inconsistency alone, invalid or ineffectual; but
>
> (b) if the act is reasonably capable of being understood or given effect to in such a way as not to be inconsistent with the proposition it shall be so given effect to.

In the first instance, sch 1.6(b) imposes a duty to observe the relevant constitutional provision (in this case s 99(3)), unless it is unreasonable to do so.[26] The language of sch 1.6(b) is reminiscent of ss 25(3) and 63(3). In the latter are the words, "... without failing to give effect to the intention of the ... in such as a way as to give effect to ...". Again, it calls for close attention to the NGDP and BSO and the three branches of government.

In addition to ss 99, a number of other provisions in the Constitution invoke the separation of powers: s 100 on legislative power, s 138 on executive

26 Other provisions in the Constitution that use the term "In principle" are s 118(1) and (4) on the committee system, s 119(2) on the chairman of the parliamentary committee, s 124(1) on parliament meetings, and s 255 on consultation.

power, and s 158 on the judiciary.[27] Each of these provisions will be examined in chapters 7, 8 and 9 to determine how they can be utilised to implement the NGDP and BSO.

The table below summarises the operation of separation of powers in Papua New Guinea.

Table on Application of Separation of Powers in Papua New Guinea

Institution	Power	Personnel	Control
National Parliament	Power to make laws	Members of Parliament elected to National Parliament	Breach of Leadership Code or expulsion from the Parliament. Judicial review
National Executive	Executive power	Ministers appointed by the Prime Minister. Must be members of the Parliament	Breach of Leadership Code or expulsion from the Parliament. Parliamentary and judicial review
The Courts	Judicial Power	Chief Justice appointed by the Executive, but other judges, including Deputy Chief Justice appointed by the Judicial and Legal Services Commission	Judges removed for breach of Leadership Code

27 Michael A Ntumy "Separation of Powers" in Anthony J Regan, Owen Jessep and Eric L Kwa (eds) *Twenty Years of the Papua New Guinea Constitution* (Lawbook Co, Sydney, 2001) 183 at 183.

Constitutional offices, such as Ombudsman Commission, Public Solicitor, Public Prosecutor and Electoral Commission	Various functions established under the Constitution	Appointment body established under the Constitution, for example the Ombudsmen are appointed by the Ombudsman Appointments Committee, which consists of the Prime Minister, Opposition Leader, a Member of Parliament, Chief Justice and the Chairman of the Public Service Commission	Constitutional office holders removed for breach of the Leadership Code. Judicial review

The table includes an additional group of public offices – constitutional offices – as they operate independently from the traditional three arms of government. This creates what has been argued to be a fourth branch of government. In *Public Solicitor*, Prentice CJ stated:[28]

> Insofar as such bodies are created independent of direction and control, they would seem to be exercising the power of the people given to them as a direct grant by the Constitution and Organic Laws and their exercise of powers could not I think be said to be an exercise of power "by the National Government" in such a sense as would by itself constitute any of them "an arm" of the National Government, or department or agency or instrumentality thereof within the meaning of s. 219 and Sch. 1.2 of the Constitution.

To reiterate a previous point: under s 99 of the Constitution, the National Government is composed of the three arms of government. So, Prentice CJ is saying that constitutional offices are outside of the traditional division of powers because they operate independently from the other arms of

[28] *Public Solicitor*, above n 20, at 350 per Prentice CJ.

government. The Ombudsman Commission has been identified from this category of constitutional offices to support the three branches of government to implement the NGDP and BSO. The Ombudsman Commission was the obvious choice from the list of constitutional offices because of its significant constitutional latitude (discussed in chapter 10) to implement the NGDP and BSO. The next part of this chapter discusses how the courts have tried to apply the principle of separation of powers to specific political and legal issues that have arisen in Papua New Guinea.

C. Practical Application of the Principle of Separation of Powers

It is important to observe the ways in which the courts have tried to apply the principle of separation of powers. The cases reflect two main approaches: a general application of the principle of separation of powers; and a more complex approach consistent with the structure of Papua New Guinea's constitutional system.

Peter v South Pacific Brewery Limited presented a general application of the principle.[29] What was in contention was s 131 of the District Court Act 1963, which allowed the District Court to hear cases in the absence of the accused for certain types of minor offences. The Court was asked to decide whether s 131 was inconsistent with the accused's right to be present in his or her trial (Constitution, s 37(5)).

The controversy over the application of separation of powers arose from Deputy Chief Justice Prentice's dissenting judgment. He not only found s 131 unconstitutional, but went further to hold that taking into account ss 25 and 32 of the Constitution and the NGDP, the courts were permitted to add words to the provision of the law, to reflect Parliament's intention as well as to implement the NGDP. His Honour said this may be undesirable in other more established constitutions, but was permissible in Papua New Guinea. The majority disagreed with Prentice DCJ on the basis that the separation of powers operated in Papua New Guinea, and the Court could only find a law unconstitutional and could not add words to the legislation, which was the province of the legislature.

---

29 *Peter v South Pacific Brewery Ltd* [1976] PGSC 28, SC109, [1976] PNGLR 345, 29 November 1976.

In *Public Prosecutor v Rooney* (No 2), the Opposition Leader Iambakey Okuk, instituted contempt proceedings against Nahau Rooney, Minister for Justice, for writing to the Chief Justice criticising him for a court decision.[30] The Court had issued an injunction preventing the deportation of a foreign national. Rooney was unhappy with the court interference over the exercise of executive power and expressed her disappointment in correspondence to the Chief Justice. Okuk cited the principle of separation of powers in his case for contempt against Rooney. However, the Court did not think this was an infringement of the separation of powers, especially of judicial independence as protected by s 157 of the Constitution. The correspondence was instead found to be contempt on the basis of scandalising the court. Subsequently, the Minister was sentenced to eight months in jail.[31] The separation of powers was the key principle behind the initiation of the case.

Another case which looked at the separation of powers generally was *SCR No 1A of 1981; Re Motor Traffic Act*.[32] This was a reference by the Public Solicitor pursuant to s 19 of the Constitution to determine the constitutional validity of certain amendments to s 19AB(2)(e)(ii) of the Motor Traffic Act 1950, s 138A(1)(b) of the District Courts Act 1963, and s 38A(1)(c) of the Local Courts Act 1963. The effect of these amendments was that if a person was fined for a traffic offence, and did not pay the fine and failed to appear in court (after service of the summons), the person would be presumed to be guilty of the offence. The Court found the amendments unconstitutional on the basis that the legislature had assumed the powers of the judiciary, and this offended the principle of separation of powers.

Public Solicitor expressed a contrary view contesting the application of the doctrine of separation of powers in Papua New Guinea.[33] But it was Pritchard J's minority decision that has spurred academic debate in Papua New Guinea. One result is the emergence of the view promoted by APW Deklin,[34] which

---

30 *Public Prosecutor v Rooney* (No 2) [1979] PGSC 23, [1979] PNGLR 448, 11 September 1979.

31 Soon after the sentence, the Prime Minister Michael Somare and his national executive council, using the executive prerogative of the power of mercy, released Rooney. This caused great controversy and a number of judges resigned.

32 *SCR No 1A of 1981; Re Motor Traffic Act* [1982] PNGLR 122.

33 *Public Solicitor*, above n 20.

34 APW Deklin "The Legal Control of the Executive in Papua New Guinea" in *Pacific Constitutions: Proceedings of the Canberra Law Workshop VI* Peter Sack (ed) (Law Department Research School of Social Science, ANU, 1982) at 173–187.

articulates an explanation of the separation of powers most likely to enable the efficient and practical implementation of the NGDP and BSO.

In *Public Solicitor*, the Court had to deal with the issue of whether the Public Solicitor was subject to the jurisdiction of the Ombudsman Commission.[35] The Constitution did not specifically identify the Public Solicitor as being subject to the Ombudsman Commission's jurisdiction. Instead, under s 219(1)(a)(ii), the jurisdiction of the Ombudsman Commission was defined as having application over all governmental bodies. The question was whether the Public Solicitor was a governmental body. Schedule 1.2(1) defines "governmental body" to include "an arm … of the National Government", and s 99(2) describes the "three principal arms" of the National Government as: (a) the National Parliament, (b) the National Executive, and (c) the National Judicial System. The majority held the Public Solicitor was not part of the National Government, which is limited to the traditional three arms of government, so the Public Solicitor fell outside the Ombudsman Commission's jurisdiction.

Pritchard J expressed a minority view. His Honour found the Public Solicitor was a governmental body within the jurisdiction of the Ombudsman Commission. He reasoned the separation of powers did not operate in Papua New Guinea. According to Pritchard J, the Public Solicitor was a "separate arm of the National Government not an instrumentality responsible or subservient to any one of the principal arms". His Honour went on to reject the traditional view of separation of powers by stating:[36]

> I say here and now, there is no such tradition [i.e. 'three traditional functions of government'] in Papua New Guinea. Except to the extent that the principles and rules of common law and equity in England are adopted under Schedule 2.2 of our Constitution, in Papua New Guinea we do not call on traditions of government from anywhere in the World at all; we look to our constitutional laws and them alone. The Constitution and the Organic Laws are the Supreme Law of Papua New Guinea and their provisions are self-executing to the fullest extent their respective natures and subject matters permit (Constitution, s 11).

---

35 *Public Solicitor*, above n 20.

36 *Public Solicitor*, above n 20, at 377 per Pritchard J.

It is unclear whether Pritchard J rejected the doctrine outright. It is more likely his Honour simply preferred the view there were more than three branches of government. On this latter view, it is also worth pointing out that Prentice CJ and Pritchard J, although reaching different conclusions, were both of the view the Constitution created an additional arm of government. When one speaks of the composition of the National Government, the composite institutions fell outside of the traditional tripartite division of power and could be considered a fourth arm of government. In Prentice CJ's view, their power is derived directly from the Constitution.[37] This was to be differentiated from other statutory bodies created by the Parliament through ordinary statute and subject to executive or parliamentary control.

Deklin, relying on Pritchard J's decision, has expounded a view of the separation of powers within Papua New Guinea's constitutional system that lays an appropriate groundwork for the implementation of the NGDP and BSO.[38] The next part presents the "interconnectedness approach". It differs to some extent from Deklin's view, and adopts a rationale similar to that of the CPC.

D. Interconnectedness Approach

This part will firstly outline Deklin's view, the main criticism of his view, and finally present the interconnectedness approach. The terminology of "interconnectedness" was inspired by Narokobi who stated that the various arms of government should work closely to ensure Papua New Guinea meets its development objectives. Narokobi preferred the term "interdependent power and mutual self-restraint".[39] Deklin provides a good starting-point to develop this idea.

1. Deklin's view

Deklin's main objective was to understand the nature of the constitutional control on the exercise of executive power in Papua New Guinea. This required him to examine the principle of the separation of powers, as it was the traditional mechanism used to control executive power. Deklin took the view

---

[37] Per Prentice CJ at 350.

[38] Deklin, above n 34.

[39] Bernard Narokobi *Law and Custom in Melanesia* (Institute of Pacific Studies of the University of South Pacific and Melanesian Institute for Pastoral and Socio-Economic Service, Goroka, 1996) at 119.

that the separation of powers did not operate in Papua New Guinea; instead he took a "composite approach". This was a system of multiple institutions with constitutional power to control the exercise of public power. The table above provides an indication of this. One of the main reasons Deklin took this view was the existence of the NGDP and BSO. There had to be a system in place to ensure the implementation of the NGDP and BSO. Section 99 of the Constitution was important to Deklin's view. As discussed above, where the Constitution states a provision is "in principle", non-compliance does not trigger possible legal enforcement. According to Deklin, the fact s 99(3) says the independence of the three branches of government was in principle only, means that the doctrine of the separation of powers had been modified in Papua New Guinea. There would be no legal consequences if one branch of government intruded into the work of another.

Two statements from the CPC played a significant role in Deklin's view. The first arose from the relationship between the legislature and the executive. The CPC envisaged a participatory democracy with a maximum emphasis on consultation and consensus.[40] The legislature would have a central role and should not be a rubber stamp for the executive.[41] Rather, the legislature was to be the executive's "full and constructive partner". Cooperation underscored the relationship between the legislature and the executive.[42] This signalled to Deklin that the traditional separation of powers was not intended for Papua New Guinea.

Although the CPC was mindful of the importance of judicial independence to the effective function of the rule of law, in terms of the courts, the importance of taking a slightly more collaborative approach influenced the CPC's recommendations for the judiciary:[43]

> In carrying out their judicial role, judges and magistrates must take full account of the goals of the society in which they live; they must be attuned to the wishes of that society and to that extent must be politically conscious (although not party politically conscious). In Chapter 2, "National Goals and Directive Principles", we have spelt out what we believe to be

---

40 CPC Report, above n 21, at 6/1 [1].

41 At 6/1 [1].

42 At 6/1 [1].

43 At 8/1 [6].

> the goals of Papua New Guinea and we have recommended that our judges uphold the Constitution and interpret the laws made under it in the spirit of those goals and principles.

The courts also have an important role to implement the NGDP and BSO, and appear to be performing an executive role, but this is sanctioned by the Constitution. Again, for Deklin, a traditional approach to separation of powers would not allow the courts to perform this role intended by the CPC. This is because the courts' function is to interpret the law and not to make policy decisions, which is the responsibility of the other branches of government.

Deklin then discussed the functions of the Ombudsman Commission, again as an institution separate from the traditional three arms of government, but as one involved in the control of the exercise of public power, to prevent abuse. As an independent institution the Ombudsman Commission has a duty to implement the NGDP and BSO under ss 23(4) and 63(4) of the Constitution. Deklin concluded Papua New Guinea had a "composite approach", which essentially was a complex power sharing scheme.

Another supporting observation from the CPC, which lends support to Deklin's thesis, was on the Leadership Code, which the Ombudsman Commission administers under the Constitution. The CPC stated:[44]

> Experience in many countries has shown that constitutional provisions and declarations have little effect by themselves. We believe that perhaps the single most important factor in determining the direction of national development is the quality of leadership. If Papua New Guinea is to have any chance of implementing its national goals and directive principles, it must ensure that its leadership has a genuine commitment to these goals.

According to the CPC, maintaining a Leadership Code, independently administered, would help foster a commitment to the NGDP (and BSO by implication). This is demonstrated in ss 25(4) and 63(4) of the Constitution. Public leadership in Papua New Guinea is composed at its highest in the legislature, the executive and the judiciary. Members of Parliament, ministers, and judges are all subject to the Ombudsman Commission's jurisdiction.

---

44 CPC Report, above n 21, at 3/2 [13].

2. *Criticism of Deklin*

Michael Ntumy has criticised Deklin, stating that if the Constitution did not require separation of powers to control exercise of public power, but instead relied on a composite approach, it would have expressly referred to it in those terms.[45] Ntumy further adds to his criticism that Deklin was proposing a view that was not readily identifiable from the text of the Constitution – an "amorphous monstrosity".[46] In Ntumy's view, there was in place a system of separation of powers, but its precise nature had not been defined by the courts. He relied on *Peter v South Pacific Brewery Limited*, which applied the principle of separation of powers, and then *Public Solicitor*, which took a different view. Ntumy concludes these approaches need to be reconciled by the courts in the future. The issue was not that Papua New Guinea did not have separation of powers, but rather the courts had not clearly defined its application.

In assessing the criticism of Ntumy, one can agree it makes practical sense. However, the criticism does not take into account one of the factors underlying Deklin's view, which was the implementation of the NGDP and BSO. Section 99 is made subject to the Constitution, and this requires compliance with ss 25 and 63. These provisions place a duty on the judiciary, the legislature, and the executive to implement the NGDP and BSO. In addition, there is the duty on the Ombudsman Commission in ss 25(4) and 63(4). All this means that while it is important to observe the separation of powers to prevent abuse, a balance must be struck to ensure each arm of government cooperates with the other arms of government to ensure implementation of the NGDP and BSO. But this is to be done within their specific sphere of influence. Implementation must, therefore, take place in a way that connects the different functions of government. This is the basic premise of the parameters that will inform the proposals presented in chapters 7 to 10.

3. *Interconnectedness approach*

According to Narokobi, the theory of the separation of powers in Papua New Guinea should be abandoned.[47] Narokobi's main objective is to work

---

45 Ntumy, above n 27.

46 Ntumy, above n 27, at 193.

47 Narokobi, above n 39, at 119.

towards reforming the law.[48] Narokobi recommended a constitutional arrangement enabling interdependent power and mutual self-restraint.[49] His recommendation was premised on the basis of exercising control to achieve predetermined goals of society.[50] But the separation of powers is a present day reality in Papua New Guinea's Constitution. However, what can be taken from Narokobi would be to consider ways in which the separation of powers in the Constitution can promote cooperation to implement the NGDP and BSO. To some extent Deklin accommodates implementation within the existing Constitution.

Whilst Deklin can be applauded for attempting to propose a view of the separation of powers that accounts for the NGDP and BSO, the fact that the Constitution expressly refers to the separation of powers and confers separate functions on the legislature, the judiciary, and the executive, means that one could not completely reject the separation of powers as Pritchard J did. But to accept Ntumy's criticism would mean that the NGDP and BSO are not given prominence. This is because the principle of non-justiciability is an effective tool of the separation of powers. That is, implementation of the NGDP and BSO should best be left to the legislative and executive arms of government without court interference. The better view would be to say that although there is a separation of powers, the Constitution creates a separate arm of government in constitutional offices and, equally significantly, all these institutions function to implement the NGDP and BSO within their sphere of influence. This naturally coincides with the indirect justiciability of the NGDP and BSO.

The idea of an interplay between the different arms of government has been highlighted as an advantage of non-justiciable directive principles in constitutions.[51] In countries without constitutional directive principles, a similar idea of constitutional dialogue has been promoted.[52] Constitutional dialogue usually takes place where courts determine the constitutionality of

---

48 At 199.

49 At 119.

50 At 199.

51 Jeffrey Usman "Non-justiciable Directive Principles: A Constitutional Design Defect" (2007) 15 Mich St J Int'l L 643 at 684.

52 Peter W Hogg and Allison A Bushel "The Charter Dialogue between Courts and Legislature (Or Perhaps The Charter Of Rights Isn't Such a Bad Thing after All)" (1997) 35 Osgoode Hall LJ 75.

legislation and Parliament replies by enacting legislation that responds to the courts' view on the law. The situation is different for Papua New Guinea, where a specific constitutional duty has been conferred on all arms of government to implement the NGDP and BSO. In a sense it is a conversation or dialogue with a specific terms of reference extending to all arms of government as well as constitutional institutions.

Deklin made a positive start by developing his view based on the NGDP and BSO. However, Deklin did not expand on how the idea of the legislature and executive being "full and constructive partners" would operate in practice, especially as it relates to the implementation of the NGDP and BSO. Deklin's view is extended by proposing the "interconnectedness approach". Fundamental to the interconnectedness approach is the requirement on each arm of government to pursue an active relationship to ensure the efficient and effective implementation of the NGDP and BSO. This is so no one arm of government is burdened with the sole responsibility of implementation, but operates cooperatively with the other arms of government to achieve the desired outcome. The best legal means of ensuring the interplay between the different arms of government is again indirect justiciability.

The main thrust of the interconnectedness approach is for each arm of government to work cooperatively. For example, Parliament can make laws which provide direction to the executive in policy formulation, and indicate to the judiciary how the NGDP and BSO can be prioritised in disputes before the court. Parliament will assist this process by mentioning explicitly in the preamble of the legislation or the objective provision of the law the particular NGDP and BSO it wants implemented. A law would be enacted to implement a particular NGDP and/or BSO. For example, in *Public Curator of Papua New Guinea v Public Trustee of New Zealand*, Prentice CJ interpreted the Wills, Probate and Administration Act in a way that promoted National Goal 2 on equality and participation.[53] There was no reference to this Goal in the legislation. Appendix Three identifies the relatively small number of laws that make explicit reference to the NGDP and/or BSO.

If Parliament had made reference to a particular NGDP and/or BSO, the court would not have as wide a discretion to choose for itself which NGDP

53 *Public Curator of Papua New Guinea v Public Trustee of New Zealand* [1976] PGNC 48, [1976] PNGLR 427, 28 September 1976.

and/or BSO to apply. The courts' mind would be directed to the NGDP and/or BSO due to their explicit reference. This leads to certainty and prominence of the NGDP and BSO. Many cases do not make reference to the NGDP and/or BSO, so a reminder from Parliament would prompt the courts to consider the NGDP and BSO. Similarly, when the government is formulating policy or carrying out laws, it would know which areas have priority based on the expressed intention of the law. It also signals to the Ombudsman Commission how it should engage the NGDP and BSO in the performance of its functions when it investigates misconduct by leaders or wrong conduct by governmental bodies.[54]

At the heart of the interconnected approach is the necessity for the legislature to assume leadership in the laws it enacts, so the executive, the courts, and the Ombudsman Commission are sufficiently guided in their functions. Whilst the absence of interconnectedness does not prevent other arms of government continuing implementing the NGDP and BSO within their present functions, its operation would ensure efficient and effective implementation.

Chapter 4 set out the limits of indirect justiciability as being subject to the Constitution. The Constitution at s 157 stipulates the independence of the judiciary. Therefore, the interconnected approach is not meant to impede on the independence of the judiciary. An independent judiciary is critical to ensuring that any failure to implement the NGDP and/or BSO by another limb of government is not left without adequate and independent supervision from the court. Without the independence of the judiciary, the supervision by the court will not be effective to ensure that each arm of government fulfils its mandate to implement the NGDP and BSO.

IV. Conclusion

When discussing the implementation of the NGDP and BSO by the traditional three arms of government and the Ombudsman Commission, it is important that each arm does so within its specific functions, and does not intrude into the spheres of influence of the other arms. That does not, however, preclude cooperation amongst the arms of government. There has to be a concept that will be able to mediate this. Such a view, based on the

54 The Ombudsman Commission is granted this power in the Constitution under ss 23(4) and 63(4) in terms of misconduct, and s 219(1)(vi) for wrongful conduct.

CPC Report and ss 99, 25 and 63 of the Constitution, is appropriately termed an "interconnectedness approach". It enables each arm of government to work cooperatively with one another in the implementation of the NGDP and BSO. The proposals for the practical application of this approach is explored in subsequent chapters.

CHAPTER SEVEN

THE NATIONAL PARLIAMENT

I. Introduction

The objective of this chapter is to present proposals for the practical and efficient implementation of the NGDP and BSO by Parliament. Parliament has a constitutional duty to implement the NGDP and BSO in the fulfilment of its specific function(s).[1] Parliament's main function is the power to make laws for the "peace, order and good government …" of Papua New Guinea.[2] This power is subject to the Constitution,[3] and it should be exercised to give effect to it.[4] Since the NGDP and BSO are constitutional law, implementing the NGDP and BSO gives effect to the Constitution.[5] Parliament has other functions, too, that will also be considered in this chapter.

This chapter has five parts. Part I is the introduction. Part II gives an overview of the two methods of implementation proposed for the Parliament. Part III presents the first proposal, direct implementation of the NGDP and BSO, and Part IV deals with the second proposal: indirect implementation of the NGDP and BSO. Part V is the conclusion.

II. Overview of the Two Methods of Implementation for the Parliament

A. Introduction

Holding Parliament to account for its performance under the Westminster system of government is traditionally done through elections and by public

---

1 Constitution, ss 25(3) and 63(3).

2 Section 109(1).

3 *Peter v South Pacific Brewery Ltd* [1976] PNGLR 537 at 542 per Frost CJ.

4 Constitution , s 109(2):

> In particular, Acts of the Parliament, not inconsistent with the Constitutional Laws, may provide for all matters that are necessary or convenient to be prescribed for carrying out and giving effect to this Constitution.

5 Constitution, sch 1.2.3.

scrutiny in the media. The CPC refers to the NGDP as the yardstick by which the public can evaluate the government's performance.[6] Although the CPC does not expressly mention the BSO in this regard, by implication the BSO is to be equally considered with the NGDP.[7] In this way, the NGDP and BSO are enforced by the people through elections. The focus, however, is on employing the existing mechanisms established under the Constitution to implement the NGDP and BSO. The implementation proposals under Parliament's various functions can be categorised into two general areas: direct and indirect. Direct implementation is provided for by ss 25(3) and 63(3) of the Constitution, and the authority for indirect implementation is found in ss 25(2) and 63(2).[8] The general difference is explained below.

B. Direct and Indirect Implementation

The manner in which Parliament enacts its laws will determine how the other arms of government, including the Ombudsman Commission, implement the NGDP and BSO.

It is therefore important to ensure Parliament performs its duty to enact legislation that promotes the NGDP and BSO. So, direct implementation refers to constitutional functions within which the court can compel Parliament to implement the NGDP and BSO when enacting laws. This is possible through the indirect justiciability of the NGDP and BSO under ss 25(3) and 63(3) of the Constitution. Sections 25(3) and 63(3) have been interpreted as rules of interpretation, but they go beyond that as chapter 4 demonstrated. It is direct in the sense the court is involved in ensuring legislation implements the NGDP and BSO.

Indirect implementation (not to be confused with indirect justiciability) is concerned with the various constitutional mechanisms Parliament can utilise to implement the NGDP and BSO; but there is no legal sanction. Be that as it may, what Parliament does under the indirect means of implementation can still impact on Parliament's attempts to implement the NGDP and BSO under ss 25(3) and 63(3) of the Constitution. Details of this interplay are

---

6 *Constitutional Planning Committee Final Report 1974* (Government Printer, Port Moresby, 1974) [CPC Report] at 2/1 [6].

7 CPC Report, at 5/1/15 [92].

8 Sections 25(3) and 63(3) of the Constitution establish indirect justiciability of the NGDP and BSO and was discussed in chapter 4.

considered further below. Again, indirect implementation is the fulfilment of the non-justiciable duty under ss 25(2) and 63(3) of the Constitution.

III. Direct Implementation

A. First Order Implementation and Second Order Implementation

In terms of direct implementation by Parliament, ss 25(3) and 63(3) provide a first order implementation and a second order implementation. First order implementation provides the platform for second order implementation to take place. Under first order implementation, the courts will consider whether Parliament has provided adequate opportunity in legislation for interpreters, implementers and enforcers of the law (courts, executive, and Ombudsman Commission respectively) to engage the NGDP and BSO. This is where the legislature has a pivotal role to direct the other arms of government.[9] To put it in another way, the executive, the courts, and the Ombudsman Commission have the primary role of interpreting and applying the laws which Parliament has enacted. Some of the practices Parliament has used, as discussed in chapter 5, include naming a particular National Goal in the long title, or the preamble of the legislation, or in the objects section of the law.[10] More direct reference in the substantive text of the legislation has been rare.[11] These are some examples of how Parliament can demonstrate that it has fulfilled its duty (in the first order sense) to implement the NGDP and BSO. But it could simply involve discussing the implications of the NGDP and BSO when enacting a Bill.

Second order implementation occurs when the legislation is being interpreted and implemented. The use of the NGDP and BSO as an interpretive aid is an example. This is the current judicial view in Papua New Guinea as expressed by the Supreme Court in *In Re Reference by the Ombudsman Commission of Papua New Guinea* (*ROCPNG*).[12] The courts have not developed the law in a way that ventures into the first order sense of implementing the NGDP and BSO by Parliament.

---

9 The pivotal role of the legislature was discussed in chapter 6 as the lynchpin for the interconnectedness approach.

10 Observation based on an analysis of current legislation.

11 Only two Acts have been identified, which take this approach: see Salaries and Remuneration Commission Act 1988 and Underlying Law Act 2000.

12 See the Supreme Court decisions in *Reference by the Ombudsman Commission of Papua New Guinea* [2010] PGSC 40, SC1088, 17 December 2010 [ROCPNG].

First order implementation allows for greater democratic legitimacy as there is political direction from Parliament to the executive, the courts, and the Ombudsman Commission about which NGDP and BSO it should prefer in implementation. The first order requirement applies only to Parliament and is not applicable to the other branches of government because their functions are determined by Parliament from the laws it enacts. The other branches' of government's duty is to implement the NGDP and BSO within the boundaries determined by Parliament.

The legal basis of direct implementation is founded on indirect justiciability under ss 25(3) and 63(3) of the Constitution.[13] It enables direct implementation in the first order sense.[14] As a noted commentary on the American Constitution states, "the explicit language of the text … [should] give effect to the underlying values and purposes that animate the Constitution …".[15] The NGDP and BSO are the underlying values and purposes that animate the Constitution. A law (the Constitution) has conferred legislative power on Parliament, and this power is to be exercised in a way that gives effect to the NGDP and BSO.[16] If Parliament does not act reasonably to fulfil its constitutional duty in a law, then that law is subject to judicial review. It is open to the court to examine whether Parliament has made reasonable attempts to implement the NGDP and BSO in legislation.[17] The manner in which the exercise of law-making power is subjected to court scrutiny is admittedly a delicate judicial process, with deference to Parliament in borderline cases.

The only law exempt from this judicial scrutiny is the annual appropriation legislation. The government is provided a certain level of discretion to prepare and present budgets to Parliament.[18] Parliament's latitude on the content of

---

[13] Indirect justiciability of the NGDP and BSO was established in chapter 4.

[14] These provisions provide for the exception to non-justiciability for the implementation of the NGDP and BSO. Chapter 4 deals with the exception to non-justiciability of the NGDP and BSO in some detail. The provisions directing a liberal interpretation of the Constitution is sch 1.2. This principle of interpretation is covered in the role of the judiciary in the implementation of the NGDP and BSO in chapter 9.

[15] Milton Handler, Brian Leiter and Carole E Handler, "A Reconsideration of the Relevance and Materiality of the Preamble in Constitutional Interpretation" (1990–1991)12 Cardozo L Rev 117 at 132.

[16] Constitution, s 109.

[17] This is the exception to non-justiciability presented in chapter 4.

[18] Constitution, s 210(2).

the budget is discussed further below, but essentially it would be impractical to allow the court to interfere with the budgetary process. If, for example, the court was to declare the annual appropriations unconstitutional, it may lead to instability in the country's economy. That, however, does not mean Parliament is exempt from implementing the NGDP and BSO in the budget. But the duty would be non-justiciable under ss 25(2) and 63(2) of the Constitution. Areas open for it to undertake this non-justiciable duty are discussed below. It is more practical to approach financial concerns in relation to the NGDP and BSO on a case by case basis. This will be addressed in chapter 8 on developing the underlying law.

B. Legal Avenue for Direct Implementation of the NGDP and BSO by Parliament

1. *Introduction*

The general provisions for ensuring compliance with constitutional duties are ss 22 and 23 of the Constitution, which provide sanctions for breaches. Nonetheless, a careful examination of ss 22 and 23 and relevant case law suggests direct enforcement of the NGDP and BSO in the manner envisaged under ss 25 and 63 of the Constitution (especially ss 25(3) and 63(3)) would not be appropriate against Parliament. Instead, s 19 of the Constitution would be more suitable. The relevance of s 22 (and also s 185 of the Constitution) to implementation of the NGDP and BSO are as ancillary provisions to the primary provision under s 19, enabling the court to tailor an appropriate remedy. It is, nevertheless, important to explain the non-application of ss 22 and 23 because, at first blush, they appear to provide the legal basis for enforcement. However, ss 22 and 23 can be used to vest power in the court to compel Parliament to observe other provisions of the Constitution.

2. *Non-application of ss 22 and 23 of the Constitution*

The Constitution may not necessarily have the supporting procedural mechanism to lead to the compulsion of entities to fulfil their constitutional duties. The Constitution anticipate this by granting the court discretion to overcome any perceived constitutional deficiencies:

> 22. Enforcement of the Constitution
>
> The provisions of this Constitution that recognize rights of individuals (including corporations and associations) as well as

> those that confer powers or impose duties on public authorities, shall not be left without effect because of the lack of supporting, machinery or procedural laws, but the lack shall, as far as practicable, be supplied by the National Court in the light of the National Goals and Directive Principles, and by way of analogy from other laws, general principles of justice and generally-accepted doctrine.

The National Court is empowered by s 22 to develop procedures to compel public authorities to give effect to the Constitution. In *SC Reference No 3 of 1999; Re Calling of the Parliament* (*Calling of Parliament*) the Supreme Court determined Parliament was a public authority within the meaning of that term in s 22.[19] The Supreme Court dealt with the issue of whether Parliament was in breach of its constitutional duty, imposed by s 124(1) of the Constitution, to meet for a minimum number of days.[20] The question which led the Court to discuss s 22 was the appropriate legal process to use when there is a breach of constitutional duty.[21] The Court held s 124(1) imposed a duty within the meaning of s 22.[22] The Court further held a person seeking to give effect to this duty may institute proceedings under the National Court Rules by way of administrative judicial review.[23]

The Supreme Court relied on the English cases of *R v Commissioner of Police of the Metropolis, ex parte Blackburn (No 1); R v Police*

---

19 *SC Reference No 3 of 1999; Re Calling of the Parliament* [1999] PGSC 55, [1999] PNGLR 285, 25 June 1999 [*Calling of Parliament*].

20 *Calling of Parliament* (see especially the decision of Kapi DCJ).

21 The relevant question the court considered in *Calling of Parliament* was:

(a) Does Section 124(1) of the Constitution impose a duty on the Parliament, as a public authority, for the purposes of Section 22 of the Constitution, to mitigate or avoid a breach of Section 124(1)?

(b) Having regard to the dates on which the 6th National Parliament has met and its adjournment on 2 December 1998, is there, for the purposes of Section 22 of the Constitution, a lack of supporting, machinery or procedural laws to give effect to that duty?

(c) If there is a lack of supporting, machinery or procedural laws, does s 22 of the Constitution give the National Court jurisdiction to supply the lack?

(d) In particular, does Section 22 of the Constitution give the National Court jurisdiction to make an order requiring the Parliament to meet on or a prescribed day for a prescribed period so as to give effect to the duty imposed by Section 124(1) of the Constitution?

22 *Calling of Parliament*, above no 19.

23 The procedures for administrative judicial review are provided for under Order 16 of the National Courts Rules.

Commissioner, ex parte Blackburn (No 3); and R v GLC, ex parte Blackburn as relevant for this conclusion.[24] In the Court's view, these English cases were helpful precedents for the procedure and the remedy of ensuring compliance with the law.[25] Alternatively, the Court proposed seeking an order in the nature of prerogative writs,[26] or to apply to the courts for specific directions.[27] It will become clear in the following discussion that these types of procedures and remedies are not appropriate to raise implementation questions against Parliament based on ss 25(3) and 63(3) of the Constitution.

The decision in *Calling of Parliament* also considered the interaction of s 22 with s 23 of the Constitution. It stated while s 22 provided for the procedures to approach the courts to secure compliance with the Constitution, s 23 set out the type of remedy the court could award against a public authority for failing to fulfil a constitutional duty.[28] Section 23 provides four main types of remedies the National Court can award depending on the circumstances of the case: imprisonment, fine, compensation and injunction. The National Court has the discretion to award any of these remedies depending on the nature of the breach of the Constitution.

The question arises whether the legal options and remedies provided in *Calling of Parliament* are appropriate procedures to review the Parliament's failure to fulfil the NGDP and BSO in enacted legislation, especially with the types of remedies offered under s 23.[29] Can the National Court declare a piece of legislation or a Bill invalid because Parliament did not make reasonable attempts to implement the NGDP and BSO? If so, the National Court will effectively be deciding the legislation or Bill is unconstitutional. There are two difficulties with this scenario, discussed below.

(a) Supreme Court has jurisdiction over constitutional issues unless the Constitution states otherwise

---

24 *R v Commissioner of Police of the Metropolis, ex parte Blackburn (No 1)* [1968] 2 QB 118 [*Blackburn (No 1)*]; *R v Police Commissioner, ex parte Blackburn (No 3)* [1973] QB 241 [*Blackburn (No 3)*]; *R v GLC, ex parte Blackburn* [1976] 1 WLR 550) [GLC].

25 *Calling of Parliament*, above n 19, per Kapi DCJ.

26 Constitution, s 155(4).

27 Section 185.

28 *Calling of Parliament*, above n 19, per Kapi DCJ.

29 See *Blackburn (No 1)*, above n 24; *Blackburn (No 3)*, above n 24; *GLC*, above n 24.

First, where laws Parliament has made are questioned in court, they are considered by a specially constituted court such as a constitutional court.[30] In Papua New Guinea, this is reserved for the Supreme Court.[31] In *SCR No 4 of 1980; Re petition by MT Somare*, Kidu CJ stated:[32]

> The rulings sought involve interpretation or application of Constitutional Laws. Subject to application of s 23, s 42(5), s 57 and s 58 of the Constitution, the Supreme Court has "original jurisdiction, to the exclusion of other courts, as to any question relating to the interpretation or application of any provision of a Constitutional Law" (Constitution s 18(1)).

The National Court is comprised of a single judge, unlike the Supreme Court where the bench is composed of three judges or more.[33] Questioning the exercise of legislative power is a serious matter and should therefore not be taken lightly.[34] As a result, the National Court would not be the proper forum.

(b) Inappropriateness of remedies under s 23 of the Constitution

The second difficulty is the appropriateness of the remedy provided by ss 22 and 23 for a case considering the constitutional duty to implement the NGDP and BSO. In *Calling of Parliament* the Court proposed an order in the nature of a mandamus to secure compliance by public authorities. Such a remedy is inappropriate against an entity like Parliament. Parliament represents diverse interests resolved by negotiations and voting to enact a law. It would be difficult for the court to effectively order Parliament to implement a particular NGDP and/or BSO. The other penalties envisaged by s 23 such as imprisonment, fine, compensation, and injunction are also inappropriate in the context of a collective entity such as Parliament. The Supreme Court recognised this issue when it stated that it could not interfere

---

30 Papua New Guinea does not have a constitutional court. All constitutional matters are heard by the Supreme Court unless the Constitution specifically confers jurisdiction on the National Court (Constitution, s 18).

31 Constitution, ss 18 and 19.

32 *SCR No 4 of 1980; Re Petition by MT Somare* [1981] PNGLR 265 at 267 per Kidu CJ [*Somare*].

33 The factor deciding the number of judges (with three being the standard Supreme Court composition) is the importance of the issue being considered, which most often relates to constitutional matters.

34 *Somare*, above n 32, at 267 per Kidu CJ.

with Parliament's law-making function when it came to issuing a remedy under s 23 of the Constitution. All it could do was to state whether a law was constitutional or not:[35]

> To me it seems that using s 23 to punish or penalize Parliament is not what the provision was intended to do. Although the court has power to rule acts of the Parliament unconstitutional, it has no power to penalize it, nor does it have power to order it to pay compensation. (See s. 115 of the Constitution.) It has no power either to stop the Parliament from making laws. The court has power only to determine whether a law made by Parliament is constitutional or unconstitutional.

Accordingly, it would be inappropriate on this ground, too, to use s 23 to secure Parliament's compliance with its duty under ss 25(3) and 63(3) of the Constitution for failing to enact a law implementing the NGDP and BSO.

3. *Use of s 19 of the Constitution for direct implementation*

(a) Introduction

If ss 22 and 23 do not provide an appropriate mechanism, then what is the appropriate legal process? This process is available under s 19 of the Constitution.[36] Section 19 grants jurisdiction to a number of authorities to file for judicial review of legislation and Bills (the common term used is constitutional references as opposed to judicial review) in the Supreme Court to determine their constitutionality. The Court identifies two other alternatives to judicial review in *Calling of Parliament*: seeking orders in the nature of prerogative writs under s 155(4) of the Constitution; and applying for directions to the Court under s 185 of the Constitution. But these alternatives would also be inappropriate as the issue of reviewing Parliament's exercise of legislative power attacks the constitutionality of a Bill or law, an outcome

---

[35] *Somare*, above n 32, at 267 per Kidu CJ.

[36] The alternative procedure, that potentially enables any person with sufficient interest (outside of the prescribed authorities under s 19 of the Constitution) to challenge the constitutionality of laws (and Bills) is by s 18(1) of the Constitution uses an originating summons (see *Re Constitutional Validity of Constitutional Amendment (Provincial Governments and Local-Level Governments)* [1995] PGSC 12, [1995] PNGLR 481, 20 September 1995; but this avenue is not pursued here because the body proposed to take up the role of examining laws to determine whether they implement the NGDP and BSO, is the Ombudsman Commission (discussed in chapter 9).

covered by s 19. That said, it is interesting to observe there is judicial authority for the proposition that a process initiated under s 19 can rely on ss 22, 155(4), and 185 to award a remedy the courts deems appropriate.[37]

Certain public authorities are granted recognition by the Constitution to initiate constitutional references before the Supreme Court for its binding opinion.[38] Most often the nature of the questions relate to the validity of legislation and Bills. But an interesting development has arisen where the Supreme Court has considered issues concerning the constitutional propriety of the election of the Governor-General under s 19 of the Constitution.[39] This has seen the expansion of the Court's jurisdiction under s 19 to compliance with constitutional processes.

(b) Sections 19, 25(3) and 63(3) of the Constitution

The question arises whether s 19 can be used to ensure Parliament complies with its constitutional duty under ss 25(3) and 63(3) of the Constitution? An examination of s 19 suggests it is sufficiently broad to mandate a constitutional challenge against Parliament on the basis of its failure to meet ss 25(3) and 63(3). Section 19(1) states:

> … on application by an authority referred to in Subsection (3), give its opinion on any question relating to the interpretation or application of any provision of a Constitutional Law, including (but without limiting the generality of that expression) any question as to the validity of a law or proposed law.

The Supreme Court has jurisdiction to provide its opinion on question(s) relating to the interpretation or application of any provision of a Constitutional Law. The NGDP and BSO are part of constitutional law, and it is therefore appropriate for the Supreme Court to determine questions relating to their

---

37 *SCR No 2 of 1978; Re Corrective Institutions Act 1957* [1978] PGSC 9, [1978] PNGLR 404, 25 October 1978 [*SCR No 2 of 1978*].

38 Some of these authorities under s 19(3) of the Constitution are:
- Parliament;
- Law Reform Commission;
- Ombudsman Commission;
- A Provincial Assembly or a Local-level Government;
- A provincial executive; and
- Speaker of Parliament.

39 *Re Re-election of the Governor General* [2010] PGSC 38, SC1089, 22 December 2010.

interpretation or application. Section 19 being the most likely provision to support implementation should be read liberally in a way that enables the fulfilment of a constitutional duty. It is important to bear in mind that where the Constitution imposes a duty, this duty is expected to be fulfilled.

(c) Present judicial view: a critique

The leading case on whether legislation can be struck down for being inconsistent with the NGDP and BSO is ROCPNG. This was a reference by the Ombudsman Commission under s 19 of the Constitution seeking the Supreme Court's opinion on the constitutional validity of the Forestry (Amendment) Act 2005 and other provisions of the Forestry Act 1991, as amended. The case concerned s 59 of the Forestry Act, which requires consultation with the customary owners of forest resources who are parties to a Forest Management Agreement (FMA).

The FMA is an agreement between the Papua New Guinea National Forest Authority (NFA) and the customary landowners of an area designated for logging. The consultation related to who should be issued a timber permit. The agreement sets out the conditions of logging. Based on the FMA, the NFA issues a timber permit to a developer to conduct logging. This is because under s 56 of the Forestry Act, the NFA acquires rights to logging in the area covered by the FMA. The customary owners were one of three groups of bodies or persons, which s 59 required the NFA to consult before a timber permit was issued to the project developer. The Reference considered whether repealing s 59 of the Forestry Act was constitutional.

The Ombudsman Commission did not raise the constitutionality of the repeal of s 59 against the NGDP directly. It first raised a question of interpretation, by asking whether s 56 could be interpreted in a manner consistent with the NGDP:

> By Section 56 of the Forest Act 1991, the Papua New Guinea forest authority may acquire the timber rights of customary owners.
>
> Does the acquisition of the timber rights of customary owners under a Forestry Management Agreement, constitute participation by the customary owners in the development of their resources within the meaning of the National Goals and Directive Principles of the Constitution, and Section 6 and 46

> of the Forestry Act 1991 or is it only a disposition of their rights and interests as in an agreement for sale and purchase for a money and/or benefits consideration?

Following this question, the constitutionality of s 59 of the Forestry Act was raised:

> Is the repeal of Section 59 of the Act which provided for meaningful consultation with and by forest resource owners with the State and the forest developer discriminatory to forest resource owners and therefore, unconstitutional within the meaning and the spirit of Section 55 of the Constitution?

Section 55 of the Constitution protects the right to equality:

> 55. Equality of Citizens
>
> (1) Subject to this Constitution, all citizens have the same rights, privileges, obligations and duties irrespective of race, tribe, place of origin, political opinion, colour, creed, religion or sex.

In answer to these questions raised by the Ombudsman Commission, the Court ruled:[40]

> The NGDP and BSO are statements of political vision and developmental aspirations on which the State is founded. They also spell out the basic principles of good governance of themselves. Their application are non-justiciable: s 25 (1) and s 63 (1) of the Constitution. Except where the Constitution itself provides the NGDP and BSO to be used as an aid to the interpretation of specific statutes, they cannot be used as a ground to strike down legislation: see s 38 of the Constitution. *The provisions of s 25 (3) and s 63(3) provide guide to exercise of power conferred by statute and of themselves do not provide a ground to invalidate an offending legislation.* Indeed we are not aware of any law or proposed law being struck down by the Court solely on the grounds that it offends the NGDP and BSO. The proposition put to us by counsel for the Applicants is

---

40 *ROCPNG*, above n 12, at [23].

> clearly against the expressed intention of the Constitution that laws should not be struck down by the Courts purely on the ground that the law offends or fails to give effect to political pronouncements on developmental aspirations and good governance [emphasis added].

There are two ways to look at *ROCPNG* in terms of the NGDP and BSO under s 25 and 63. First, the question did not attack the Parliament's law-making powers, or first order category of implementation. It merely focused on interpreting the legislation in light of the NGDP. The question could have been asked: "Is the repeal of s 59 of the Forest Act 1991 a derogation by Parliament of its duty to implement the NGDP through its legislative power under s 25(3) of the Constitution?" A question put this way meets the terms of ss 25(3) of the Constitution, which requires any law or power, be it legislative, judicial, executive, or administrative to be exercised in a way that gives effect to the NGDP. In this instance, the issue questioned the exercise of legislative power. It was unsurprising, therefore, that the Court refused to answer the question. It must also be noted that Parliament has the authority to expressly derogate from the NGDP and BSO for a legitimate (or reasonable) reason.[41]

Second, the Court also failed to apply its own definition of the meaning of s 25(3) (and s 63(3)). It is true the Court was only interested in restricting the role of the NGDP (and BSO) to being an interpretive aid, that is, the second order sense. But even on this score, the Court did not make any judicial pronouncement on whether s 56 can be interpreted in a way that promotes the NGDP. The Court simply made a blanket statement that the NGDP were non-justiciable. Perhaps if the Supreme Court had addressed the question, it could have interpreted s 55 of the Constitution in a manner consistent with the NGDP and/or BSO so the constitutionality of s 59 of the Forest Act would have been considered.

(d) Proposals for Parliament to fulfil its constitutional duty to directly implement the NGDP and BSO in a reasonable manner

If the courts have the power to strike down legislation for non-implementation of the NGDP and BSO, it is important for Parliament to have clear guidelines on how it should exercise its power in a constitutionally-

41 Discussed in chapter 4. What is reasonable depends on the circumstances of each case.

compliant manner. However, there is presently no guidance on how Parliament should go about fulfilling its constitutional duty. All the Constitution suggests is to use legislative power to implement the NGDP and BSO unless it would be unreasonable to do so.[42]

The often used test of reasonableness was established in *Associated Provincial Picture Houses Ltd v Wednesbury Corporation.*[43] Where an authority has power to do something, it must do it in a way that is reasonable. If it fails to act reasonably, the courts can step in. The usual test proceeds on the basis of whether a reasonable person in a similar situation would have made such a decision. While *Wednesbury* dealt with the exercise of administrative power, and not judicial review of legislation, the idea that the duty to act reasonably must be within the parameters of the law is apposite. It is difficult to set a single test of what would be a reasonable means for Parliament to enact laws that implement the NGDP and BSO. Matters to be considered include Parliament's collective nature, the complexity of the Bill's subject matter, and the availability of resources. Tying down a particular view of what a "reasonable person" would have done in the circumstances is challenging. The most practical option would be to suggest procedural guidelines to provide opportunities for Parliament to meaningfully address implementation.

Another case that might provide a useful comparative lesson is *Government of Republic of South Africa and Others v Grootboom and Others.*[44] The Constitutional Court reviewed the South African government's legislative and policy efforts to implement the right to housing under s 26 of the South African Constitution. The Court determined the government's legislative effort, policy initiatives, and budgetary allocations failed to make reasonable provision for the affected people's right to housing. Granted South Africa recognises housing as a right as opposed to a directive principle, the comparison is appropriate because of the positive duty conferred by ss 25 and 63 of the Constitution. The factors which the court in Papua New Guinea could examine to determine reasonableness include legislative, policy, and budgetary decisions.

---

42 The term "reasonable" appears in the Constitution, ss 25(3) and 63(3).

43 *Associated Provincial Picture Houses Ltd v Wednesbury Corporation* [1948] 1 KB 223 (CA).

44 *Government of the Republic of South Africa v Grootboom* (CCT11/00) [2000] ZACC 19, [2001] 1 SA 46 (CC), [2000] 11 BCLR 1169, 4 October 2000.

(e) Determining what is reasonable for Parliament to fulfil its duty to implement the NGDP and/or BSO

A two-stage approach for Parliament to implement the NGDP and BSO in a way that can be said to be reasonable relying on ss 22 and 185 of the Constitution is available. The authority to enable the courts to devise such a procedure is *SCR No 2 of 1978; Re Corrective Institutions Act 1957*, where the Supreme Court, on the basis of s 19 of the Constitution, considered the validity of s 30 of the Corrective Institutions Act 1957.[45] This provision prevented prisoners from appealing conviction for offences committed in custody. The Supreme Court found this was inconsistent with s 37(15) of the Constitution which deals with the right to appeal. As a result, the Court devised a procedure to correct this constitutional deficit until such time Parliament enacted the procedure to enable appeals. It did this on the basis of ss 22 and 185 of the Constitution. While s 22 referred to the National Court only, the Supreme Court did not see that as an obstacle to devising appropriate remedies for a case initiated under s 19.

The procedure (presented below) the courts may consider sanctioning would be authorised by ss 22 and 185 to enable Parliament to fulfil its constitutional duty.[46] Such procedure would not be mandatory, but Parliament can use it to demonstrate to the court its efforts to implement the NGDP and BSO. Nevertheless, it is well supported by the Constitution and is presently provided for under the Standing Orders; although not in so far as considering the NGDP and BSO. It must be stressed that following this process is not the only legal avenue for Parliament to satisfy its duty under ss 25 and 63 of the Constitution, but this process has the advantage of enabling Parliament to avail itself of relevant documents to make a considered decision on a Bill in an environment of wide consultation.

(f) Centrality of the committee system

The centrality of parliamentary committees to this process is crucial and a short overview will be presented below to demonstrate its importance.[47]

---

[45] *SCR No 2 of 1978*, above n 37.

[46] In chapter 10, it is proposed the Ombudsman Commission undertake this role.

[47] The different types of committees operating as at present are listed in the National Parliament website: National Parliament of Papua New Guinea <www.parliament.gov.pg> [National Parliament website].

Parliament should as a matter of good practice refer all Bills to a relevant parliamentary committee. The committee system is established under the Constitution.[48] It is designed to ensure all Members of Parliament are involved in the work of the government and should cover all areas of government activity.[49] Committees are either permanent or sessional.[50] An example of the former is the Public Accounts Committee.[51] Sessional committees are set up by Parliament for a specific purpose and cease to exist after fulfilling their terms of reference. Committees form an important part of the work of Parliament in Papua New Guinea.[52]

The CPC believed the parliamentary committee system was the most significant of the proposals it made for Parliament to properly discharge its functions.[53] The CPC considered it so important that they proposed that every Bill presented to Parliament should be referred to an appropriate committee after the first reading.[54] Referral to the relevant committee would be a formal matter. But the attention the committee devotes to studying the advantages and disadvantages of a Bill is important to ensure good legislation is enacted. At this stage the committee can ask for public submissions to ensure its final report to Parliament is broadly representative of the people's views.

The CPC's strategy to ensure that laws conform to the NGDP and BSO revolved around the committee system and the Law Reform Commission.[55] The reason for the CPC's approach is not entirely clear, but it may well reflect the fact that much of the legislation adopted at independence were pre-independence laws that had to be reviewed for conformity with the Constitution.[56] Implementation would be a gradual process. This recommendation demonstrates that not only the courts, but each arm of government, too, has a responsibility to ensure implementation of the NGDP and BSO.[57]

---

48 Constitution, s 118. See also chapter 4, which discusses the committee system in general.

49 Constitution, s 118(1).

50 National Parliament website, above n 47.

51 Constitution, ss 118 and 121.

52 National Parliament website, above n 47.

53 CPC Report, above n 6, at 6/9 [66].

54 At 6/11 [71].

55 At 5/1/34 [23].

56 At 2/25 [3].

57 See discussion on interplay of the arms of government in chapter 5.

To date, Parliament has not established a particular committee to implement the NGDP and BSO; nor has the Law Reform Commission been given a specific mandate to consider the compatibility of existing legislation with the NGDP and BSO.[58] Since the focus is on the legislature, the executive, the courts, and the Ombudsman Commission, the work of the Law Reform Commission is not considered. But as a governmental body, there is no doubt it could (and should) make an important contribution. Its role is particularly important because much (if not all) of the pre-independence legislation was merely adopted at independence to fill a legal vacuum, with no careful assessment of their compatibility to the Papua New Guinea's stated national Goals and Obligations.[59] As an indication, those laws that refer to the NGDP and BSO, includes only one pre-independence Act, the Harbours Act 1963 (adopted in 1975 at independence), which refers to the NGDP and BSO.

No specific parliamentary committee is required to be established to promote the implementation of the NGDP and BSO in laws. The existing committees can each separately undertake this role, which helps ensure all parliamentarians can be involved in the process (as they should be). The reason why it should not be a specific committee is mainly practical. For example, there is an Industry and Industrial Relations Committee. Presumably it will deal with matters/Bills relating to industrial relations, and could promote the NGDP and BSO in the context of industrial relations. Likewise, there is an Economic Affairs Committee, which can deal with laws relating to creating economic opportunities for Papua New Guineans consistent with Goal 2 of the NGDP.

---

[58] One of the earliest attempts the Law Reform Commission made to consider proposals for the implementation of the NGDP and BSO was a seminar conducted in 1976 in Goroka, Eastern Highlands Province. It was highlighted there was a lack of cooperation between politicians and bureaucrats and there was a need to educate them on the National Goals: see JK Gawi, YP Ghai and A Paliwala "National Goals and Law Reforms: A Report on the Goroka Seminar" (1976) 4 Melanesian LJ 259 at 269.

[59] Immediately after independence (1976), the Law Reform Commission set about recommending laws that would be relevant to Papua New Guinean circumstances fulfilling the NGDP and BSO. Two pieces of legislation it recommended were the Fairness of Transaction Bill (see Fairness of Transaction Act 1993) and the Underlying Law Bill (see Underlying Law Act 2000). It was not until in 1993 and 2000 respectively that Parliament enacted these laws.

(ii) Mandatory consideration of NGDP and BSO

After the relevant committee has a Bill referred to it, it should consider and record its recommendation noting how the referred Bill can implement the NGDP and BSO within its subject matter, and report its findings to Parliament. Parliament then votes on the Bill taking into account the report. This is an opportunity for Parliament to demonstrate to the Supreme Court its attempts to implement the NGDP and BSO through its specific instruments. With time, a culture of NGDP and BSO implementation will hopefully be inculcated into Parliament's practices as well as influencing other governmental bodies.

Subsidiary legislation is enacted by the executive; s 116 of the Constitution requires it to be tabled in Parliament for ratification. The relevant committee that deals with the primary legislation on the particular subject matter would be best placed to review the subsidiary legislation and report to Parliament whether it should confirm the subsidiary legislation.

There may be good reasons for not considering the NGDP and BSO relevant to a Bill. The area of foreign aid is one example. Papua New Guinea relies heavily on foreign aid, especially from Australia. Accepting the aid may run contrary to Goal 3 of the Constitution on National Sovereignty and Self-Reliance.[60] Nevertheless, there may be overriding economic reasons for accepting aid, for example, in a time of natural disaster. Such reasons should be stated clearly when the committee reports to Parliament.

The use of Hansard in the context of Parliament discharging its duty to implement the NGDP and BSO would be an extension of the present position where Hansard is used as an interpretive aid:[61]

> In general, proceedings of Parliament are protected by Parliamentary privilege. An exception is the Court's use of Hansard records to resolve ambiguities or competing meanings in statutory provisions, and their application to the circumstances of the case at hand. Recourse to the Hansards for statutory interpretation is not a breach of Parliamentary privilege … .

---

[60] See for example Directive Principle 8 of Goal 3.

[61] *Re Reference to Constitution section 19(1) by East Sepik Provincial Executive* [2011] PGSC 41, SC1154, 12 December 2011 at [24] per Injia CJ [*East Sepik*].

Hansard records useful information to assist the court to make an assessment on whether the efforts of Parliament have been reasonable or not in the implementation of the NGDP and BSO.[62] This would add another dimension to the general rule on Hansard's use as an interpretive aid. Since courts can already refer to Hansard, there should not be any legal obstacles to extending the manner in which the courts can use Hansard to implement the NGDP and BSO pursuant to ss 25 and 63 of the Constitution.

Useful lessons may be drawn from the New Zealand Bill of Rights Act 1990 (NZBORA) and the Human Rights Act 1998 (UK), which enacts the European Convention on Human Rights in domestic law.[63] Under NZBORA, s 7, the Attorney-General is required to report to Parliament if a Bill is inconsistent with NZBORA.[64] The Attorney-General's opinion is tabled for Parliament to consider, but Parliament is sovereign and it can choose to enact laws that are inconsistent with NZBORA.[65] In the United Kingdom a Minister of the Crown is required to make a statement before a Bill's second reading that, in the Minister's view, the Bill is compatible with Convention Rights.[66] The important point for Papua New Guinea would be that Parliament has considered a Bill in light of the NGDP and BSO, and expressed a view on its compatibility with the NGDP and BSO.

For Papua New Guinea it is appropriate for a committee of Parliament to undertake this role. In New Zealand, it has been suggested assessing compatibility with human rights is not only a legal exercise but has a political dimension, and relying solely on the Attorney-General's view is unduly legalistic.[67] A committee review would incorporate political views

---

62 Use of debates in Parliament to interpret the Constitution is allowed especially the pre-independence Constituent Assembly debates and the CPC Report, based on s 24 of the Constitution. See Chapter 5. Access to Hansard maintains that position.

63 For a useful comparison between the Human Rights Act 1998 (UK) and the New Zealand Bill of Rights Act 1990 on the issue of Parliament clearance of Bills vis-à-vis human rights: see Janet McLean "The New Zealand Bill of Rights Act 1990 and the Constitutional Propriety" (2013) 11 NZJPIL 19.

64 New Zealand Bill of Rights Act 1990, s 7.

65 New Zealand Bill of Rights Act 1990, ss 4 and 7; and see Petra Butler "15 Years of the NZ Bill of Rights: Time to Celebrate, Time to Reflect, Time to Work Harder?" [2006] HRR 1 at 5.

66 Human Rights Act 1998 (UK), s 19.

67 Janet L Hiebert "Rights-Vetting in New Zealand and Canada: Similar Idea, Different Outcomes" (2005) 3 NZJIPL 63 at 98.

on the Bill for compatibility with the NZBORA. Since the NGDP and BSO may have implications on current government policy, the committee is best placed for undertaking the task of reviewing Bills for compatibility with the NGDP and BSO. Such assessments by a parliamentary committee have been considered by the courts in the United Kingdom. The House of Lords was impressed by the level of parliamentary scrutiny on the compatibility of the Communications Act (UK) with human rights.[68] In *R (Animal Defenders International) v Secretary of State for Culture, Media and Sport*, the House of Lords noted the attention which a committee of Parliament addressed to the issue of human rights, despite the requirement that issues of compatibility are in the purview of a Minister of Crown.[69] Papua New Guinea would not be acting alone, as it has these common law experiences to draw from.

The committee can be composed of members from the government, the opposition, various parties, and also from the different regions in the country. For example, the CPC was a committee of a parliament-like body, the House of Assembly, which was representative of the various regions, political parties, interests groups, and opinions from conservative to radical.[70] A committee would give due attention to the Bill, while at the same time being representative of Parliament and society in general. Details of the committee's study should help Parliament decide on a Bill's merits and demerits, especially in light of the NGDP and BSO.

How the committee performs its task will evolve over time. Two immediate possibilities are that after the committee studies a Bill, it recommends a particular NGDP and BSO the Bill should implement, perhaps by inserting it in the preamble and/or objectives section. Another possibility is to recommend that the Bill explicitly highlights the NGDP and BSO (either generally or specifically) as factors a public authority (established under the proposed law) has to take into account when it has discretion to make a decision. An example is the Salaries and Remuneration Commission Act 1988. This Act establishes the powers and functions of the Salaries and

---

68 *R (Animal Defenders International) v Secretary of State for Culture, Media and Sport* [2008] UKHL 15, [2008] 1 AC 1312.

69 *R (Animal Defenders International) v Secretary of State for Culture, Media and Sport* was discussed in McLean, above n 63, at 25.

70 Bernard Narokobi "The Constitutional Planning Committee, nationalism and vision" in Anthony Regan, Owen Jessep and Eric Kwa (eds) *Twenty Years of the Papua New Guinea Constitution* (Lawbook Co, Sydney, 2001) 25 at 25.

Remuneration Commission (SRC). The SRC sets the terms and conditions of important public office holders in Papua New Guinea, including Members of Parliament. Section 14 of that Act stipulates the guidelines the SRC should take into account, one of which is the NGDP.[71] In this way the body making the decision is required to turn its mind to the NGDP.

(iii) Nature of constitutional challenges for failure to implement the NGDP and BSO

The challenge to Bills and/or legislation is an example of implementation in a first order sense. It considers whether Parliament has made reasonable attempts to implement the NGDP and BSO in the law. Constitutional challenges to laws and Bills under s 19 of the Constitution are not about whether the law or Bill is inconsistent with the NGDP and BSO, but rather whether the law or Bill has made provision for implementing the NGDP and BSO. There is a slight difference to the traditional way the Supreme Court deals with constitutional questions. While this may appear to be a judicial encroachment into the legislative sphere, the CPC envisaged that although the court would be considering political questions, it should not retreat from dealing with such issues:[72]

> The courts do not, however, exist in a vacuum. Like other institutions of the government of a country they are caught up in political realities, and often their decisions have important political consequences.

The court must consider carefully extent to which it can interfere with Parliament's law-making power on the basis of ss 25(3) and 63(3). Unlike other specific provisions of the Constitution, the NGDP and BSO are cast as principles. Parliament would be allowed a greater level of discretion. There could be instances where a particular NGDP is thought to be more appropriate (or not at all). What is important is that those reasons are discussed and recorded. For example, in the United Kingdom, in cases which deal with public authorities such as the police, courts have stated the police

---

71 14. Guidelines in Fixing Salaries, etc.
(1) In fixing the salaries, allowances, pensions and other benefits (financial and otherwise) for all or any members of the Parliament, the Parliament shall give full and proper consideration to—
(a) the National Goals and Directive Principles; … .

72 CPC Report, above n 6, at 8/1 [5].

were not entirely free and had a legal duty to the public to enforce the law, but if it was exercised reasonably, the court would not interfere.[73] In Canada in 2005, the Supreme Court revised the minimum constitutional requirements of judicial financial security and "confirmed the need for curial deference to government decisions on judicial compensation".[74] In the context of Papua New Guinea, such experiences point to the need to develop the law on a case-by-case basis in this potentially new area of constitutional law. Other arms of government also have a role to play in implementation, with direction from Parliament to assist them.

It is important the documents and reports Parliament relies on to arrive at its decisions are available to the court to consider. Papua New Guinea has adopted the position advanced in *Pepper v Hart*.[75] Hansard is available to the courts to ascertain Parliament's intentions, but only in certain circumstances.[76]

IV. Indirect Implementation

Parliament can record its decisions and intentions in a number of ways. This would be primary legislation, subsidiary legislation, committee reports, and Hansard.[77] The legal aspect of implementation comes into play when these documents are made available to the courts to ascertain Parliament's intentions when question(s) relating to the implementation of the NGDP and BSO arise. The court will use these "records of Parliament's intentions" to determine whether Parliament has discharged its duty. A three-point plan is presented here for Parliament to indirectly implement the NGDP and BSO. However, this study does not intend to suggest these options are the only avenues available to Parliament in this respect.

The first proposal is to make greater use of the NGDP and BSO in the preamble and/or objective statement of legislation. The second proposal argues for the Plans and Estimates Committee to recommend to the National Executive Council, prior to the formulation by the NEC of the budget, areas

---

[73] *Blackburn (No 3)*, above n 24.

[74] Lori Sterling and Sean Hanley "Judicial Independence Revisited" (2006) SCLR (2d) 34 at 57.

[75] *Pepper (Inspector of Taxes) v Hart* [1992] UKHL 3, [1993] AC 593. This case was cited with approval in *East Sepik*, above n 62.

[76] See *East Sepik*, above n 62.

[77] Hansard is available to the court to consider the reasons and circumstances in which a Bill was enacted. See *East Sepik*, above n 61, at [24] per Injia CJ.

where the government can spend more resources to implement the NGDP and BSO. The third proposal is that Parliament should consider in the debates during question time whether decisions made by the executive fulfil the NGDP and BSO.[78] Parliament's interaction with the executive, the courts, and the Ombudsman Commission as it undertakes these functions will be considered in chapters 8, 9 and 10 respectively. The plan also demonstrates the interplay between the legislature and the courts, discussed in chapter 6. The three proposals are considered in more detail below.

A. Preambles/Objective Section of Legislation

The Constitution requires a purposive approach to the construction and interpretation of legislation enacted by Parliament. Section 109(4) states:

> Each law made by the Parliament shall receive such fair, large and liberal construction and interpretation as will best ensure the attainment of the object of the law according to the true intent, meaning and spirit … .

Parliament can assist the courts to fulfil their constitutional duty to interpret laws liberally by stating their purpose clearly in the preamble or in the objectives section. An example of the use of this means to indirect implementation is the Environment Act 2000, but this approach is not common. Its preamble states:

> Being an Act to provide for and give effect to the National Goals and Directive Principles and in particular—
>
> (a) To provide for protection of the environment in accordance with Fourth National Goal and Directive Principle (National Resources and Environment) of the Constitution;

It is evident from the preamble to the Environment Act that its purpose is to ensure sustainable use of the environment advocated by Goal 4 of the Constitution. When this law is being implemented by its administrators, such as the Director of Environment, this Goal will guide how the legislation is applied.[79] Similarly, where any decision the Director of Environment makes

[78] Question time is provided for in the Standing Orders of Parliament.

[79] Director of Environment is appointed under s 15 of the Environment Act 2000 and is responsible for the office of environment and conservation matters. One of the director's function is to administer the Act (s 16(1)(a)).

is contested by an aggrieved person, the Goal will assist the court in resolving the issues. A liberal and purposive approach to interpretation ensures this.[80]

In terms of the current legislation surveyed, this approach to legislative enactment is not universal in Papua New Guinea; it is in fact atypical.[81] It is recommended Parliament should undertake a specific and consistent approach to enacting laws. There may be special reasons or particular situations where Parliament considers the NGDP and BSO should not apply to a particular piece of legislation. However, any intention not to implement the NGDP and BSO should be expressed in the Act. Alternatively, Parliament should clearly record in its pre-enactment deliberations the reasons for not entertaining the NGDP and BSO.

Situating the NGDP and BSO clearly in the preamble or the objectives section of legislation displays Parliament's efforts at implementation. It allows for "indirect application", as it will determine how rules are applied when the particular legislation enacted by Parliament is enforced by the court.[82] Enacting legislation with clear preambles and objective statements is consistent with the role proposed for the courts in chapter 8.

Rather than the court relying directly on the Constitution to determine for itself which NGDP and/or BSO to apply, as it did in *Public Trustee of New Zealand v Public Curator of Papua New Guinea*, it can do so relying on Parliament's express view.[83] An example is provided by the Wills, Probate and Administration Act 1966 which made no reference to the NGDP and BSO in its preamble. The Court took it upon itself to refer to Directive Principle 4 of Goal 2 to interpret s 43 of the Act.[84] Had Parliament provided for the NGDP and/or BSO it thought were applicable in the preamble of the Act, the Court would have been guided by Parliament's expressed intentions.

---

80 Constitution, s 109(4).

81 This is from a survey of legislation in Papua New Guinea. Results are summarised in Appendix Three.

82 Another term that could be equally used is "indirect justiciability," which was discussed in chapter 4.

83 *Public Curator of Papua New Guinea v Public Trustee of New Zealand* [1976] PGNC 48, [1976] PNGLR 427, 28 September 1976.

84 Directive Principle 4 of National Goal 2 states:

> (4) equalization of services in all parts of the country, and for every citizen to have equal access to legal processes and all services, governmental and otherwise, that are required for the fulfilment of his or her real needs and aspirations; and … .

This does not mean the court was wrong to rely on the NGDP directly from the Constitution. Rather, Parliament would have assisted the Court by stating which principles it thought were applicable to the Wills, Probate and Administration Act, thereby limiting the unwarranted exercise of court discretion as well as giving greater political legitimacy to its decisions.

B. Control of Finance

Parliament has ultimate control for raising revenue and public expenditure in Papua New Guinea.[85] This is done annually through an Appropriations Bill commonly referred to as the "Budget". This is an avenue for Parliament to ensure resources are allocated to areas that promote the NGDP and BSO.

The executive is responsible for preparing and implementing the Budget.[86] The Constitution provides the executive arm of government certain latitude to develop the Budget.[87] The annual Budget is presented to Parliament for debate and approval. Parliament can reduce, but not increase or re-allocate, the amount and purpose of any proposed taxation, loan or expenditure.[88] But Parliament can help ensure the executive allocates resources to areas that focus on the NGDP and BSO.

Section 209(3) of the Constitution provides very clear roles for a parliamentary committee to be involved in this process:

> Before any Budget or appropriation is prepared for submission to the Parliament, the National Executive Council shall consult with any appropriate Permanent Parliamentary Committee, but this subsection does not confer any right or impose any duty of consultation after the initial stages of the preparation of the Budget or appropriation.

The legal implications if the relevant committee is not consulted are unclear, but the government does not have any duty to consult after the Budget's initial stages. When the initial stages end is similarly unclear as

85 Constitution, s 209.

86 The role of the executive will be considered in chapter 8.

87 Constitution, s 210, following the CPC Recommendations: see CPC Final Report, above n 6, at 9/2 [10].

88 Section 210(2). CPC Final Report 1974, above n 6, at p 9/2 [10].

there has not been any cases on this point. This is important because the Parliamentary Committee must know at what point it can contribute to the Budget formulation process. Interestingly, though, Parliament has debated the constitutionality of a Budget after a failure to consult the relevant committee.[89] Another aspect is the form of the consultation between the committee and the executive branch. The Constitution provides guidance on what consultation should entail:

> 255. Consultation.
>
> In principle, where a law provides for consultation between persons or bodies, or persons and bodies, the consultation must be meaningful and allow for a genuine interchange and consideration of views.

Such explicit consultation requirements place the relevant committee in a strong position to have its views taken seriously by the National Executive Council.

The relevant committee with this function is the Plans and Estimates Committee, established to fulfil s 209(3) of the Constitution.[90] The Plans and Estimates Committee has the following main function:[91]

> 1. The Committee shall be established at the commencement of each Parliament and for the purposes of consulting with the National Executive Council before any budget or appropriation is prepared for submission to the Parliament, in accordance with Section 209 (3) of the Constitution.

In terms of the NGDP and BSO, the Plans and Estimates Committee would be responsible for proposing to the executive arm of government areas where resources can be spent to fulfil the NGDP and BSO. The committee would not have to start from scratch. Most of the institutions directly funded by the government through the annual appropriations cycle are established by law. For example, the Department of Education is established by the Education Act 1983. This Act has in its objectives Goal 1 of the NGDP on Integral

89 Graham Hassall "The Parliamentary Committee System in Papua New Guinea, 1975–1997" (2011) 17 CLJP-RJP 29 at 33–34.

90 National Parliament website, above n 47.

91 National Parliament website, above n 47.

Human Development.[92] If, for some reason, the Department of Education is underfunded, Goal 1 can be used as the basis for the Plans and Estimates Committee to recommend an increase in funding. The complementarity between the roles of Parliament and the executive on implementing the NGDP and BSO are made possible through the active reference to the NGDP and BSO in the preamble of legislation. Funding of organisations like the Department of Education will fulfil the NGDP and BSO as the NGDP and BSO are explicitly stated as an objective in the relevant legislation.

The Plans and Estimates Committee's report, if not taken seriously by the National Executive Council, can be the subject of debates on the Budget. Parliament's role as ultimate overseer of public funds is thematic rather than addressing individual claims, which can be pursued through other avenues.[93]

C. Parliamentary Debates

The Constitution protects free speech and parliamentary debate.[94] It is important for Parliament to constructively debate the implication of legislation and government policies on the NGDP and BSO.[95] Parliament, as a governmental body, ought to use its functions to promote the NGDP and BSO. Parliament, through its discussion around the NGDP and BSO and the steps it takes to implement them, has an important role to play in promoting a culture of implementation for other arms of government to follow.

---

[92] Education Act 1983:

> 4. Objects of the National Education System.
>
> (1) Bearing in mind the National Goals and Directive Principles of the Constitution, and subject to a provincial law and this section, the objects and purposes of the National Education System, by means of the maximum involvement and co-operative effort by persons and bodies interested in education in the country (including the State, the teaching profession, Provincial Governments, Local-level Governments, churches and the community as a whole) and the maximum utilization of the resources available from all sources are—
>
> (a) for the integral human development of the person; … .

[93] As will be seen in chapter 9 on the underlying law, there is the possibility (and potential) of making a claim against the government on the basis of the right to development under Goal one on Integral Human Development. If a claim of this nature succeeds in court, it would be factored into the budget by the executive for approval by the legislature to satisfy the court order.

[94] Constitution, s 115 (2).

[95] The CPC argued the NGDP and BSO should be the yardstick by which the performance of the government is measured: see CPC Report, above n 6, at 2/1 [6].

Reports on parliamentary committees' deliberations are eventually tabled in Parliament. Such reports can suggest how Parliament can best implement the NGDP and BSO within the scope of the Bill the committee deliberated on. Members of Parliament should refer to committee reports and the NGDP and BSO when debating Bills in Parliament. Hansard then records these exchanges. If the Bill becomes law, the courts may refer to Hansard to clarify Parliament's intentions to resolve any ambiguity in interpretation.[96] The reference to Hansard will be necessary only to determine whether Parliament has considered the NGDP and BSO in the enactment of the legislation.[97] Where it is clear from the text, it may not be necessary to refer to Hansard. This enables a constitutional exchange to take place between the court and the Parliament on common ground but at the same time respecting the specific functions of each arm of government.

There is no direct legal enforcement should Parliament fail to debate the NGDP and BSO. But this lack of attention to the NGDP and BSO will be exposed when the court interprets legislation or formulates new underlying law.[98] The court will be imposing its view on how the legislation promotes the NGDP and BSO, and little weight is given to Parliament's view. This may be a disincentive to Parliament enacting legislation without appropriate reference to the NGDP and BSO. As a result, it should prompt Parliament to address this constitutional deficit in its deliberations.

For example, Parliament may wish to debate the issue of resource development. It is an important subject where implications involving the NGDP and BSO can be addressed. Two relevant Goals that may come into conflict when discussing mining are Goal 3 on National Sovereignty and Self-Reliance and Goal 4 on Natural Resources and Environment. Parliament may feel it needs to encourage mining projects to support its revenue raising. This will help Papua New Guinea to be economically self-reliant pursuant to

---

96 Refer to chapter 4.

97 Chapter 4 states House of Assembly debates should be considered in constitutional interpretation and used where relevant. Here the situation is different. Hansard will only be referred to if Parliament's intention is not clear from the law.

98 Underlying law is used in the sense of new case laws developed from existing laws that are inappropriate. Chapter 9 discusses the use of the NGDP and BSO to develop the underlying law.

Goal Three. But mining can have disastrous environmental consequences.[99] Pursuing economic self-reliance may come into conflict with Goal 4 on Natural Resources and Environment.

This balancing exercise seems to have weighed heavily in the mind of the Court in *Medaing v Ramu Nico* when it considered whether it should issue an order compelling the mining company Ramu Nico to construct a tailings dam.[100] Had the Court issued such an order, the mining project was likely to stop operations, as the construction costs would not have made the project feasible. While the Court relied on Goal 4 in issuing a non-binding declaration noting the waste discharge would damage the environment, the economic advantage outweighed the environmental harm. In practice, the Court conducted a balancing exercise. Parliament can assist the courts by debating these matters itself so the courts will have the benefit of its views when deciding a case that touches on related and conflicting NGDP and BSO. The courts will refer to Hansard to determine which NGDP and/or BSO Parliament prioritised.

V. Conclusion

The legislature's constitutional functions to make laws, approve the national Budget, and debate Bills and policies can be used either directly or indirectly to implement the NGDP and BSO.

In terms of direct implementation, regard must be had to the exception to non-justiciability under ss 25(1) and 25(3) and ss 63(1) and 63(3). It presents the view a governmental body (which includes Parliament) is subject to court intervention if it does not exercise its power in a way that implements the NGDP and BSO. The issue is whether Parliament has been reasonable or not in enacting legislation that fulfils the NGDP and/or BSO. There is no guidance on what this may entail, but an active engagement of Parliament's committee system to fulfil this constitutional duty will help. Depending on

---

99 One of Papua New Guinea's largest gold and copper mine, Ok Tedi Mine caused widespread environmental damages to the various river systems that run off from the mine because its tailings are directly discharged into them. As part of the settlement for these damages BHP Biliton the major shareholder, transferred its shares to PNG Sustainable Development Ltd, a trust company to use the proceeds of the mine for the benefit of the affected people: see Mining (Ok Tedi Mine Continuation (Ninth Supplement) Agreement Act 2001.

100 *Medaing v Ramu Nico Management (MCC) Ltd* [2011] PGNC 95 N4340, 26 July 2011. Refer to chapter 10 for a discussion on the aspect of non-binding declaration of the court.

a Bill's subject matter, the relevant committee (permanent or select) will prepare its report in light of the NGDP and BSO, and submit its report to Parliament to consider before Parliament votes on the Bill.

A number of proposals have been offered for Parliament in terms of indirect implementation. If Parliament has attempted any of these proposals for indirect implementation before enacting a Bill, Parliament can argue with confidence that it has satisfied its duty in respect of the NGDP and BSO under ss 25(3) and 63(3). An example discussed was referring to the NGDP and BSO in the preamble or objects section of the legislation. The courts would then have recourse to these guiding principles and obligations in the way legislation is interpreted using the contextual role of preambles in statutory interpretation. The executive is similarly assisted when implementing the legislation on a day to day basis.

CHAPTER EIGHT

ROLE OF THE NATIONAL GOALS AND DIRECTIVE PRINCIPLES AND BASIC SOCIAL OBLIGATIONS

I. Introduction

The executive arm of government has a constitutional duty to implement the NGDP and BSO.[1] The effective unit in the executive is the National Executive Council (NEC), headed by the prime minister.[2] The non-implementation of the NGDP and BSO by governmental bodies as a significant issue in Papua New Guinea's constitutional development and[3] the NEC is a governmental body.[4] Proposals to address this issue have been suggested for the legislature in the previous chapter.[5] What can be done for the executive to enable it to fulfil its duty to implement the NGDP and BSO?

The proposals in this chapter come in three parts. Part II (after the introduction) provides a brief overview of the chapter. Part III presents the proposal for an NEC manual, discussing its necessity to implement the NGDP and BSO. It covers justifications for the manual, proposed content in light of the NGDP and BSO, and legal status. Part IV concludes the chapter with a summary of the main points.

---

1 Constitution, ss 25(3) and 63(3).

2 The ceremonial head of the Papua New Guinea executive is the Queen of England, represented by the Governor-General: see Constitution, ss 86(2) and 139.

3 The issue of impediments to implementation is discussed in chapter 5.

4 Constitution, s 139.

5 Refer to chapter 7 on the legislature and chapter 9 for the judiciary.

II. Brief Overview

This chapter recommends the NEC should adopt a manual that explicitly spells out in the decision-making process the duty to implement the NGDP and BSO with other constitutional principles.[6] The manual would emphasise linkages with the proposals for implementation of the NGDP and BSO by the judiciary,[7] the legislature,[8] and the Ombudsman.[9] There is at present no such publicly available document undertaking this role.[10]

This book proposes a constitutional document to facilitate proper conduct of cabinet meetings following the New Zealand and United Kingdom tradition, instead of the Australian model. The chapter spells out why a Cabinet manual could be an important step to ensuring the implementation of the NGDP and BSO. This proposal cannot set out in detail the manual's specific content, but key focus areas where the NGDP and BSO can be incorporated into the NEC policy and decision-making process are suggested.[11] These areas include responding to judicial review challenges,[12] formulating legislation,[13] preparation of the annual supply Bill,[14] avoiding wrongful conduct, and observing the Leadership Code.[15] By explicitly recognising principles, the manual would require the NEC to develop new policies consistently with them.[16] It would offer an important tool for the interplay between the various arms of government in the implementation of the NGDP and BSO.

---

6 For example, compliance with the principles of the rule of law and separation of powers.

7 Refer to chapter 9 for discussions on proposals for the judiciary.

8 Refer to chapter 7 for discussions on proposals for the legislature.

9 Refer to chapter 10 for discussions on proposals for the Ombudsman.

10 Papua New Guinea National Executive Council [NEC] does not have a manual at present. This is confirmed from official email correspondence with the Papua New Guinea Department of Prime Minister and National Executive Council and from the Prime Minister's official website: <www.pm.gov.pg>.

11 See Lanse Minkler "Economic Rights and Political Decision Making" (2009) 31(2) Hum Rts Q 368.

12 The application of the NGDP and BSO in judicial review is considered in chapter 8.

13 Formulating legislation to take account of the NGDP and BSO was discussed in chapter 6.

14 Engaging the NGDP and BSO in formulating the annual supply Bill was discussed in chapter 7.

15 Wrong conduct and misconduct are discussed in chapter 9 on the Ombudsman Commission.

16 A useful analogy can be drawn from Dworkin's argument for court and government decisions to conform to principles. For Papua New Guinea the principles are the NGDP and BSO: see Ronald Dworkin *Taking Rights Seriously* (Harvard University Press, Cambridge, 1978) at 82–84.

III. A Proposal for the National Executive Council - Cabinet Manual

A. Introduction

What follows is a justification for a manual as a useful NEC aid, not only in terms of implementing the NGDP and BSO, but also to ensure transparent and constitutionally sound decisions. The manual (or handbook as used in Australia) would be an easily accessible public document.[17]

Part III has five sections. After section A, Introduction, section B provides an outline of the Australian Handbook, and the New Zealand and United Kingdom Cabinet Manuals. It explains why there are good grounds for comparison. Section C considers the legal status of the present NEC decision-making process, and how a manual would impact on it. In section D justifications for a manual are presented. The proposed contents of the manual are outlined in section E. Finally, in section F, the legal status and accessibility of the Manual are discussed.

B. Relevance of Comparison

Papua New Guinea has a political system similar to Australia, New Zealand and the United Kingdom, popularly described as the Westminster system of government. Papua New Guinea's Constitution professes to have separation of powers and a parliamentary democracy. The latter features principles of collective responsibility and representative government. These common elements Papua New Guinea has with Australia, New Zealand and the United Kingdom can facilitate comparisons.[18] Papua New Guinea's colonial links to Australia and the United Kingdom, as well as their continuing influence on Papua New Guinea's political system lend support to this view.[19] These countries have a stable and vibrant

---

[17] Manual or handbook is used interchangeably, but where there is a need for use of a particular term, it will be pointed out. In this book, a manual records a country's interpretation of the fundamental laws from the point of view of the executive, and is more formal with broader subject matter and higher labels; a handbook, being less formal, provides a procedural guide for conducting a cabinet meeting.

[18] Tony Blackshield and George Williams *Australian Constitutional Law and Theory* (5th ed, The Federation Press, Sydney, 2010) at 1.

[19] Whilst Papua New Guinea was determined to have a home-grown constitution, its content retained much of Westminster parliamentary democracy.

system of government, and keenly observe a culture of transparency and accountability.[20]

The Cabinet Manual (New Zealand and the United Kingdom) or Handbook (Australia) are an important tool these three countries employ to aid the executive government's performance. The Cabinet Manual guides the conduct of Cabinet affairs.[21] Since the Handbook/Manual are public documents in each of these countries, the public is informed on how Cabinet makes decisions. Similarly, public accessibility of the proposed NEC Manual is recommended for Papua New Guinea.

Having publicly accessible rules in one document under which the government operates helps promote a culture of transparency because the public has a set of guidelines to hold the executive to account. The public and/or Parliament can point to the manual where the executive oversteps its mark. The executive (including civil servants and ministers), and not only the Cabinet, knows what is expected and conduct official affairs accordingly.

In the Foreword to the 2008 New Zealand Cabinet Manual, Prime Minister Helen Clark wrote:[22]

> The Cabinet Manual is an authoritative guide to central government decision making for Ministers, their offices, and those working within government. It is also a primary source of information on New Zealand's constitutional arrangements, as seen through the lens of the executive branch of government.

The Manual is not governed by statute, but aims to reflect in one document the various constitutional arrangements that obtain in New Zealand. Important sources of constitutional law, such as the Treaty of Waitangi and the New Zealand Bill of Rights Act 1990 (NZBORA) are identified. The executive branch of government is alerted to the principles promoted by

---

20 In the 2013 Transparency International Corruption Perception Index (from least corrupt), out of 171 countries Australia is ranked 9th, New Zealand is ranked 1st and the United Kingdom is 14th. Papua New Guinea is 144th: see Transparency International, Corruption Perception Index 2013 <www.transparency.org>.

21 See: Australia <www.dpmc.gov.au>; New Zealand <http://cabinetmanual.cabinetoffice.govt.nz>; United Kingdom <www.gov.uk>.

22 Cabinet Office *Cabinet Manual 2008* at xv [NZ *Cabinet Manual*].

these sources of constitutional law, to make decisions consistent with them where appropriate.

The United Kingdom Prime Minister, David Cameron, expressed similar views in the Foreword to the United Kingdom Cabinet Manual:[23]

> The Cabinet Manual sets out the internal rules and procedures under which the Government operates. For the first time the conventions determining how the Government operates are transparently set out in one place.

A manual may be more useful for countries with unwritten constitutions such as New Zealand and the United Kingdom. But even for Canada, a country with a written Constitution, it has been suggested that following the United Kingdom model of cabinet Manual may be appropriate.[24] What Canada presently has is quite detailed. The Manual of Official Procedure of the Government of Canada is some 1,500 pages long.[25] It is mainly intended for use by senior civil servants, the Prime Minister and Ministers, and has the following function:[26]

> These practitioner's handbooks compile historical precedents and provide justifications in a more exhaustive format, designed to present decision-makers with the relevant information required to make informed decisions. Their sheer bulk and technical nature, however, make them inaccessible to a general audience who would want to learn about parliamentary government.

The advantage of the New Zealand and United Kingdom model over what Canada has is their brevity and accessibility:[27]

> In contrast, "cabinet manuals" like the British Cabinet Manual and the New Zealand Cabinet Manual are presented in shorter, more accessible formats, describing general principles and

---

23 Cabinet Office *The Cabinet Manual* (1st ed, October 2011) at iii [UK *Cabinet Manual*].

24 Fraser Harland "Constitutional Convention and Cabinet Manuals" (2011) 34(2) Canadian Parl Rev 25.

25 Nicholas A MacDonald and James W Bowden "The Manual of Official Procedure of the Government of Canada: An Exposé" (2011) 20(1) Constit Forum 33.

26 At 37.

27 At 37.

> constitutional conventions of the parliamentary system and the basic roles and functions of its main components, rather than listing historical precedents that justify current positions.

The reasons advanced for Canada to shift to the New Zealand and United Kingdom model is appropriate for Papua New Guinea, which like Canada, has a written constitution. A manual as operates in New Zealand and United Kingdom would also aid the implementation of the NGDP and BSO as will be explained below.

Australia has a written Constitution, but its Cabinet is not expressly referred to in the constitutional text.[28] Instead of a manual, the Australian government has a handbook. The difference between a manual (New Zealand and the United Kingdom) and a handbook (Australia) is not only semantic but also substantive as is evident in this statement from Prime Minister Julia Gillard and the Cabinet Secretary, Mark Dreyfus, in the Foreword to the Australian Cabinet Handbook:[29]

> The Handbook outlines the underlying principles of Cabinet government and general expectations for Cabinet business and meetings, with detailed arrangements included in Annexes. The Handbook should be used as a resource for all ministers, ministerial staff and public officials involved in the development and progression of Cabinet business.

The Handbook helps the Prime Minister organise the affairs of the Cabinet, but does not reflect other constitutional principles on the executive government's relationship with the other arms of government in the way the New Zealand and the United Kingdom manual does. The use of the word "manual", going by current practice in the Commonwealth, has a greater constitutional and political implication.

For Papua New Guinea, something more in the nature of the New Zealand and United Kingdom model may be relevant. What is proposed is a document that will have constitutional implications for the way the government conducts its affairs.

---

[28] Australian Constitution, Chapter II, The Executive Government, ss 61–70 inclusive.

[29] Australian Government Department of the Prime Minister and Cabinet, *Cabinet Handbook* (7th ed, 2014) at 6 [Australia *Cabinet Handbook*].

It is important to set out clearly, simply, and briefly, the main constitutional principles that determine the executive's relationship with other organs of government. The focus would be on implementing the NGDP and BSO in the executive's relations with other government branches.

C. The Legal Status of the NEC Decision-Making Process

The Constitutional Planning Committee (CPC) recommended establishing specific decision-making procedures for the NEC. The Constitution was to define the manner in which the NEC would make its decisions.[30] Did the CPC want this to be a mandatory requirement? The CPC Report does not say so directly, but because it details a specific process, it is reasonable to infer their view was the NEC's modus operandi should be spelt out in the law. The Constitution did not take up this option, leaving the process open-ended.[31] Furthermore, the process was left non-justiciable.[32] However, where the NEC is directed to observe a law, failure to comply enables an aggrieved person to seek redress in the court. Non-justiciability does not prevent, for example, judicial review of NEC decisions.[33] A number of these decisions relate to appointments to public offices.[34]

The Prime Minster and National Executive Council Act 2002 is the main law governing NEC procedures.[35] The legislation deals with two main subjects – appointing an acting Prime Minister in the event of a vacancy, and the roles and functions of specific NEC committees such as the National

---

[30] Constitutional Planning Committee *Constitutional Planning Committee Final Report, Part One* (Government Printer, Port Moresby, 1974) [CPC Report] at 7/2–7/3 [17].

[31] Constitution, s 149(5) states: "Subject to any Organic Law or Act of the Parliament, the procedures of the Council are as determined by it".

[32] Constitution, s 153(2) states: "The question, whether the procedures prescribed for the National Executive Council have been or are being complied with, is non-justiciable".

[33] The most recent high profile case was over the government decision to host (and process) asylum seekers seeking entry into Australia on Manus Island of Papua New Guinea. The case was initiated by then Opposition Leader Belden Namah on the basis the arrangement was unconstitutional. The case is on-going.

[34] For example see *Lupari v Somare* [2008] PGSC 33, SC951, 10 November 2008.

[35] The Prime Minster and National Executive Council Act 2002 was the subject of the "two prime minister's saga". The issue was the Act's non-observance in removing Michael Somare from office, which became the subject of intense constitutional litigation: see Vergil Narokobi "The Papua New Guinea 'Two Prime Ministers' Saga': Parliament Testing the Supremacy of the Constitution" (2013) 24 PLR 92.

Security Council, the National Security Advisory Committee, and the Central Agencies Co-ordination Committee. Apart from the NEC, general procedures are not governed by any other laws.[36] Since the NEC can create its own procedures, it can also adopt a manual for the public to appreciate its decision-making process.

The Standing Orders of Parliament provide another useful comparison for determining the legal status of a proposed manual for the NEC. Compliance with the Standing Orders is non-justiciable.[37] But the Standing Orders provide a comprehensive guide to the Parliament to conduct its affairs in a legally compliant manner. Furthermore, it provides an indication of whether Parliament has complied with other justiciable provisions, such as the procedures for enacting constitutional laws and amendments. For example, "Part XIXA – Constitutional Laws" of the Standing Orders, prescribes procedures for constitutional amendment consistent with ss 14 and 17 of the Constitution. Parliament's non-compliance with ss 14 and 17 in enacting laws can result in the Supreme Court declaring such laws unconstitutional.[38]

D. Justification for a Manual

1. *Introduction*

There are obvious advantages and disadvantages in having a manual. However the advantages of a manual for Papua New Guinea that expects the fulfilment of broad constitutional principles, appears to outweigh the disadvantages. The main point underlying the various reasons for a manual would be a more user friendly guide for decision-making consistent with constitutional principles, rather than insisting the NEC resort directly to constitutional laws and case law for direction. As alluded to earlier, a manual would combine in a single, publicly accessible document all the main principles of government, especially as it pertains to the executive's functions and its relations to other organs of government and thus support transparent practices.

---

[36] There are specific laws the NEC is required to consider when dealing with a particular subject matter such as the Organic Law on the Provincial Governments and Local Level Governments 1995, s 57 on suspensions of provincial governments.

[37] Constitution, s 134.

[38] *In the Matter of Constitutional Validity of Constitutional Amendment (Provincial Governments and Local-Level Governments)* [1995] PGSC 12; [1995] PNGLR 481, 20 September 1995.

New Zealand introduced a Cabinet Manual in the late 1970s to consolidate the principles of various laws (such as the Constitution Act 1986) and conventions pertaining to the executive.[39] The United Kingdom adopted a Manual in 2009. The United Kingdom did not have a Cabinet Manual before that.[40] The United Kingdom drew heavily from the New Zealand experience as neither country has a written constitution.[41] Three advantages of a Cabinet Manual in these two countries are:[42]

- It allows for codification of constitutional conventions without making them law;
- It clarifies key conventions to help prevent a constitutional crisis following the election of a minority government; and
- It is relatively simple to implement – at least from a logistical perspective.

A Cabinet Manual may be more suited to countries with unwritten constitutions as a means to document unwritten constitutional conventions. Like other written constitutions, there are aspects of the Papua New Guinea Constitution left undefined. Resorting to the provision's historical antecedents may aid interpretation. Section 149(3) places responsibility on the NEC for the executive government of Papua New Guinea. However, there is no definition of "executive government"[43] apart from the requirement to observe collective responsibility.[44] So whilst Papua New Guinea has a written constitution, there is a large area of government functioning left for convention to fill, based on countries with similar government systems, including those with

---

39 Rebecca Kitteridge "The Cabinet Manual: Evolution with Time" (paper presented to the 8th Annual Public Law Forum, Wellington, 20–21 March 2006).

40 There were separate manuals for different departments, but no manual specifically for the Cabinet as a collective entity.

41 House of Commons Political and Constitutional Reform Committee *Constitutional Implications of the Cabinet Manual* Sixth Report of Session 2010–11, Volume 1 (29 March 2011) at 5.

42 Harland, above n 24.

43 John Goldring "Responsibility of the Executive Government – To Whom and for What" (1981) 9 Melanesian LJ 116 at 117–118.

44 Constitution, s 141. For an interesting piece on ambiguity in the courts constitutional review jurisdiction see: Law Reform Commission of Papua New Guinea *Occasional Paper No 16: Constitutional Review Jurisdiction in Papua New Guinea* (September 1981).

Westminster traditions.[45] In addition, when ss 25(3) and 63(3) refer to the exercise of executive power to implement the NGDP and BSO, no guidance is provided to the executive. A manual would satisfy this expectation.

A disadvantage would be setting up a manual can confuse Ministers, who can refer directly to laws to determine an issue. In the United Kingdom the proliferation of codes has been identified as a potential challenge.[46] But principles of government modelled on a Westminster system can sometimes be wrongly assumed to be understood by all key stake-holders from resorting to the Constitution. The realities in Papua New Guinea militate against making such assumption.[47] The two Prime Minister's saga is one example.[48] A manual which provides a ready chart for leaders to navigate the complex constitutional system would go a long way to avoid misunderstandings. Further, there could be a gap, or an issue in the law, and the manual would not confuse the Ministers, but actually help clarify the issue.

Another argument against a manual is the difficulty of reaching consensus on its content. In Canada, it was observed that codifying conventions is a contested field, and it would be difficult to get parties to agree on the terms of a particular convention to include in a manual.[49] In the United Kingdom, the process was initiated by the legislature, and driven by a specific committee. Ultimately it would be for the executive to determine whether it accepted the parliamentary committee recommendation.[50] If there is wide

---

[45] Goldring, above n 43, at 117–118. For a Supreme Court decision drawing on relevance of Westminster comparison with Papua New Guinea: see *Special Reference by Fly River Provincial Executive Council; Re Organic Law on Integrity of Political Parties and Candidates* [2010] PGSC 3, SC1057, 7 July 2010, at [209].

[46] Andrew Blick "The Cabinet Manual and the Codification of Conventions" (2014) 67 Parl Aff 191 at 193.

[47] In *Public Prosecutor v Rooney (No 2)* [1979] PGSC 23, [1979] PNGLR 448, 11 September 1979, Minister for Justice Nahau Rooney was found guilty of contempt of court for writing a letter directly to the court criticising the court over its decision. Rooney was imprisoned for six months but was soon released by the National Executive Council exercising its prerogative power of mercy. A number of judges resigned from office, in protest against the interference by the executive over the independence of the judiciary.

[48] Narokobi, above n 35.

[49] Bruce Hicks "Advice to the Ministers of democratic reform: Senate reform, constitutional amendments, fixed election dates, and a Cabinet Manual" Constit Forum (Fall, 2012) 23.

[50] For example in New Zealand, it has been customary for each incoming government to declare its support for the Cabinet Manual. This point was observed by Kitteridge, above n 39.

stake-holder consultation prior to adoption of a manual (as there should be), various and often conflicting views are bound to arise, compounding the difficulty. The response to this would be that a manual is a statement of the executive's intent, understanding and commitment to government under constitutional law. Whatever differences there are can be resolved when the matter is contested in court. An example could be in the context of litigating a justiciable provision of the Constitution and the scope of a related constitutional practise(s) arises.[51] Such differences and ambiguities should not prevent the executive from establishing a manual. In the United Kingdom, the problem of ambiguity was addressed by simply stating the uncertainty in the Manual.[52]

2. *Non-justiciability versus justiciability*

A strong reason for a Cabinet Manual is that a manual clarifies conventions,[53] and demonstrates a government's commitment to what cannot be enforced by law.[54] A Manual would as a result reduce the opportunity for arbitrary government because it provides a tool for the government to follow, especially in areas where the law confers powers with wide discretion.

In the context of social rights enforcement, it has been suggested in New Zealand the Cabinet Manual can be amended to cater for the consideration of social rights by Cabinet alongside the Treaty of Waitangi for instance.[55] Due to the prevailing position in Papua New Guinea that the NGDP and BSO are non-justiciable, this proposal warrants serious consideration.[56] Despite the United Kingdom Manual's non-binding nature, David Cameron expected Ministers and officials would comply with it.[57] The sanction for non-compliance is political, but it may eventually lead to a "legitimate

---

[51] For example in *Board of Inquiry appointed under Public Service (Interim Arrangements) Act 1973 Re Alleged Disciplinary Offences in Office by Mr Phillip Bouraga* [1982] PGSC 11, [1982] PNGLR 178, 23 March 1982, the court has to define what the executive function entailed.

[52] House of Commons Political and Constitutional Reform Committee, above n 41, at [22].

[53] Harland, above n 24.

[54] A convention is a rule that is not supported by the force of law: see Blick, above n 46, at 191.

[55] Claudia Geiringer and Matthew SR Palmer "Human Rights and Social Policy in New Zealand" (2007) Soc Pol J NZ 12.

[56] *Reference by the Ombudsman Commission of Papua New Guinea* [2010] PGSC 40, SC1088, 17 December 2010 at [23].

[57] UK *Cabinet Manual,* above n 23, at iii.

expectation" to comply.[58] A Manual would evince a commitment from the NEC to implement the NGDP and BSO, therefore demonstrating it has taken its constitutional duty seriously.

Since the procedures of the NEC are non-justiciable, a Manual primarily concerned with the procedures of the NEC would be non-justiciable as well; much like the status of the Parliament's Standing Orders.[59] The non-justiciability of the NEC procedures is provided for in the Constitution.[60] But the Manual would contain important constitutional principles (as expressed in the Constitution) pertaining to the executive government. Non-compliance with these provisions is justiciable without the manual, but the Manual would draw the NEC's (and the public's) attention to the requirements of the law. An example discussed below relates to the Prime Minister's referral by the Ombudsman Commission to the Public Prosecutor for breach of the Leadership Code.[61]

3. *Contribution towards general constitutional compliance*

It is not only the lack of implementation of the NGDP and BSO that poses a constitutional issue, but there have been differences in the understanding of the Constitution between the legislature and the executive. Having a manual would also serve a greater purpose of general compliance with the Constitution and contribute towards avoiding the constitutional strains that the country has experienced. Two cases will be highlighted to make the point.

In 1994, Prime Minister Pius Wingti attempted, with another 18 months in office to circumvent the constitutional process to avoid a vote of no-confidence.[62] Under the Constitution, a Prime Minister is immune from a

---

[58] Elizabeth McLeay "What is the Constitutional Status of the New Zealand Cabinet Office Manual?" (1999) PLR 10 at 13.

[59] Constitution, s 134.

[60] Constitution, s 153(2).

[61] The basis of the allegation was the Prime Minister committed Papua New Guinea to a loan without approval from Parliament contrary to Constitution, s 209. The loan was for about US$400 million from the Union Bank of Switzerland to purchase shares in Oil Search Limited, which part owns a Liquefied Natural Gas project in the highlands of Papua New Guinea.

[62] *Haiveta, Leader of the Opposition v Wingti, Prime Minister, Attorney-General, and National Parliament* [1994] PGSC 6, [1994] PNGLR 197, 25 August 1994 [Haiveta]. This case was also discussed in chapter 6 on the legislature on the manner in which the judiciary can incorporate the NGDP and BSO in constitutional interpretation.

vote of no confidence for a period of 18 months from the time he is elected.[63] By resigning and getting re-elected again on the same day, Wingti planned to surprise his political opponents and retain additional life (another 18 months) in power. This move was contested, and the Court decided against Wingti declaring it unconstitutional. The Court relied heavily on the NGDP and BSO to justify its decisions:[64]

> Sections 25(3) and 63(3) of the Constitution direct the courts to interpret and apply the law in such a way to give effect to the National Goals and Directive Principles and to encourage compliance with the Basic Social Obligations, without failing to give effect to the intention of the Parliament or the Constitution. These goals, principles, and obligations are subject to the intention of the Parliament or the provisions of the Constitution … .
>
> I bear all these principles in mind in interpreting the provisions of s 142 of the Constitution.

The court held the view that the surprising manner in which Wingti used Parliament to extend his political rule did not allow Papua New Guineans to participate meaningfully in the decision-making process through their elected representatives consistent with Goal 2 on equality and participation. This decision demonstrates a powerful interaction between the NGDP, BSO and the Constitution. The principles of that case are important, especially as regards meaningful participation by elected representatives in decision-making. Those principles should be captured in a Cabinet Manual, to alert the NEC to such matters when making decisions.

The lesson from the experience of 1994 seems not to have been learnt. In 2011, Papua New Guinea was caught up in a constitutional and political stand-off where two members of Parliament declared they were the Prime Minister, in what is now popularly described as the "two Prime Minister's saga".[65] In that case, Prime Minister Michael Somare was ousted from office by Parliament, in defiance of constitutional procedures, including the Prime Minister and National Executive Council Act 2002. Despite the court's ruling

---

63 Constitution, s 145.

64 *Haivetta*, above n 62.

65 Narokobi, above n 35.

that Somare's unseating was unconstitutional, Peter O'Neil continued to hold office.[66] Both sides claimed to act within the Constitution. The often used phrase was "court appointed prime minister versus parliament appointed prime minister".

This demonstrates the need for the NEC to capture the major principles of the Constitution and of the laws that have legal consequences for the NEC, and reduce them to a single document guiding the NEC in its decision-making process. Obviously there may still be areas the Manual may overlook, but it reduces the opportunity for arbitrary behaviour.

4. Recording constitutional development

Despite a number of amendments, Papua New Guinea has retained the main features of its Constitution enacted in 1975.[67] There have been important constitutional developments affecting the distribution of power between the various government arms. It is important to clarify, simplify and combine these decisions in the document that will help the NEC in its deliberations. It will provide clear guidance on how the NGDP and BSO can be implemented without compromising functions of other arms of government. Important cases in Papua New Guinea's constitutional development can be expressly referred to in the manual. For example, the United Kingdom Cabinet Manual refers to the case of *Pepper v Hart* as a case with the status of constitutional law.[68]

Court decisions on important constitutional matters lend support to a cabinet manual. The courts (especially the Supreme Court) are designated as the guardian of the Constitution.[69] In interpreting the Constitution, the courts actually lay down new laws. New precedents are created on how the

---

66 See *Re Reference to Constitution section 19(1) by East Sepik Provincial Executive* [2011] PGSC 41, SC1154, 12 December 2011; and *Re Reference Pursuant to Constitution section 19(1) by Allan Marat* [2012] PGSC 1, SC1149, 23 January 2012.

67 Two of the major amendments (of the 22) to the Constitution was the introduction of the provincial government system in 1976, and the creation of the Autonomous Region of Bougainville in 2006.

68 *Pepper (Inspector of Taxes) v Hart* [1992] UKHL 3, [1993] AC 593 determined courts can have recourse to Parliamentary records (Hansard) to determine the intention of Parliament when the objective of legislation is ambiguous and it cannot be resolved by reference to the texts of the legislation alone.

69 *Haiveta*, above n 61, per Amet CJ.

Constitution should be interpreted and applied. This adds to the complexity of the constitutional arrangement, especially for non-lawyers. Distilling the main principles of the court's decision along with other important aspects of the Constitution would aid the NEC. A number of cases that have influenced the constitutional development of the country will be discussed below. These cases show two things – firstly the necessity to appreciate constitutional process and secondly, that the experiences of these constitutional developments should not be lost, but continue to influence the behaviour of future governments.

The Constitution is said to speak from time to time, meaning that an interpretation of the Constitution in one period of time may differ when circumstances change in the future.[70] Such changes are important to document. An example is s 124 of the Constitution on the number of sitting days of Parliament.[71] In 1990 the Supreme Court determined that s 124 was only a guide and not mandatory.[72] There would be no legal sanction against Parliament if it did not comply with s 124. Nine years later, the Supreme Court interpreted the provision differently stating that failure to sit the minimum number of sitting days in a year was a breach of the Constitution, making the Parliament liable to enforcement proceedings in the court.[73] Such changes in the interpretation of the Constitution should be recorded in a manual; the NEC has control of the majority of Parliament, and should observe changes in constitutional understanding. The Manual would be produced by the NEC as a statement of its intent in constitutional understanding; but does not prevent consultations with the public to develop a manual. This is a challenging area for Papua New Guinea as often the executive, having control of Parliament would postpone sittings to avoid potential votes of no confidence.[74]

---

70 Constitution, sch 1.2.4.

71 Constitution, s 124.

72 *SCR No 4 of 1990; Reference by the Acting Principal Legal Adviser* [1994] PGSC 17, [1994] PNGLR 141, 11 January 1991 [*Acting Principal Legal Advisor*].

73 *SC Reference No 3 of 1999; Re Calling of the Parliament* [1999] PGSC 55, [1999] PNGLR 285, 25 June 1999 [*Calling of Parliament*]. Despite this ruling there has been no enforcement proceedings against the parliament, and concerns continued in 2010 because parliament was not sitting the required number of sitting days: see Solomon Kantha "Papua New Guinea" (2011) The Contemporary Pacific 23.

74 This behaviour of Parliament has resulted in a number of constitutional cases; see *Acting Principal Legal Adviser*, above n 70, and *Calling of Parliament*, above n 71.

What has emerged over time in Papua New Guinea is important policies have been developed by the government on an ad hoc basis. The reason is government formation depends on coalitions and no single party has been able to secure an outright majority to run a single party government to implement the party policies. Policies are often a result of compromises. These policies are not law, but have assumed a level of importance and permanence. One can categorise them as part of Papua New Guinea's constitutional commitments. Papua New Guinea has adopted a key set of goals in Vision 2050. The primary objective of this policy is to enable Papua New Guinea to improve its human development index to at least a rank of 50 by the end of 2050. Vision 2050 sets some guidance on how this can be done, by focusing on key development priorities. Being an important policy objective of the government, it is given prominence.[75] Vision 2050, however does not have any legal status as does the NGDP and BSO. But a Manual could incorporate it as part of the directional focus of the country.

5. *Whole of government approach*

The Papua New Guinea Constitution's definition of constitutional law extends to organic laws, which have an entrenched status almost the same as the Constitution itself.[76] The Constitution establishes the main organs of the state, their functions and responsibilities, but provides for the specific details of these constitutional institutions to be enacted under separate organic laws. For example, the Constitution established the Ombudsman Commission, but its specific powers and organisational structure is provided for in two Organic Laws: the Organic Law on the Ombudsman Commission; and the Organic Law on the Duties and Responsibilities of Leadership. In addition to this, the types of laws existing in Papua New Guinea are set out in s 9 of the Constitution and include the Constitution, Organic Laws, provincial government laws, ordinary legislation, subsidiary legislation and the underlying law.[77] Such a complex statutory framework presents a formidable task for any decision-maker, let alone the NEC, to steer through to ensure

[75] The Prime Ministers Department website refers to *PNG Vision 2050* as an important policy it tries to implement <www.officeofprimeminister.com>.

[76] Constitution, sch 1.2 defines constitutional law as composed of the Constitution, organic law and amendments to the Constitution; s 13 to 17 of the Constitution set out the enactment (of organic laws), amendment and repeal process of the Constitution and organic laws.

[77] The Underlying Law Act, s 4 defines the sources of the underlying law as customary law and common law and equity.

that its decisions are legally correct, and at the same time implement the NGDP and BSO. Capturing the main principles of these laws as they pertain to the NEC in a single document would enable a more effective guide for the NEC to operate within the parameters of the law.

Another example where a manual would enable effective governance is in the area of devolution of power. In the United Kingdom, devolution of power to Northern Ireland, Scotland and Wales is regulated by legislation[78] and expressly identified in the Manual.[79] In Papua New Guinea there are 21 provinces and one autonomous region (Bougainville). The political head of a province is the governor. He or she is a member of the provincial assembly and concurrently a member of the national Parliament. The provincial assembly is made up of presidents of local level governments. Each local level government has its own assembly consisting of ward members. For the former, the Organic Law on Provincial and Local Level Government sets up the legislative areas of competence for each of the provinces. Furthermore, there are local level governments in each of the provinces, which have law-making powers over certain subject areas.[80] It is important that the national government does not make laws for a subject that is designated for a province or a local level government. Bougainville, with its special relationship to Papua New Guinea and a higher degree of autonomy than the other provinces, is regulated by a separate Organic Law.[81] A manual would help the government identify the various limitations on its powers on certain subject matters and help the NEC steer through this complex area.

The complexity of the level of legal compliance with the constitutional obligation to implement the NGDP and BSO requires a measure of guidance that can bring all these diverse pieces of legislation together for a common objective.

---

78 Northern Ireland Act 1998; Scotland Act 1998; and Government of Wales Act 2006 (superseding the Government of Wales Act 1998).

79 UK *Cabinet Manual*, above n 23, at [8.1].

80 Organic Law on the Provincial Governments and Local-level Governments, s 42 sets out the subject areas for provincial laws and s 44 sets out the areas for local level government laws. Essentially a subject not distributed to the province or the local level government remains with the national government, unless the matter is of national interest (s 41).

81 Organic Law on Peace-Building in Bougainville-Autonomous Bougainville Government and Bougainville Referendum 2002.

E. The Content of the Manual

1. Introduction

This part of the chapter first conducts a comparison of the contents of the manuals/handbook from Australia, New Zealand and the United Kingdom and, second, makes specific suggestions for Papua New Guinea.

2. Contents of manual: Australia, New Zealand and the United Kingdom

The Australian Cabinet Handbook has the following content, reflecting its practical orientation:

- Cabinet Government in Australia;
- Cabinet business; and
- Cabinet meetings.

There are three main subjects and the specific details are set out in 11 annexes, specifying the roles and responsibilities of each of the stakeholders in preparing Cabinet documentation amongst other requirements. The Handbook guides ministers' preparation of submissions to Cabinet and also helps prevent confusion over ministerial subject areas. Persons singled out in the Handbook are the Prime Minister, ministers, Cabinet secretary and Cabinet committees.

The New Zealand Cabinet Manual covers the following areas:

- Governor-General and the Executive Council;
- Ministers of the Crown: Appointment and Role;
- Ministers of the Crown and the State Sector;
- Ministers and the Law;
- Cabinet Decision Making;
- Elections, Transitions and Government Formation;
- The Executive, Legislation and the House; and
- Official Information.

New Zealand's Manual is more detailed than the Australian Handbook, because it captures the main principles of the country's constitutional arrangements. It sets out in some detail how Cabinet is to conduct itself, and simultaneously maintain a compliant constitutional relationship with other arms of government.

In the United Kingdom, there is the following:

- The Sovereign;
- Elections and government formation;
- The Executive – the Prime Minister, ministers and the structure of government;
- Collective Cabinet decision-making;
- The Executive and Parliament;
- The Executive and the Law;
- Ministers and the Civil Service;
- Relations with Devolved Administration and Local Government;
- Relations with the European Union and other international institutions;
- Government finance and expenditure; and
- Official information.

Comparing the United Kingdom model to New Zealand, the former's content is quite exhaustive, attempting to capture the essence of the country's complex constitutional structure. There is a level of complexity apparent in Papua New Guinea's government system such that a manual as it operates in New Zealand and the United Kingdom may be helpful. Papua New Guinea has three levels of government (national, provincial and local), and an autonomous region in Bougainville. Coordinating these complex relationships from guidelines out of a single document is practically beneficial to the NEC.

3. *Contents of a NEC manual*

A Cabinet Manual for Papua New Guinea can be an important device to concurrently reflect the country's constitutional arrangements and focus attention on the NGDP and BSO. The following subjects are recommended:

- Main Principles of Government;
- The Executive and the Law;
- The Executive and the Parliament;
- The Executive and the Ombudsman Commission; and
- Government Finance and Expenditure.

Each of these areas links up with the other government arms, including the Ombudsman Commission. A Cabinet Manual with principles guiding how the government operates places all ministers, civil servants, provincial (including the Autonomous Region of Bougainville) and local level governments, on equal footing to appreciate the process of governance and the separate areas of responsibilities. Some comments will now be offered for each of these proposed subject areas for the NEC manual.

(a) Main Principles of Government

The beginning of the cabinet manual should outline the NGDP and BSO and state clearly that the executive is committed to fulfilling them in the performance of its functions. All decisions of the government would be weighed against the standards of the Basic Rights and the NGDP and BSO.[82] Where a decision of the NEC can fulfil the NGDP and BSO, it should do so. This is not only a non-justiciable duty, but also a justiciable one.[83] This dual non-legal and legal nature of the NGDP and BSO is provided for in ss 25 and 63 of the Constitution.[84]

If the NGDP and BSO are stated clearly at the commencement of the manual, it would draw the attention of the NEC to them. For example, in New Zealand, the fundamental principles governing New Zealand constitutional arrangement, touching on matters such as the decisions of the courts, the

---

[82] CPC Report, above n 30, see ch 2 generally, especially at 2/1 [6].

[83] Constitution, ss 25(3) and 63(3).

[84] This is the interpretation of ss 25(3) and 63(3) defended in chapter 4.

Treaty of Waitangi and conventions are marked out clearly in the manual.[85] In the United Kingdom, the manual refers to the role of the Sovereign, the idea of parliamentary democracy and statutes such as the Magna Carta 1215.[86] Papua New Guinea's manual could demonstrate an appreciation of its home-grown Constitution by making express reference to the NGDP and BSO as first, the country's founding principles and second, the Constitution's underlying aims.[87]

Significantly, the preamble to the Papua New Guinea Constitution states clearly that all power belongs to the people and that it is exercised through the people's representatives. Leaders must be constantly reminded of this. This power is to be exercised to fulfil the NGDP and BSO.

(b) The executive and the law

Two legal avenues are considered here, where the executive's decision (including the NEC) can be reviewed in court against the basis of the NGDP and BSO. They are first, judicial review of administrative action and second, matters of statutory and constitutional interpretation. Detailed discussions on these two aspects of the judiciary will be taken up in chapter 9. What follows is a brief overview of the main points of these two matters, to set the context for the proposal to incorporate provisions in the manual alerting the NEC to this level of judicial scrutiny.

(i) Judicial review

When the executive implements legislation, it exercises decision-making powers and this can be subject to judicial review.[88] If the executive is not able to promote the NGDP and BSO in a decision, then it should state the reasons for it. A person aggrieved by such a decision can seek review on the basis of ss 25(3) and 63(3) of the Constitution using the *Wednesbury* test of reasonableness under the National Court Rules.[89] If the courts adopt this approach, it would require the executive and the NEC in particular as the head of the executive in Papua New Guinea to adequately defend its decisions when it is judicially reviewed. The Manual for the NEC would provide this guide in decision-making.

---

[85] NZ *Cabinet Manual*, above n 22, at 2.

[86] UK *Cabinet Manual*, above n 23, at 2.

[87] See chapter 3.

[88] The grounds of judicial review are discussed in chapter 9.

[89] This point was discussed in chapter 7.

Reviewing a NEC outcome requires court access to the materials the NEC relied on to make its decision. But documents used in the NEC decision including the NEC submission may be privileged. What can be made available would be the minutes of the decision recording separately the manner in which the NGDP and BSO were considered and the reasons either for their implementation or not. The minutes would be made available to the court when it undertakes its process of review on the basis of *Wednesbury* reasonableness. The manner of recording the engagement of the NGDP and BSO in the decision-making process ought to be stated clearly in the Manual.

(ii) Interpretation and application of laws

The other legal avenue for the court's intervention in the executive function is the interpretation and application of the Constitution, Organic Laws and legislation. Chapter 7 recommended that the legislature enacts laws with specific reference to the NGDP and BSO in the preamble and/or in the objectives provision. If the courts then use a contextual role of preambles in statutory interpretation they will naturally engage the NGDP and BSO. This is an indication to the executive as to the manner in which its decisions will be reviewed by the court. It therefore requires the executive to respond accordingly to both the direction of the legislature in implementing Acts and the attitude of the courts in statutory interpretation. It is submitted that the best means of ensuring a harmonious relationship with the other arms of government in implementing the NGDP and BSO would be through a manual which explicitly proposes the consideration of the NGDP and BSO.

The executive operates by virtue of law, primarily legislation. Chapter 7 recommended Parliament adopts consistent reference to the NGDP and BSO in legislation more consistently. If Parliament regularly adopts the proposal of engaging the NGDP and/or BSO in the legislation, it will consequently provide a clear direction to the executive of which Goals or Obligations it should promote in implementing the relevant legislation. The end result would be a recording of this practice in the Manual. A greater implementation effort by both the legislature and the executive would have been achieved.

(c) The executive and the parliament

The NEC is politically responsible to the Parliament under the principle of collective responsibility.[90] Parliamentary question time and debates

---

[90] Constitution, s 141.

are avenues to hold the executive to account for its decisions (or lack of). Conversely, it is also an opportunity for the executive to promote its performance. Parliament also has the opportunity to inquire about laws it has enacted from the executive whether it has fulfilled the NGDP and BSO in implementing these laws. The ultimate control that the Parliament has over the executive is to remove it from office through a vote of no confidence.[91]

In countries like Australia, New Zealand and the United Kingdom, the Cabinet Handbook/Manual states clearly that the executive's existence is by virtue of the legislature's confidence.[92] Papua New Guinea has witnessed a great degree of executive dominance over the legislature.[93] For example, of the 111 members of Parliament, the Opposition currently has fewer than 10 MPs. Despite the executive's overwhelming majority, it is a requirement of the Constitution that it justifies its decisions to Parliament. A manual that demonstrates the executive's commitment to a sense of accountability to the legislature is important to help maintain an appropriate balance between the legislature and the executive.

Much of the legislative programme of the Parliament in a Westminster government system is determined by the executive and Papua New Guinea is no exception. The Manual would take up the proposal for any legislation initiated by the executive to specifically have a preamble and/or objective section stating which NGDP and/or BSO the legislation intends to implement. This connects the two arms of government – the executive and the legislature. In chapter 7 it was recommended that if the legislature did not enact legislation that took due account of the NGDP and/or BSO it would be liable to a constitutionality challenge. A statement in the Manual capturing this proposed requirement would reflect the legal obligation of the legislature.

The level of engagement by laws with the NGDP and BSO would increase if the NEC's attention is drawn to sponsoring Bills which expressly identify and promote a particular NGDP and/or BSO. The flow on effect on the implementation of the laws by the executive and the interpretation of the law by the judiciary using a contextual role of preambles in statutory

---

91 The use of the motion of no confidence is discussed later in the chapter.

92 Australia *Cabinet Handbook*, above n 29, at [13]; NZ *Cabinet Manual*, above n 22, at 3; UK *Cabinet Manual*, above n 23, at [5.2].

93 Bal Kama "Can PNG democracy survive without the Opposition?" (3 September 2014) Dev Policy Blog <http://devpolicy.org>.

interpretation (discussed in chapters5 and 9) should help fulfil the NGDP and BSO.

(d) The executive and the Ombudsman Commission

The Ombudsman Commission has an important accountability role in the government system. Members of the NEC are subject to the twin jurisdictions of the Ombudsman Commission: the administrative complaints function and the Leadership Code. In both these matters, the Ombudsman Commission takes account of the NGDP and/or BSO.[94] Drawing the attention of the NEC to the requirements of the Ombudsman Commission makes sense, too, as Ministers are alerted to these requirements before decisions are made. For the purposes of the Leadership Code, the NGDP and BSO are justiciable that is, enforceable in a Leadership Tribunal.[95] Having clear guidelines stating what type of conduct and behaviour are expected of the leaders who are subject to the jurisdiction of the Ombudsman Commission is important.

The Manual should outline matters which are potentially the subject of the Ombudsman Commission investigation for wrong conduct.[96] It would remind leaders of what good administration entails. Ministers can then encourage their departments to meet these requirements. An example which is discussed in detail in chapter 10 was the Peter Yama case.[97] Yama unfairly and inequitably distributed public funds under his control contrary to the NGDP, particularly Goal 2 and was found to have committed misconduct in office by the Leadership Tribunal. A Manual which guides the conduct of the Minister may help the leader avoid running foul with the Leadership Code.

An important limitation on the power of the executive is stated in s 219(3) of the Constitution:

> (3) The Commission shall not inquire into the justifiability of a policy of the National Government or a Minister or a provincial government or a member of a provincial executive, except insofar as the policy may be contrary to law or to the National Goals and Directive Principles, the

---

94 Constitution, ss 25(3), 63(3) and s 219(1)(B).

95 Constitution, ss 25(3) and 63(3).

96 For definition of wrong conduct: see Constitution, s 219(2).

97 *In the matter of Peter Yama, Member of Parliament* [2004] PGLT 2, N2746, 1 December 2004.

Basic Rights or the Basic Social Obligations, or of any act of the Parliament.

It is imperative that this requirement is set out clearly in the Manual so the NEC will be guided as it carries out its duties.

Australia, New Zealand and the United Kingdom have ombudsman institutions, but these institutions do not have the role of supervising and enforcing a Leadership Code. In Australia, New Zealand and the United Kingdom, the Handbook or Manual sets out requirements for integrity in office, and avoiding conflict of interests, including the process for dealing with a conflict of interest during a Cabinet meeting.[98] Papua New Guinea has a Leadership Code, where the NGDP and/or BSO are justiciable.[99] The Leadership Code refers specifically to ministerial behaviour, especially to avoiding conflicts of interest.[100] A Manual which draws the attention of the members of the NEC to this requirement encourages a collective approach to compliance instead of leaving it to the conscience of the individual Minister.[101] Responsibility is placed on the Prime Minister as chairperson of the NEC to routinely remind Ministers.

(e) Government finance and expenditure

Parliament has ultimate authority to approve the annual supply Bill or the budget under s 209 of the Constitution. In *Norah Mairi v Alkan Tololo, Secretary for Education*[102] and *Saleng Mileng v Alkan Tololo Secretary for Education*[103] the Court, relying on the English case of *Attorney-General v Wilts United Dairies Ltd*,[104] held certain fees imposed on students purportedly under the Education Act 1970 were in reality taxes and an illegal exercise of power by the executive, as it was only the legislature that has the power to

---

98 Australia *Cabinet Handbook*, above n 29, at 25–34; UK *Cabinet Manual*, above n 23, at 26.

99 Constitution, ss 25(4) and 63(4).

100 Organic Law on the Duties and Responsibilities of Leadership, s 9.

101 For example former Public Service Minister Peter Peipul was referred for misconduct in office by the Ombudsman Commission for failing to declare his interest in the appointment of his brother to an important public office. See *Peipul v The Leadership Tribunal* [2002] PGSC 1, SC706, 24 May 2002.

102 *Mairi v Tololo, Secretary for Education* [1976] PGSC 9, [1976] PNGLR 125, 15 April 1976 [*Mairi*].

103 *Mileng v Tololo* [1976] PGSC 12, [1976] PNGLR 447, 6 October 1976.

104 *Attorney-General v Wilts United Dairies Ltd* (1921) 37 TLR 884.

impose taxes. The Court's decision also referred to the English Bill of Rights of 1689 for its historic relation to s 209.[105] This is an important area, because in August 2014 the Prime Minister was referred to the Public Prosecutor by the Ombudsman Commission for misconduct in office.[106] The basis of the allegation was that the Prime Minister had committed Papua New Guinea to a loan from an international financier without obtaining approval from Parliament. On its face, it is a clear requirement of the Constitution which the Prime Minister appears not to have complied with. This constitutional requirement has its roots in the historical tradition of the Westminster system emanating from the Glorious Revolution of 1688, where parliament successfully wrested financial powers from the monarchy.

The Treasury Department of Papua New Guinea has a Manual that refers to s 209 of the Constitution among other laws to guide governmental bodies to prepare budget submissions for funding, reporting and accountability.[107] It also spells out the budget cycle and approval process. Interestingly, the Treasury Manual does not refer to the NGDP and BSO. Allocating resources to fulfil the NGDP and BSO is an important step to fulfilling them. The NEC should have its own Manual that connects with that of the Treasury Department. Both Manuals should make reference to the NGDP and BSO.

When the NEC is formulating the budget for submission to Parliament for approval, the Manual should state that the NEC ought to allocate resources to matters that fulfil the NGDP and BSO.[108] Government institutions are established by legislation, and such laws refer to the NGDP and/or BSO.[109] Funding these statutory institutions will result in these organisations achieving the NGDP and/or BSO.[110]

Another area where the Manual can draw the attention of the NEC to the NGDP and BSO is the need to pay attention to any report a committee of

---

105 *Mairi*, above n 102, at 130 per Frost CJ.

106 Prime Minister Peter O'Neil was referred to the Public Prosecutor to consider a prosecution before the Leadership Tribunal for alleged misconduct in office in August 2014.

107 Papua New Guinea Department of Treasury *Budget Manual* (10 September 2014) <www.treasury.gov.pg>.

108 The NEC is required by the Constitution to formulate the budget (s 210(1)). Parliament has sole authority to approve, but this approval is restricted to either not approving the budget in total or to reduce certain items; it cannot change or increase (s 210(2)).

109 Refer to chapter 7 for an elaboration of this point.

110 This proposal was made in chapter 7.

the Parliament may make in terms of reviewing the previous year's finance and expenditure. The NEC will be required to consider any such reports in formulating the following year's budget. In chapter 7, it was pointed out that the Plans and Estimates Committee could take up this role. The Manual can be an important link between the role of the parliamentary committee and the NEC in terms of the latter giving due regard to the recommendations in the committee's report.

F. Legal Status and Accessibility of the Manual

Although the NEC procedure is non-justiciable, the manual proposed for the NEC would be documentary evidence of constitutional and legal expectations.[111] It would not only demonstrates to the public the executive's commitment to upholding the country's constitution and the fundamental principles underlying it, but what the NEC does in fact. The public is informed of the executive's understanding of the present state of the Constitution. From the many varied pieces of constitutional laws and policies, the NEC Manual brings them together in one document and supports the NEC in coordinating these commitments so that there is an overall policy and legal compliance.

However, that does not mean the matters it refers to, especially the fulfilment of the NGDP and/or BSO are non-justiciable. It will be recalled that a decision of the NEC can be reviewed by the courts for not making reasonable attempts to implement the NGDP and/or BSO.[112] Such judicial scrutiny against the terms of the NGDP and/or BSO should not come as a surprise to the NEC. The Manual would set out the extent to which the NGDP and BSO are justiciable in the decision-making process.

What is important, as noted above, is while NEC procedure is non-justiciable, the NEC should still demonstrate to the court its attempts to implement the NGDP and/or BSO within the dual confines of the particular law on the subject and reasonableness.

The proposed Manual should be publicly available to ensure transparency in government decision-making. For example in 2014, the NEC awarded a K71 million contract (about NZ$30m) to a foreign pharmaceutical company

---

[111] Constitution, s 153(2).

[112] This argument was presented in chapter 6.

to distribute medicines throughout the country. Originally, the Tender Board indicated bidding companies had to comply with International Standards Organisations (ISO) benchmarks to ensure they were qualified and reputable.[113] During the tender process, the NEC dropped this requirement. The contract was awarded to a company that did not satisfy the ISO standards, leading to widespread complaints about the government's decision. One of the strongest criticisms was from the Papua New Guinea National Doctors Association.[114] The government indicated it would not reverse its decision to award the contract to this company.

A NEC Manual would require the NEC to deliberate on how this medicine supply contract would interact with the NGDP and BSO. National Goal 1 calls for integral human development. Under Directive Principle 4 of this Goal, it calls for "… improvement in the level of nutrition and the standard of public health to enable our people to attain self-fulfilment …". Taking into account this principle would require the NEC to consider the purpose of the contract and its beneficiaries, the ordinary people, especially in the rural areas. In aid of the position of the NGDP the BSO states:

> (c) to exercise the rights guaranteed or conferred by this Constitution, and to use the opportunities made available to them under it to participate fully in the government of the Nation; …

A person who intends to review such a decision by way of judicial review would ask the NEC how it took into account relevant Goals and Obligations. The public would be participating in the governance of the country through the ability to scrutinise the decision because of a transparent process. Such scrutiny would portray a message to the government not to take the views of the public for granted in important decisions. It would ensure active participation by the people in the governing process. In the United Kingdom it

---

113 Rowan Callick "High-cost bid secures tender for drug distribution in PNG" *The Australian* (online ed, Surry Hills, NSW, 14 March 2014).

114 Martyn Namarong "The Regime, the Drug Company and the 'murder' of #PNG Citizens!" (14 January 2014) Namarong Blog Spot <http://namorong.blogspot.com.au>. The Papua New Guinea National Doctors Association states:

> The Medical Society of PNG appeals to the Prime Minister to reject the recommendation from the CSTB (Central Supplies and Tenders Board) in this case, and insist that tenders for the nation's medicines only be accepted from ISO Quality Management System accredited companies who promise to only supply medicines from GMP accredited manufacturers.

is possible to challenge inconsistent allocation of funds to government policy. For example, a civil society organisation has challenged government decisions because of apprehension of aid being applied for undesirable purposes.[115] In that case, potential aid recipients with questionable backgrounds were prevented by civil society organisation through successful litigation. Such cases provide useful guidance for Papua New Guinea on the extent of judicial review of government policy and resource allocation.

It may be that over time, a new legal doctrine may emerge together with a legitimate expectation that the manual should be complied with.[116] This angle is not taken up here. The Manual proposed, as in New Zealand will be non-justiciable. *Te Waka Hi Ika O Te Arawa v Graham* provides perhaps the most recent view on the New Zealand Cabinet Manual.[117] The Cabinet Manual "outlines conventions and procedures of Cabinet government but without a statutory basis".[118] However, it can be used to establish the proper process of government.[119] Accepting the New Zealand legal position as appropriate for Papua New Guinea, the Manual, as a constitutional document, helps the NEC coordinate its functions amongst the complex government machinery to ensure the NGDP and BSO are implemented. Some of these requirements to implement the NGDP and BSO are potentially justiciable, and the NEC must be conscious of them in its decision-making process.[120]

IV. Conclusion

This chapter recommended the NEC adopts a Cabinet Manual that demonstrates the executive's constitutional understanding and commitment to the NGDP and BSO underlying the Constitution as well as the substantive Constitution. A Manual would help the NEC link up its functions with that of the other governmental bodies that also have the duty to implement the NGDP and BSO.

---

115 *R v Secretary of State for Foreign and Commonwealth Affairs, ex parte World Development Movement Ltd* [1995] 1 All ER 611.

116 House of Commons Political and Constitutional Reform Committee, above n 41, at 12.

117 *Te Waka Hi Ika O Te Arawa v Graham* CA556/96, 27 November 1996 [*Te Waka*].

118 *Te Waka*, per Richardson P, referred to by Grant Duncan "New Zealand's Cabinet Manual: How Does It Shape Constitutional Conventions?" (2014) Parl Aff 1 at 8.

119 House of Commons Political and Constitutional Reform Committee, above n 41, at 12.

120 For example, the use of NGDP and BSO in judicial review discussed in chapter 1, and constitutionality challenges against the legislature for not making reasonable attempts to implement legislation proposed in chapter 7.

There are many reasons that justify the adoption of a Manual for the NEC. They include the fact it can enable the effective implementation of the NGDP and BSO in a non-justiciable manner, consistent with ss 25(2) and 63(2) of the Constitution. A Manual can also help the NEC comply with its constitutional obligations by distilling main principles of government as they apply to the NEC. Another reason is the developing nature of constitutional law. A Manual may help state in a clear but simple manner the current state of the law.

What is important is the content of the Manual, which brings together the various proposals presented in this book. The proposed Manual should be available publicly and would have a clear statement expressing the NEC's commitment to fulfilling the NGDP and/or BSO. The public is then made aware of the fact that the NEC has made a serious commitment to fulfilling the NGDP and BSO. Other measures which are proposed for the legislature, the judiciary and the ombudsman are brought to the attention of the NEC in the Manual.

The Manual itself would be non-justiciable but it would contain a clear statement on how the NEC should adopt specific procedures to demonstrate to an aggrieved person how it has engaged the NGDP and/or BSO in its decision and for the courts too, if the decision is judicially reviewed.

CHAPTER NINE
THE JUDICIARY

I. Introduction

This chapter will focus on the judiciary and how its functions under the Constitution can be used effectively to implement the NGDP and BSO. The judiciary is one of the authorities required to implement the NGDP and BSO.[1] Under the Constitution, the judiciary consists of the Supreme Court, National Court and other statutory courts.[2] The Supreme Court is the highest court of appeal and also hears cases on constitutional issues unless the Constitution grants jurisdiction to another court. The National Court is the court of first instance in most civil disputes including judicial review of administrative matters and underlying law causes of action (which has customary law and common law as its source), except where statute confers jurisdiction on another court or tribunal such as the District Court. This is not to say other courts like the Village Court and the District Court have no role to implement the NGDP and BSO. The Supreme Court and the National Court lie at the apex of the court system in Papua New Guinea and their decisions have significant legal and political implications for the operation of other branches of government.[3]

This chapter has seven parts. Part I is the introduction. Part II presents the contextual role of preambles as the appropriate rule of statutory interpretation to implement the NGDP and BSO. Part III makes a proposal for the development of the underlying law by the court in a way consistent with the NGDP and BSO. Part IV makes proposals for the implementation of the NGDP and BSO in the judicial review of administrative action. Part V will look at weak-form judicial review and how it could have been properly

---

1 Constitution, ss 25(3) and 63(3) refer to exercising judicial power (amongst legislative, administrative and other powers) to give effect to the NGDP and BSO respectively.

2 Constitution, s 155 (1).

3 For Village Courts: see Village Court Act 1989; and for District Court: see District Court Act 1963.

grounded in the Constitution to enable the courts to better implement the NGDP and BSO. Part VI discusses the protection and enforcement of human rights and freedoms and its interaction with the NGDP and BSO. Part VII concludes the chapter.

II. Contextual Role of Preambles and Indirect Justiciability

A. Introduction

Chapter 4 argued the courts have incorrectly limited the NGDP and BSO to an interpretation aid and have not ventured into examining the implication of a positive duty to implement the NGDP and BSO. Chapter 4 also highlighted the difference between the two approaches (interpretive aid versus indirect justiciability). But even if the NGDP and BSO are considered as an aid to interpretation, there is scope for the courts to make greater use of them in the context of indirect justiciability.

The NGDP and BSO are situated in the preamble of the Constitution.[4] Although the Constitution applies the common law case of doubt approach on the use of preambles, the NGDP and BSO are distinguished by ss 25 and 63.[5] This suggests the NGDP and BSO should always be considered in appropriate cases to provide the context of the Constitution and legislation in the court's interpretive function. This is unless the Constitution or Parliament's intention is expressed otherwise. A proper meaning cannot be ascribed to words in the Constitution and legislation unless the judicial mind is "enlightened" by the NGDP and BSO.[6]

B. Contextual Role of Statutory Interpretation

Chapter 5 highlighted the two competing views courts take of preambles and the difficulty this may cause for implementing the NGDP and BSO. The views were constructive and contextual. The latter was found to be more compatible with implementation. The contextual role of preambles in statutory interpretation also works well with active reference to the NGDP and BSO in the preamble and/or objectives section of the legislation, recommended in chapter 7. Interpreting legislation will require automatic

4 Constitution, sch 1.2.3 "Form of the Constitutional Laws".

5 Schedule 1.2.3.

6 *SCR No 3 of 1986; Ref by Simbu Provincial Executive* [1987] PGSC 17, [1987] PNGLR 151, 10 April 1987 at 174 per Barnett J [Simbu].

reference to the NGDP and BSO as part of the process of having recourse to its context. In the English case of *Attorney-General v Prince Ernest Augustus of New Hanover (Prince Ernest of Hanover)* the Court stated preambles are an integral part of the Act:[7]

> For words, and particularly general words, cannot be read in isolation: their colour and content are derived from their context. So it is that I conceive it to be my right and duty to examine every word of a statute in its context, and I use 'context' in its widest sense, which I have already indicated as including not only other enacting provisions of the same statute, but its preamble, the existing state of the law, other statutes in pari materia, and the mischief which I can, by those and other legitimate means, discern the statute was intended to remedy.

The meaning of words and phrases in legislation are derived from a context of which the preamble is an important element. Use of the preamble in statutory interpretation should therefore not be restricted to instances of ambiguity only.[8] Legislation having a particular NGDP and BSO will have its provisions interpreted to promote them.

This statement from *SCR No 3 of 1986; Ref by Simbu Provincial Executive* (*Simbu*) best expresses the contextual approach in Papua New Guinea:[9]

> When interpreting the details of a provision in a constitutional law ... an essential pre-requisite [is] for the judicial mind to be enlightened by the spirit of the Constitution itself. This enlightenment comes from developing a thorough understanding of the National Goals and Directive Principles, by taking an overview which will place the particular provision in the context of the total legislative scheme of which it forms a part and by seeking to understand the intention of the founding fathers as they expressed it on behalf of the people, when enacting the Constitution and subsequent amendments.

---

7 *Attorney-General v Prince Ernest Augustus of Hanover* [1957] AC 436 (HL) [*Prince Ernest Augustus*].

8 *Prince Ernest Augustus*, at 174.

9 *Simbu*, above n 6, at 174 per Barnett J.

The reason why the preamble should be referred to in statutory interpretation to either confirm the meaning of legislation or resolve an ambiguity is because it provides a good indication of the intention of the legislation, its scope or purpose, and the values it seeks to promote.[10] This view of the preamble follows a line of common law authority such as *Prince Ernest of Hanover*, which have held a preamble is part of the Act.[11]

C. Indirect Justiciability and the Contextual Approach

1. *Introduction*

The chapter proposes an area in which the courts can use the contextual approach to implement the NGDP and BSO. This approach places the onus on the parties to the case, and the manner in which they frame constitutional issue(s), to point the court to using a contextual approach to interpret the law and determine the issue based on the cause of action pleaded before the court.

2. *Framing constitutional issues for the courts using NGDP and/ or BSO – Indirect justiciability*

A survey of the Supreme Court cases dealing with constitutional interpretation under s 19 of the Constitution revealed framing constitutional questions to couch the NGDP and BSO is not common. Ordinarily, the cases that have had made reference to the NGDP and/or BSO in the decision do so on the Court's initiative. But a pro-active use of the NGDP and BSO in framing questions is a permissible exercise of indirect justiciability. It can draw the Court's attention to using the contextual method of statutory (or constitutional) interpretation.

An example of actively framing constitutional issues to engage the NGDP and BSO was the case of *Reference by the Ombudsman Commission of Papua New Guinea* (*Ref by OCPNG*).[12] A short background to this case is necessary to understand the nature of the constitutional issues determined by the court. Papua New Guinea has three levels of government: local, provincial and national. The Constitution (under Part VIA) provides for an Organic

10 Anne Winckel "The Contextual Role of a Preamble in Statutory Interpretation" (1999) 23 MULR 184 at 185.

11 *Prince Ernest Augustus*, above n 7, at 467.

12 *Reference by the Ombudsman Commission of Papua New Guinea* [2010] PGSC 10, SC1058, 4 June 2010 [*Ref by OCPNG*].

Law to establish a provincial government system. This is the Organic Law on Provincial Government and Local Level Government 1995 (OLPGLLG). A provincial government is made up of the Provincial Assembly, the Provincial Executive and the Head of the Provincial Executive. Section 187C(2)(a) of the Constitution states a Provincial Assembly must be constituted by a mainly elective body.

In reality, the Provincial Assembly representation is nominal. There are no directly elected members of the Provincial Assembly being composed of elected local government level Presidents and national Members of Parliament. The provincial executive is selected from the Provincial Assembly (except for the head of the province, the Governor, who is directly elected by the province). In 2000, Parliament made amendments to the OLPGLLG. These amendments (s 18) removed members of the local level government (Presidents) from the Provincial Assembly and, as a result, of the executive too (because one had to be a Member of the Provincial Assembly before appointment to the executive arm of the Assembly). This amendment became the subject of court proceedings initiated by the Ombudsman Commission which has power under the Constitution to challenge laws or proposed laws in the Supreme Court.[13]

The OLPGLLG, the subject of the constitutional litigation, had in its preamble the purpose of fulfilling Goal 2 on equality and participation. The Referrer (Ombudsman Commission) framed the question for the Supreme Court, thus:

> Whether Sections 1 and 2 of the Organic Law on Provincial Governments and Local-Level Governments (Amendment No 10) Laws 2006, in removing:
>
> (1) Heads of the rural Local-Level Government as Members of the Provincial Assembly; and
>
> (2) One representative to represent the heads of both urban authorities and urban councils as member of the Provincial Assembly; and
>
> (3) Either the heads of the rural Local-level Government or the representative of the heads of both urban authorities

[13] Constitution, s 19.

> and urban councils from contesting the post of Deputy Governor
>
> is contrary to the requirements of Section 187C(2)(a) of the Constitution to have "an elective or mainly elective legislature", as understood, applied and enforced within the meaning of the Second National Goal (Equality and Participation) of the National Goals and Directive Principles and therefore unconstitutional?

Two observations can be made about this question. The first is the Ombudsman Commission correctly identified the second National Goal on equality and participation in the way it raised the question for the court, because this goal is in the preamble of the OLPLLG. The question also brings attention to the purpose (or context) of the OLPLLG, which is to fulfil the NGDP. The second observation is in order for the court to determine the constitutionality of the amendments to the OLPLLG if it had to choose an interpretation of s 187C(2)(a) that is consistent with the NGDP. Such an approach is supported by a contextual approach to interpretation. The Court decided in *Ref by OCPNG* the amendments were contrary to the Constitution and declared them invalid. No doubt the NGDP played an important role in reaching this outcome:[14]

> The *Amendment Law* is inconsistent with the meaning, purpose and spirit of *Constitution*, s 187C 2) (a) and the whole purpose of provincial government system in the *Constitution*. The *Amendment Law* effectively removes people at the provincial, district and community level from participation in the legislative process and important policy decisions through the provincial legislature … . It is contrary to the intentions and aspirations of the people, expressed through the *Constitution*, of a participatory democracy where the people at all levels of the community; in their own diverse way; in all matters that concern them at their own level; are active participants in decision-making at all levels of government; and not mere spectators and recipients of goods and services delivered by the national government.

---

[14] *Ref by OCPNG*, above n 12, at [68] per Injia CJ.

This approach of highlighting the NGDP and BSO in framing questions has two consequences. First, courts are compelled to refer to the NGDP and BSO in the course of their decision, because they are raised directly in the issue(s) for determination; and second, and importantly, it demonstrates the indirect justiciability of the NGDP and BSO.

3. *Conclusion*

The use of the contextual approach to statutory interpretation enables the court to engage with the context of the legislation, by considering its preamble. Since the NGDP and BSO are part of the preamble of the Constitution, using the contextual rule of interpretation provides an opportunity to implement the NGDP and BSO meaningfully.

III. Developing the Underlying Law

A. Introduction

The sources of the underlying law of Papua New Guinea consists of customary law, common law and equity of England prior to 1975, and court made law.[15] In 2000 Parliament passed the Underlying Law Act 2000 to fulfil the constitutional dictate to enact such a law. This legislation was based on the recommendations of the Law Reform Commission in 1977, but did not get much attention from the Parliament until 2000.[16] The Law Reform Commission's recommendation had an extensive preamble that referred strongly to the NGDP.[17] This section looks at the role of the NGDP and BSO in the development of the underlying law in the Act passed in 2000.

There have not been many cases on the Underlying Law Act. The case of *New Britain Oil Palm Ltd v Sukuramu* exposed the practical limitations of the Act and prompted the courts to rectify the situation.[18] In the view of the Supreme Court, a court could not develop new principles of the

---

15 Underlying Law Act 2000, ss 3 and 7. The underlying law has new case law, developed using either custom or the common law as a source (Underlying Law Act 2000, s 3). It also relates to new law developed by the courts, where no existing law applies to the particular facts (Underlying Law Act, s 7).

16 Law Reform Commission of Papua New Guinea *Role of Customary Law in the Legal System* (Law Reform Commission, Waigani, 1977) vol 7.

17 At 15.

18 *New Britain Oil Palm Ltd v Sukuramu* [2008] PGSC 29, SC946, 30 October 2008.

underlying law without the parties expressly pleading this claim in the originating process. Soon after this decision, the Court (under its delegated authority), enacted the Rules of the National Court of Justice (Underlying Law Amendment) 2011 (Underlying Law Rules). Persons going to court now have more certainty in pleading their claim under specific court rules.

B. Proposals for Implementing the NGDP and BSO in the Development of the Underlying Law

1. NGDP and BSO as a shield

(a) Introduction

There are two proposals to enable implementation of the NGDP and BSO in the development of the underlying law. The first proposal concerns the utilisation of the NGDP and BSO in the application of custom and the common law. The second proposal is to develop new case law (also defined as part of the underlying law under the Act) where no law applies to an issue, relying on a number of factors, including the NGDP and BSO. One could explain the situation using the analogy of "shield" and "sword" as used in equitable estoppel.[19] In the first proposal the NGDP and BSO are used as a "shield" and in the second as a "sword".

(b) NGDP and BSO as a shield

The Underlying Law Act recognises customary law and the common law as sources of the underlying law of Papua New Guinea. But their recognition is not automatic, depending on a number of criteria.[20] The criteria for recognition of custom as underlying law are a little less rigorous than for the common law. But they both include the necessity to be consistent with written law, human rights and freedoms and the NGDP and BSO. This places the NGDP and BSO on equal footing with other directly justiciable provisions in the legal system. Issues of justiciability arise as a result of this, but as it is a

---

[19] Prior to the case of *Walton Stores (Interstate) Ltd v Maher* (1988) 164 CLR 387, equitable estoppel was used as a "shield" and not as a "sword." That is to say that it could not be used to assert justiciable rights, but could be used to prevent the strict enforcement of existing contractual rights to prevent injustice: see John Philips and Louis Proksch "*Walton Stores (Interstate) Ltd v Maher*: Implications for the Law of Contract" (1989) 19(1) UWA L Rev 171 at 175.

[20] Underlying Law Act 2000, s 4.

specific intention of Parliament to treat the NGDP and BSO in this manner, ss 25(3) and 63(3) would permit this interaction.[21]

In a review of cases on the underlying law, Chief Justice of Papua New Guinea, Sir Salamo Injia, observed that courts routinely apply the common law without specifically measuring its relevance against the standards of the Underlying Law Act.[22] It is therefore important to consider carefully the requirements of the Underlying Law Act before applying custom or the common law.

The NGDP and BSO are used as a "shield" in the general sense of societal protection from either inappropriate foreign values or customs repugnant to present day values. A certain vision of the country is promoted in the Constitution. The NGDP and BSO would ensure the progressive realisation of this vision. The concept of a shield is not used directly in the sense of protecting a person from strict application of another person's legal rights as was observed in *Central London Property Trust Ltd v High Trees House Ltd* by Lord Denning.[23] In *Central London Property Trust Ltd* there was an existing lease agreement between the tenant and the landlord, but the acquiescence by the landlord not to insist on the full original rental amount created an estoppel in favour of the tenant against the landlord. The idea was that it acted as a "shield" against an otherwise legitimate claim under contract law. The application of the term "shield" in the development of the underlying law is to rely on the NGDP and BSO to prevent application of common law or new case law that is inconsistent with the NGDP and BSO.

One of the earliest cases to consider the Underlying Law Act was *Magiten v Beggie*.[24] The plaintiff commenced proceedings by originating summons, alleging his wife, the first defendant, had illegally married his brother, the second defendant. The plaintiff claimed the defendants' marriage was in breach of the East Sepik (a province of Papua New Guinea) customary law,

---

21 Vergil Narokobi "The Justiciability of the National Goals and Directive Principles and Basic Social Obligations in the Context of the Underlying Law Act 2000" (2015) The Underlying Law Journal Developments in the Underlying Law of Papua New Guinea (forthcoming).

22 Salamo Injia "Presentation by the Chief Justice to the Underlying Law Conference, Alotau, December 2010 (2012) 8 The Underlying Law Journal Developments in the Underlying Law of Papua New Guinea 3.

23 *Central London Property Trust Ltd v High Trees House Ltd* [1947] KB 130 (HC).

24 *Magiten v Beggie* [2005] PGNC 75 N2880, 21 April 2005 [*Magiten*].

to which all parties were subject. The plaintiff sought a declaration that the defendants' marriage was prohibited by custom and void, and also requested consequential orders for damages. After considering the provisions of the Act, the Court decided against the plaintiff because he did not state clearly the custom being relied on, who it applied to, and did not provide details of its requirements in clear, precise and adequate terms. If the case had proceeded, the Court would have had to assess the applicability of the custom at issue against the provisions of the Act.

If the plaintiff in *Magiten v Beggie* had satisfied the procedural requirements the Court would have had to apply the custom of the parties that prohibited a woman marrying her husband's brother.[25] But the custom would not have applied if:[26]

(a) it is inconsistent with a written law; or

(b) its application and enforcement would be contrary to the National Goals and Directive Principles and the Basic Social Obligations established by the Constitution; or

(c) its application and enforcement would be contrary to the basic rights guaranteed by Division III.3 (*Basic Rights*) of the Constitution.

The Court would have had to examine the custom preventing a woman from marrying her husband's brother against the factors stated above including the NGDP and BSO. Would such a custom be sanctioned by the NGDP and BSO, for example with Directive Principle five of Goal 1?:

(5) the family unit to be recognized as the fundamental basis of our society, and for every step to be taken to promote the moral, cultural, economic and social standing of the Melanesian family;

Or would such a custom run contrary to Directive Principle 12 of Goal 2?:

(12) recognition of the principles that a complete relationship in marriage rests on equality of rights and duties of the

---

[25] At the time of *Magiten*, the Rules of the National Court of Justice (Underlying Law Amendment) were not adopted yet. The Underlying Law Act 2000 alone determined the application of customary law.

[26] Underlying Law Act, s 4(2).

partners, and that responsible parenthood is based on that equality.

The court would be required to perform a delicate balancing process. If the Court took the view the particular custom was applicable, it would have proceeded to declare the marriage of the two defendants was illegal by virtue of underlying law (customary law transforms into underlying law, once it satisfies the requirements of the Underlying Law Act).

If the *Magiten v Baggie* case was decided after 2011, the Underlying Law Rules would have regulated how the case would have been pleaded. An interesting feature of the Underlying Law Rules is the way it describes the NGDP and BSO as "constitutional rights".[27] Equally interesting is the fact the Rules deem the custom, common law or equity being pleaded is consistent with the NGDO and BSO (and the written law and human rights) unless the contrary is shown. A plaintiff would automatically plead the underlying law sought to be relied on; and the burden shifts to the defendant to argue that the particular custom or common law should not be recognised as part of the underlying law for inconsistency with the NGDP and/or BSO.[28] So in *Magiten v Baggie*, the custom preventing a woman from marrying her husband's brother would have been deemed to be applicable, unless the defendants could demonstrate its application would be contrary to the NGDP and BSO.

(c) Remedy for NGDP and BSO as a Shield

The remedy an aggrieved person would seek when arguing a particular custom or common law is not applicable based on the NGDP and BSO would be straightforward. The court would consider the NGDP and BSO (amongst other factors) and make a ruling that the custom or common law is inapplicable to the circumstances of Papua New Guinea. A new rule would as a result emerge where such customs and common law is no longer applicable in Papua New Guinea.

---

27 Rules of the National Court of Justice (Underlying Law Amendment) 2011 [Underlying Law Rules], Order 8, rule 20A(1)(c):

> In this rule the term "*Constitutional rights*" means the National Goals and Directive Principles and Basic Social Obligations established in the *Constitution* and the basic rights guaranteed by Division III.3 (Basic Rights) of the *Constitution*.

28 As seen in s 4(2) of the Underlying Law Act above, other reasons to refute the application of custom in addition to the NGDP and/or BSO are inconsistent with the written law and human rights and freedoms.

In a scenario such as this, the court would be making a declaration. Before making the declaration, the court will consider a host of factors, which, as noted above, are found in the Underlying Law Act. One of the criteria is whether the common law is consistent with the NGDP and/or BSO.

(d) Conclusion

The NGDP and BSO are used as a shield when they do not create legal rights, but shape how rights emanating from custom and the common law are used. It is a balancing exercise, and the court would be using its discretion to determine which principles should prevail in this process. This feeds into the idea of indirect justiciability discussed in chapter 4.

2. *NGDP and BSO as a sword*

(a) Introduction

On the reverse side is the question of the extent to which the NGDP and BSO can be used as a cause of action in the underlying law, hence the sword analogy. The NGDP and BSO are used to create legally enforceable rights.

(b) NGDP and BSO as a sword

A factual scenario may help bring the issue into perspective. Imagine a village that has had its only road destroyed by earthquake. It is a village of about 1,000 people. The village is some 500 metres above sea level. The only access to schools, hospitals and the market is by road. The distance is not far compared to other more remote places, but the slope is steep and makes transport of heavy store goods and housing materials almost impossible. Sick and deceased persons rely on human carriers for transportation to and from the village. It is almost 20 years since there was a road. Despite numerous promises from elected representatives, there has been no assistance. So the people decide that they will institute a class action against the state compelling it to provide budgetary allocation to build their roads. They argue they have a right to development and that this is provided for under National Goal 1 (Integral Human Development).

Under s 7 of the Underlying Law Act, the court would have to consider whether there is a written law that applies to the facts the plaintiffs say gave rise to a cause of action. In this case the plaintiffs claim a right to development. If there is no written law, the next question is to consider custom and the common law. Assuming there is neither, it would be an appropriate case for the development of the underlying law. The court could start by looking at Goal 1 on integral human development – for every person to have the opportunity to develop as a whole person in relationship with others. A road would enable better access to education, good health services and stimulate economic activities. Following Goal 1, Goal 2 requires the state to provide equal opportunity for the people to participate in the development of the country. A road would meet the expectation of Goal 2 for equal opportunity.

Further, a road would also ensure greater prospects of self-reliance (third National Goal). This could happen by enabling efficient means for the people to bring their proceeds to the market through vehicles, resulting in increased production levels. Additionally, the BSO places an obligation on the people to contribute to the revenue of Papua New Guinea. A road is a means to help them fulfil this obligation to the country. All in all, by taking into account the NGDP and BSO as discussed here, the court would be required to develop a new underlying law requiring the government to take all reasonable measures to provide the people appropriate development. To decide whether the government was reasonable in its efforts, the court would consider whether the circumstances of these people were dire and furthermore, determine if the state had overlooked them in the previous annual budgetary allocations.

While the factual and legal scenario may appear fanciful or novel, the heritage of the NGDP and BSO suggest otherwise. The idea of having Directive Principles in a Constitution has travelled to Papua New Guinea via India and Ireland. In India, the legal status of the Directive Principles of State Policy is defined as "not enforceable by the court".[29] In *Bandhua Mukti Morcha v Union of India*, the petitioner approached the court on behalf of a group of children under the age of 14, arguing that the children's employment violated their rights under the Constitution.[30] What is interesting about this case, is firstly, the petitioner took the case on behalf of the children; and secondly, the defendant was the state, not the alleged offender. The petitioner sought a mandamus to compel the state to put in place programmes to protect the children from child labour. The Court in granting the petition, interpreted the right to life in a way consistent with

---

[29] Constitution of India, art 7.

[30] *Bandhua Mukti Morcha v Union of India* (1984) 3 SCC 161, [1984] AIR 802 [*Bandhua*].

the Indian Constitution's Directive Principles. The Court held the right to life:[31]

> [was the] most precious human right … [and] …must therefore be interpreted in a broad and expansive spirit so as to invest it with significance and vitality which may … enhance the dignity of the individual and the worth of the human person.

The state was therefore required to investigate the abuse of children and implement programmes to prevent child labour. This demonstrates the potential of Directive Principles to enable an innovative use of the law.

The NGDP and BSO have been identified by constitutional commentators such as Kwa as providing economic, social and cultural rights similar to the International Covenant on Economic, Social and Cultural Rights.[32] As noted previously, the recent amendments to the National Court Rules recognise the NGDP and BSO as "constitutional rights".[33] In South Africa, cases such as *Government of the Republic of South Africa and Others v Grootboom and Others* have attempted to directly enforce social rights like the right to housing.[34] The main question the court examined was whether the government housing programme had been reasonable in the circumstances. The necessity to ascertain rights compliance on the test of reasonableness is by virtue of the requirement of the South African Constitution.[35] Such an approach does not directly compel the government to act, but examines whether it has discharged its mandated role properly. The advantage is that the court does not interfere with government functions but reviews the latter's actions as an independent but interested observer.

---

[31] *Bandhua*, cited in Malcolm Langford "The Justiciability of Social Rights: From Practice to Theory" in Malcolm Langford (ed) *Social Rights Jurisprudence* (Cambridge University Press, Cambridge, 2008) at 6.

[32] Eric Kwa *Constitutional Law of Papua New Guinea* (Law Book Co, Sydney, 2001) at 169. There is nothing directly on point in the CPC Report to suggest the analogy to social, economic and cultural rights, but there is a strong suggestion of comparison to these types of rights because ss 38 and 39 of the Constitution require consideration to be had to the NGDP and BSO when qualifying rights and freedoms in the Constitution.

[33] Underlying Law Rules, ord 20A, r (1)(c).

[34] *Government of the Republic of South Africa v Grootboom* (CCT11/00) [2000] ZACC 19, [2001] 1 SA 46 (CC), [2000] 11 BCLR 1169, 4 October 2000.

[35] Constitution of South Africa, art 26, which after recognising the right to housing (art 26(1)) requires the state to put in place reasonable means to progressively realise the right (art 26(2)).

The NGDP and BSO must also be taken into account where the court finds that a particular underlying law (for example, common law) is no longer relevant.[36] There have not been many cases on this aspect of the Act. *Sukuramu v New Britain Palm Oil Ltd*, which was overruled in the Supreme Court is one example of the court attempting to use its jurisdiction under s 9.[37] The National Court had held the common law right to hire and fire was no longer appropriate to the circumstances of Papua New Guinea, and proceeded to develop a new principle of the underlying law that took into account natural justice principles, the constitutional right to protection against harsh and oppressive actions (Constitution, s 41), and the NGDP and BSO.[38] The case went on appeal to the Supreme Court and the decision of the National Court was overturned. In the Supreme Court's view, a court could not develop new principles of the underlying law without the parties expressly pleading this claim in the originating process. The rationale was to provide an opportunity to opposing parties to respond to the new underlying law in their defence. It appears this decision prompted the court under its delegated authority to enact the Underlying Law Rules. Persons going to court now have more certainty in pleading their claim under specific court rules.

(c) Remedy for NGDP and BSO as a sword

Where the NGDP and BSO are used as a sword it will determine the parties' rights and interests. In a sense this is a more direct application of the NGDP and BSO. This is allowed for by Parliament's specific intention in the Underlying Law Act. In the example above, the right to development would be considered as a new underlying law, and aggrieved parties can rely on that new law in future cases.

In this type of situation, where the court will be proactive, it should be wary of its limitations as a judicial body. The court would look firstly at how the relevant government body took into account the NGDP and/or BSO in the decision-making process. Appropriate deference should be given to the decision-making body. The court would be limited to determining whether decision was reasonable in the circumstances. In that regard, a procedural lens best allows the court to mediate between the aggrieved and the decision-maker. A more substantive approach, for example, by specifically ordering

---

36 Underlying Law Act, s 9.

37 *Sukuramu v New Britain Palm Oil Ltd* [2007] PGNC 21, N3124, 16 February 2007.

38 At [96]–[106] per Cannings J.

allocation of resources to fulfil the NGDP and/or BSO, could result in the court assuming the role of another arm of government.

The types of remedies applicable would be firstly a declaration of a new underlying law (as opposed to common law). Depending on the nature of the new underlying law, consequential remedies would be applied to alleviate its breach. For example, if the court declared there was a new right to development, that in and of itself would not mean the court would order the government, by way of a mandatory injunction, to provide this right. The court would have to bear in mind the governmental body's available resources, its institutional capacity, and the process it used to determine priority. The court could probably ask the government body to provide information on the criteria it used to determine which village or group of people deserved a road over another. From such information the court may decide whether government efforts were reasonable or not in the circumstances of each case.[39]

(d) Conclusion

Under the framework of the Act, and supported by a liberal reading of s 25 and s 63, it is quite possible that the present view of the NGDP and BSO as being entirely non-justiciable may be reviewed to allow for greater interaction in directing the way society develops consistent with the vision of the Constitutional Planning Committee (CPC).

This change would see the incorporation of the NGDP and BSO in the development of the underlying law.

IV. Judicial Review of Administrative Action

A. Constitutional Basis for Using Existing Judicial Review Procedures to Implement NGDP and BSO

1. Introduction

The phrase "judicial review" is not understood in the same way as one moves from jurisdiction to jurisdiction. In the American tradition, it refers to the Supreme Court's power to review the constitutionality of legislation. Judicial review in the United Kingdom, where the Parliament is purportedly supreme, refers to the process where the exercise of statutory powers by a public body can be reviewed by the court, being initiated by person(s) adversely affected.

---

[39] See *Grootboom*, above n 34, also discussed in chapter 4.

The scope of judicial review in Papua New Guinea is determined by whether a decision-maker's power is established by statute and the relationship sought to be reviewed is governed by legislation and not under contract or tort.[40] As most, if not all powers exercised by the executive are prescribed by statute, its decisions would as a matter of course be subject to judicial review. Papua New Guinea has adopted the English version of judicial review, and it is in this tradition the term judicial review is used here.[41]

Many of the decisions that concern the NGDP and BSO are made by the government. After Parliament enacts law, it is subsequently removed from the picture, leaving the executive (and the administration) to implement the law. As a result, consideration should be given to the administration of the law too for implementation of the NGDP and BSO. For example, in New Zealand, placing too much attention on the actions of Parliament on human rights issues can be misleading, since much of the infringement of human rights occurs within the administration of law:[42]

> ... this vision of rights does not seem to address the needs of those living under regimes most likely to perpetrate the worst rights abuses, it is also an incomplete description of the modern western democratic legal order. More than ever, public power is exercised through the use of discretion and delegated legal instruments, organisations at arms-length from the state, and even contracts, rather than directly through legislation.

Judicial review of administrative action is an opportunity for the courts to ensure the effective implementation of the NGDP and BSO through adequate judicial scrutiny of the exercise of public power.

---

40 Michael A Ntumy *Administrative Law of Papua New Guinea, Cases Texts and Materials* (2nd ed, CBS Publishers, New Delhi, 2003) at 221. See also *Bari v Governing Council, St Paul's Teachers College, Vunakanau; Chairman, National Education Board Appeal Committee; Minister for Education; Ministry for Education and The State* [1994] PGNC 158, [1995] PNGLR 364, 6 April 1994; and *Ragi and State Services & Statutory Authorities Superannuation Fund Board v Maingu* [1994] PGSC 3, SC459, 29 June 1994.

41 The National Court Rules which regulates the judicial review process is adopted from the United Kingdom Supreme Court Practice 1967 (The White Book).

42 Janet Mclean "Legislative Invalidation, Human Rights Protection and s 4 of the New Zealand Bill of Rights Act" (2001) 4 NZ L Rev 421 at 424.

2. *Constitutional basis for engaging the NGDP and BSO in judicial review*

The court's jurisdiction to review the exercise of executive power against the requirements of the NGDP and BSO is guided by an integrated reading of a combination of constitutional provisions – ss 22, 25(3), 63(3) and 60.[43] What these provisions provide is that where the Constitution confers a duty, the duty should be implemented notwithstanding the fact that there is a lack of implementing legal procedural mechanisms (s 22). The court should have regard to legal developments in other jurisdictions to help it formulate appropriate procedures to respond to the constitutional duty.

In answer to this stipulation, the courts have stated that judicial review is the most appropriate legal avenue to enforce constitutional duties.[44] Section 60 connects the NGDP and BSO to the executive and the judicial review process. In developing the rules of natural justice, the court should have regard to the NGDP and BSO. This Part asserts judicial review can ensure the executive is held accountable for non-implementation of the NGDP and BSO.

Section 22 has been used to provide a jurisdictional basis for the court to protect existing rights. In *State v Alan Woita (No 2)*, the accused (Alan Woita) was allowed to sit next to his counsel during trial. The court was said to have a duty, stemming from ss 22 and 57, to see the court process does not render inoperable the exercise an accused's constitutional right to effective legal representation.[45] In *SCR No 2 of 1978; Re Corrective Institutions Act 1957*, the Court ruled provisions of legislation which prevented an inmate from appealing an offence committed in prison were invalid for offending a person's right to appeal. On the basis of s 22 of the Constitution, the Court then proceeded to establish procedures to enable Woita to exercise his right of appeal.[46] The strongest view for the use of judicial review procedures to enforce constitutional duties comes from *SC Reference No 3 of 1999; Re*

---

[43] These provisions were covered under chapter 7, except for s 60 of the Constitution.

[44] *SC Reference No 3 of 1999; Re Calling of the Parliament* [1999] PGSC 55, [1999] PNGLR 285, 25 June 1999 [*Calling of Parliament*].

[45] *The State v Alan Woita (No 2)* [1978] PNGLR 113, at 117 per Kearney J, cited in Brian Brunton and Duncan Colquhoun-Kerr *The Annotated Constitution of Papua New Guinea* (University of Papua New Guinea Press, Port Moresby, 1984) at 61.

[46] *SCR No 2 of 1978; Re Corrective Institutions Act 1957* [1978] PGSC 9, [1978] PNGLR 404, 25 October 1978.

Calling of the Parliament.[47] The Court held the remedy of mandamus can be obtained against Parliament to ensure it performs a particular function conferred on it.

3. *Grounds for judicial review of administrative action*

The procedures and grounds to review decisions of public bodies are primarily regulated by Order 16 of the National Court Rules 1983 and the National Court Judicial Review (Amendment) Rules 2005.[48] At present, the grounds for review include decisions where the authority:[49]

- Exceeds its power;
- Commits an error of law;
- Commits a breach of natural justice;
- Reaches a decision which no reasonable tribunal could have reached; or
- Abuses its power.

These are based on common law principles. Sections 25(3) and 63(3) state where public power can be exercised in a manner to implement the NGDP and BSO,

it should be exercised accordingly. Four different types of public powers (legislative, executive, judicial and administrative) are referred to. Executive and/or administrative powers are considered here. Section 60 of the Constitution lends additional weight to the case for the inclusion of NGDP and BSO in judicial review:

> 60. Development of Principles.
>
> In the development of the rules of the underlying law in accordance with Schedule 2 (adoption, etc., of certain laws) particular attention shall be given to the development of a system of principles of natural justice and of administrative law specifically designed for Papua New Guinea, taking special

---

47 *Calling of Parliament*, above n 44.

48 *Kekedo v Burns Philip (PNG) Ltd* [1988-89] PNGLR 122, 13 April 1989.

49 National Court Judicial Review (Amendment) Rules 2005, ord 16, r 13, "Purpose." The grounds for judicial review are not limited to what are stated in ord 16, r 13.

> account of the National Goals and Directive Principles and of the Basic Social Obligations, and also of typically Papua New Guinean procedures and forms of organization.

Courts will not make the decision, but ensure the process was fair. The position follows closely the principles enunciated in *Associated Provincial Picture Houses Ltd v Wednesbury Corporation.*[50] *Wednesbury* recognises the courts' jurisdiction to review decisions of public bodies on the grounds of reasonableness, but only within the ambit of the decision-making process or the four corners of the power. Separation of powers is implicit in this process; courts do not make the decision but review the process.

Another English case which applied *Wednesbury* may be apposite for Papua New Guinea when it comes to implementing the NGDP and BSO, especially where legislation make direct reference to the NGDP and BSO. This is *R v Minister of Agriculture ex parte Padfield.*[51] A decision by a Minister was overturned, because the reasons for his decision did not promote the underlying policy of the legislation. This was considered by the court to be unreasonable. Ntumy discusses *Padfield* generally in his comprehensive text on Papua New Guinea's administrative law, but did not explore the opportunity it presented for using s 60 of the Constitution to implement the NGDP and BSO.[52]

Going by the interconnectedness approach, if an NGDP and BSO is stated to be the objective of the legislation, the court can determine whether a decision-maker has fulfilled the objective of the law in their decision. On a liberal interpretation of the Constitution, public bodies should explicitly take into account the NGDP and BSO in the exercise of their public functions anyway, even if the NGDP and BSO are not stated in the law.[53] The question of what is reasonable is a balancing exercise and should depend heavily on which outcome favours the NGDP and BSO. Following *Padfield* would oblige the courts to decide whether the public authority has promoted the NGDP and/or BSO.

---

50 *Associated Provincial Picture Houses Ltd v Wednesbury Corporation* [1948] 1 KB 223 (CA) cited with approval in *Dusava v Justice Doherty* [1999] PGSC 43, [1999] PNGLR 419, 1 October 1999.

51 *R v Minister of Agriculture ex parte Padfield* [1968] AC 997 (HL).

52 Ntumy, above n 40, at 802–803.

53 Constitution, ss 25(3) and 63(3), sch 1.5.

4. *Remedy for Administrative Judicial Review*

The traditional types of remedy available when a claim is made to court through administrative judicial review include certiorari, prohibition, mandamus and declaration. There would be no new remedies proposed for indirect justiciability in administrative judicial review. However, it may mean the court orders a governmental body's decision is quashed, and it should go back and make a decision that demonstrates compliance with, and/or implementation of the NGDP and BSO. In that sense the court would be taking a procedure based approach to implementing the NGDP and BSO.

In a case such as that discussed below (*Medaing*), where a governmental body is required to consider the NGDP and/or BSO, the court can order it to take them into account. Then by using the remedy of mandamus, the court could order the governmental body take such a course of action. But as discussed in the section on the Development of the Underlying Law, the court would take great care, and show appropriate deference to the authority before taking such an approach.

5. *Case study on incorporating the NGDP and BSO in the judicial review process – Medaing v Ramu Nico*

(a) Introduction

It is appropriate to consider how instantiating the NGDP and BSO in the context of judicial review would operate in practice. A review of *Medaing v Ramu Nico (Medaing)* will provide comments on how the NGDP and BSP may have been given prominence through judicial review instead of the civil process initiated by the parties.[54]

(b) The facts of *Medaing* and the subsequent appeal

The plaintiffs in *Medaing* were persons who had customary interests in the Astrolabe Bay of Madang Province. The plaintiffs, numbering 1,083 individuals were led by Louis Medaing. They were concerned about the potential environmental damage to the marine life by the planned waste disposal system from Ramu Nico Management (MCC) Ltd, a mining company. Ramu Nico's mining operations were being constructed further inland. In Ramu Nico's view, the commercially viable option to dispose of the

---

[54] *Medaing v Ramu Nico Management (MCC) Ltd* [2011] PGNC 95 N4340, 26 July 2011 [*Medaing*].

mining waste would be to discharge it into the coastal waters rather than to retain it in a tailings dam. Medaing instituted a claim seeking a permanent injunction against direct discharge into Astrolabe Bay. The defendants were Ramu Nico, the Independent State of Papua New Guinea, and Dr Wari Iamo in his capacity as the Director of the Environment. The basis of the plaintiffs' case was threefold: (a) the common law tort of nuisance, (b) breach of the Environment Act 2000, and (c) breach of National Goal 4 of the Constitution. Based on scientific evidence the court was able to find the common law tort of nuisance was made out and there was a breach of National Goal four of the Constitution. But there was no breach of the Environment Act. While the court found that the defendants were tortfeasors, it did not grant the remedy the plaintiffs sought.

The plaintiffs appealed the National Court decision refusing the injunction and the defendants also cross-appealed in *Medaing v Ramu Nico Management (MCC) Ltd (Medaing on appeal)*.[55] The Supreme Court, on a two-to-one majority, held public and private nuisance could only be made out if there was actual damage suffered by the plaintiffs. In this case the project had not commenced and as a result there could not be nuisance. The Court may have been correct on this point following English authorities, according to which, the damage has to be substantial and not trivial.[56] As to the Court of first instance finding the discharge was contrary to Goal 4 on natural resources, the appellate Court said the court below lacked jurisdiction to make declarations on the NGDP and BSO as they were non-justiciable. It would seem the best means of ensuring compliance with the NGDP and BSO would have been the administrative law judicial review process.

(c) Judicial review: a better option

Under the Environment Act 2000, a development project that would have significant impact on the environment is required to obtain an environmental permit from the Director of Environment. Before the Director of Environment is satisfied that a permit should be granted, the project proposal is advertised and the public is called to make submissions on the likely impact of the project on the environment.[57] This was an opportunity the

55 *Medaing v Ramu Nico Management (MCC) Ltd* [2011] PGSC 40, SC1144, 22 December 2011 [*Medaing on appeal*].

56 *Medaing on appeal* at [158] per Sawong and Hartshorn JJ.

57 Environment Act 2000, s 55.

plaintiffs should have availed themselves of to make known their views to the Director of Environment. In *Medaing* the plaintiffs had amassed a credible group of expert witnesses to give evidence to support their case the project would cause irreparable harm to the environment and as such contrary to National Goal 4 on sustainable use of the environment. The Court concluded from the scientific evidence that it was likely the tailings would harm the area it was deposited into and not behave as the defendants' scientific experts predicted.[58] This avenue was open to the plaintiffs to make their views known to the Director of Environment at the initial stage of the project.

The Director of Environment is required by law to advertise a proposed mining project and request public submissions before it decides to issue the developer an environmental permit.[59] As the Environment Act 2000 recognises Goal 4 of the Constitution in its long title, the Director would have to make its decision in a manner consistent with the NGDP. The scientists' views accompanying the plaintiff's submissions to the Director of Environment would have to be verified by the Director of Environment's technical experts to verify the plaintiff's submissions. The Director would consider the submissions and make his or her decision and the reasons for it. There would be no law impeding the Director of Environment from recording whether the decision to grant the environmental permit promoted Goal 4 or not.

If notwithstanding the plaintiff's submission, the Director of Environment awarded the permit to Ramu Nico, the plaintiffs could seek judicial review of the decision in the National Court. The plaintiff would argue as one of its grounds, the Director did not give sufficient consideration to Goal 4 of the NGDP and adduce as its evidence the scientific report. The court could apply *Padfield* to support the proposition that the Director's actions did not promote the objectives of the legislation and were therefore unreasonable. The plaintiff would then be required to seek an appropriate remedy from the court, which may include a condition on the environmental permit, not to discharge waste into the Bay but instead to construct a tailings dam. Another option could have been a declaration that the permit granted was unreasonable and should be nullified and the Director of Environment reconsider an alternative avenue to discharge the waste that meaningfully takes into account Goal 4.

58 *Medaing*, above n 54, at [47]–[61], especially [61].

59 Environment Act 2000, s 55.

Use of judicial review would have provided a better approach to securing the NGDP. Promoting the NGDP would not happen in isolation from the legislation in issue, but in tandem with it, and in this case, the Environment Act 2000. Such a position respects each arm of government's sphere of operations. There was nothing problematic with the decision in the Court of first instance as it was recommendatory in nature, but it did not have the desired effect of preventing a potentially environmentally disastrous project.[60]

V. Weak-form Judicial Review

A. Constitutional Basis of Weak-form Judicial Review

1. Introduction

Weak-form judicial review is proposed for the courts as it meets the dual constitutional demands of ss 25 and 63 of the Constitution of implementation and non-justiciability.[61] It is a useful way for the courts to be engaged in the political discourse of implementation of the NGDP and BSO without being directly implicated by making a legally enforceable decision. Weak judicial review is usually associated with the enforcement of rights and freedoms.[62] The courts point out that a particular law or provision of the law inconsistent with a right or freedom, but do not invalidate the law, leaving it to the legislature to correct the error. Gardbaum has described weak-form judicial review as the new model of Commonwealth constitutionalism after studying the constitutional developments of Australia (state of Victoria for instance), Canada, New Zealand and United Kingdom.[63] Gardaum distinguishes this new model of Commonwealth constitutionalism from the model of constitutionalism as it operates in the United States, as in the latter the judiciary has the ultimate power to invalidate legislation on grounds of unconstitutionality.

Weak-form judicial review has been in operation in Canada since the Bill of Rights 1960; in New Zealand since the New Zealand Bill of Rights Act

---

60 This position was advanced in chapter 7.

61 See Mark Tushnet "New Forms of Judicial Review and the Persistence of Rights – and Democracy-Based Worries" (2003) 38 Wake Forest L Rev 813; and Stephen Gardbaum "The New Commonwealth Model of Constitutionalism" (2001) 49 Am Comp L 707 at 710.

62 Judicial review as used here in the context of courts power to invalidate legislation as opposed to administrative judicial review of government decisions.

63 Gardbaum, above n 61.

1990 (NZBORA); and in the United Kingdom since 1998. A typical feature of this approach noted in New Zealand and the United Kingdom is that the court may declare the incompatibility of a law with the Bill of Rights but has no power to invalidate the law.[64] Weak-form judicial review is therefore a middle ground in constitutionalism between parliamentary supremacy and ultimate judicial power on constitutional issues.

Comparative constitutional scholars such as Tushnet propose this method to deal with the counter majoritarian argument when promoting non-justiciable social rights.[65] In weak-form judicial review, the judiciary points out the offending provision of law and allows the legislature to remedy the situation.[66] Weak-form judicial review is recommended as an alternative to the other proposals presented in this chapter. Obviously, the first line of choice is to use the NGDP and BSO as indirectly justiciable under ss 25(3) and 63(3). The strength of weak-form judicial review is to sensitise public discourse to issues directly affecting the NGDP and BSO so as to influence the political process. It is not a directly justiciable approach as was seen in one of the first cases in Papua New Guinea to sanction it.[67] The application of weak-form judicial review in *Medaing* is taken up below. Weak-form judicial review would help the court use the NGDP and BSO more proactively.

B. Applying Weak-form Judicial Review to Papua New Guinea's Context

Although the terminology of weak-form judicial review is used here, there are a number of fundamental differences with regard to the use of that term in Canada and New Zealand. Civil rights and freedoms are not being considered, but instead the NGDP and BSO. NGDP and BSO are in a sense considered as part of social, economic and cultural rights.[68] In Papua New Guinea, civil and political rights and freedoms are directly justiciable,

---

[64] See s 4 of New Zealand Bill of Rights Act 1990 [NZBORA] and s 4 the Human Rights Act 1998 (UK). For a New Zealand case that considered s 4 of NZBORA see *Moonen v Film and Literature Board of Review* [2000] 2 NZLR 9 [*Moonen*].

[65] Tushnet, above n 61.

[66] New Zealand legislates this means of judicial review into the New Zealand Bill of Rights Act 1990.

[67] *Medaing*, above n 54.

[68] Kwa, above n 32, at 69.

following the model of American constitutionalism.[69] Applying weak-form judicial review to the protection and promotion of the NGDP and BSO follows legal developments in Canada, New Zealand and the United Kingdom in human rights legislation.

The object of the court's observation on the compatibility of a law with rights and freedoms in weak-form judicial review is usually the legislature, but for Papua New Guinea it could also include the executive or any other governmental body. Essentially, the NGDP and BSO applies to all governmental bodies under the Constitution, which covers the traditional three arms of government. What is important is the court's constitutional ability to make declarations on the compatibility of a law, decision or policy with the NGDP and BSO.

C. The Constitutional Basis

What would be the constitutional basis for the courts in Papua New Guinea to make declarations of inconsistency with the NGDP and BSO? In New Zealand, *Moonen v Film & Literature Board of Review* suggested the courts have the power to make a declaration of inconsistency.[70] This power was not exercised until July 2015 when a provision of a law which disenfranchised sentenced prisoners was declared to be inconsistent with s 12 of NZBORA (the right to vote).[71] The effectiveness of court declarations depends on the legislature acceding to the court as the courts have no power to invalidate offending law under s 4 of NZBORA.[72] In the United Kingdom, the law is more specific: s 4 of the Human Rights Act 1998 enables the court to declare legislation incompatible with the European Human Rights Convention if it is not possible to construe it consistently with the Convention. It is then up to the legislature to correct the inconsistency.

For Papua New Guinea, s 25(2) (and s 63(2) in similar terms), which states "Nevertheless, it is the duty of all governmental bodies to apply and give effect to them as far as lies within their respective powers", provides the constitutional basis for weak-form judicial review. The court is included in

---

[69] Constitution, ss 57 and 58.

[70] *Moonen*, above n 64.

[71] *Taylor v Attorney-General* [2015] NZHC 1706.

[72] Andrew Butler "Judicial Indications of Inconsistency – A New Weapon in the Bill of Rights Armoury?" (2000) NZ L Rev43 at 59–60.

the definition of governmental bodies and should, therefore, apply its specific functions to give effect to the NGDP and BSO. The issuing of declaratory orders falls within court functions. Since the constitutional duties of governmental bodies under ss 25(2) and 63(2) are non-justiciable, it would be in the discretion of the legislature to decide whether to accept the court's decision or not.

The focus of court decisions on ss 25 and 63 of the Constitution in Papua New Guinea have centred on non-justiciability and ss 25(3) and 63(3).[73] The courts have not explored the possibility of ss 25(2) and 63(2) in relation to weak-form judicial review. While the principle of non-justiciability is consistent with weak-form judicial review, governmental bodies (such as the courts) are not prevented from insisting on compliance with the NGDP and BSO. If the court asserts a statement without making it legally binding, it would meet the demands of the Constitution under ss 25(2) and 63(2).

D. Case study on Medaing

The view was taken above that the better approach to achieve justiciable outcomes consistent with the NGDP and BSO would be to use judicial review of administrative action. Be that as it may, there was no error in the final outcome of *Medaing*. What the Court did, it is submitted, was to fail to cite the correct constitutional basis for its decision on the application of the NGDP.

In *Medaing*, the National Court, after considering the evidence on the potential harm to the marine ecology, made the following observation on Goal 2 on Natural Resources and the Environment based on s 25(3) of the Constitution:

> It amounts to a breach of our duty of trust for future generations for this to happen. It is a course of action that shows deafness to the call of the People through Directive Principle 4(2) to conserve and replenish our sacred and scenic marine environment in Astrolabe Bay. It puts other coastal waters of Madang Province at risk. Inadequate protection has been given to our valued fish and other marine organisms.

---

73 This discussion took place in chapter 4.

On appeal to the Supreme Court, the majority ruled the National Court's declaration on the actions of the state was inconsistent with the NGDP:[74]

> The extent provided in *Constitution* s 25(3) for the National Goals and Directive Principles to be heard or determined is in relation to whether a law can be reasonably enforced to give effect to or not derogate from the National Goals and Directive Principles. It is not provided in s 25(3) that the National Court can give an opinion or make a declaration as to whether a law or power conferred by a law is contrary to a National Goal.

The Supreme Court had relied on a previous decision of the same Court upholding the non-justiciability of the NGDP and BSO.[75] In that decision the Court had only considered s 25(1) (and s 63(1)) to arrive at its conclusion. The Court had not adequately dealt with s 25(2) (and s 63(2)). Justice Davani (minority Supreme Court decision) agreed with Cannings J ruling in the Court below and commented directly on s 25(3) (and s 63(3)):[76]

> Section 25(3) of the *Constitution* cannot be any clearer. If given its fair and liberal interpretation, states in no uncertain terms that a Judicial power, which includes the power to issue any declaration by a Court and which is also a judicial power to issue administrative relief being a Declaration, is issued to give effect to the National Goals and Directive Principles because it must be enforced in that way. (s.25(3) of the *Constitution*).

Davani J went on to say:[77]

> I agree with the Trial Judge's findings that he is not contradicting or contravening the non-justiciability of the NGDP. The power to issue a Declaration is discretionary, subject to s.25(2). He proceeded under s.25(3) of the *Constitution*, which provision in my view is an exception to the general rule on the non-justiciability of s.25 of the *Constitution*.

---

74 *Medaing on appeal*, above n 55, at [166] per Hartshorn and Sawong JJ.

75 *Reference by the Ombudsman Commission of Papua New Guinea* [2010] PGSC 40, SC1088, 17 December 2010.

76 *Medaing on appeal*, above n 55, at [123] per Davani J.

77 At [127].

Even Davani J focused on s 25(3) and did not consider s 25(2).

In *Medaing* the principal relief the plaintiff sought was a permanent injunction to prevent the discharge of waste into the Astrolobe Bay of Madang Province. The plaintiffs further sought to compel the defendant through the court proceedings to construct a tailings dam to contain the waste. The National Court, despite finding that the waste discharge method was contrary to Goal 2 of the NGDP, did not grant the remedy sought. In the view of the National Court the tremendous national economic significance of the project dictated against the grant of the remedy. What the National Court did was to prioritise the goals of the state, although it focused on the Goal dealing with the environment. It could instead have justified its position by considering other NGDP Goals such as the Goal 3 on "National Sovereignty and Self-Reliance", and decide which Goal was to be given priority in such a situation. This would have granted greater legitimacy to the goals in legal and social development, but at the same time address the counter-majoritarian apprehension of courts enforcing social rights. This conclusion is that ss 25(2) and 63(2) authorises the court to make non-justiciable observations.

E. Conclusion

Weak-form judicial review provides a constitutional opportunity for the court to express an opinion on whether another governmental body has exercised its powers in a manner consistent with the NGDP and BSO. The constitutional basis for this can be found in ss 25(2) and 63(2) of the Constitution. Although the party's rights are not to be determined by the court, they are nevertheless sensitised by the decision to the NGDP and BSO, which in most cases includes the government. Further, it creates a situation for a conversation on the NGDP and BSO by different governmental bodies.

VI. Human Rights and Freedoms and the NGDP and BSO

A. Introduction

Securing civil and political rights should be done in a manner consistent with the NGDP and BSO. Basic rights in the preamble of the Constitution highlight the importance of considering rights and freedoms together with the NGDP and BSO. In areas of inconsistency, human rights and freedoms (given their directly enforceable status) would prevail.

It is appropriate to provide a general overview of how the Constitution protects human rights and freedoms. There are three main procedures.[78] The first relates to inconsistency of laws with human rights and freedoms provisions in the Constitution. The Supreme Court has jurisdiction to declare laws and even executive decisions invalid for offending the Constitution.[79] Human rights and freedoms are expressly recognised as constitutional laws (and justiciable), which other laws must conform to.

The second relates to the question of limiting or qualifying human rights and freedoms provisions. This is permissible under ss 38 and 39 of the Constitution. The general test is whether the law is reasonably justifiable in a democratic society having proper regard for the rights and dignity of mankind. Certain rights and freedoms in the Constitution can be qualified. The Supreme Court has jurisdiction to invalidate a law for not meeting the stipulations of ss 38 and 39.

The third is enforcement through ss 57 and 58 of the Constitution. Under this procedure, persons whose rights have been infringed can claim damages against human rights abusers and also seek preventative orders against potential abuse to avoid future breaches. The police feature prominently in many of these abuse cases.

B. NGDP and BSO on Questions of Inconsistency with Human Rights Provisions

Much legislation and many Bills have been declared invalid by the Supreme Court for having violated human rights and freedoms in the Constitution.[80] The question of inconsistency is one of constitutional interpretation. This would require consideration of the NGDP and BSO. Surprisingly, many of the leading cases dealing with inconsistency of laws do not consider the NGDP and BSO.

---

[78] HA Amankwah "Chapter 11: Human Rights in the Superior Courts" in Rudy James and Ian Fraser (eds) *Legal Issues in a Developing Society* (Faculty of Law, University of Papua New Guinea, Port Moresby, 1992) 170 at 171.

[79] Constitution, ss 10–11.

[80] One of the earlier cases on this aspect of protecting human rights was *SCR No 2 of 1978; Re Corrective Institutions Act 1957* [1978] PGSC 9, [1978] PNGLR 404, 25 October 1978 where the court held s 30 of the Corrective Institutions Act 1957, which prevented prisoners right of appeal against convictions for corrective institution-related offences was inconsistent with s 37(15) (right to review of conviction or sentence by a higher court) of the Constitution, and therefore invalid.

Karingu, Enforcement of Rights Pursuant Constitution S57 provides a useful opportunity to discuss how the NGDP and BSO could have been involved more prominently but were not.[81] Karingu (a lawyer) challenged the constitutionality of the Lawyers Act 1986. That legislation created a body called the Law Society, and made it mandatory for lawyers to join this organisation and obtain professional indemnity insurance before he or she can practise law. Karingu claimed the compulsory membership of the Law Society and requirement for professional insurance breached his right to freedom of employment protected by s 48 of the Constitution. The court concluded s 48 guaranteed the right to choose, and not entitlement to employment. The dual requirements for a practising certificate under s 35 of the Lawyers Act and for evidence of professional indemnity insurance under s 43 of the same Act were "qualifications (if any) lawfully required" within s 48(1).

The court could have elaborated on why it thought the Lawyers Act met the standards of s 48(1) in light of the NGDP and BSO. For example, it could have been argued that a professional organisation set up by law would help develop better skilled lawyers pursuant to Goal 3 on national sovereignty and self-reliance. This would be a sufficient basis for a rationale consistent with the constitutional scheme. It is equally true that a different conclusion may be possible, also relying on the NGDP and BSO.

However, what is important is the courts should actively promote the NGDP and BSO through discussion and prioritisation. This will provide an opportunity for a more open and engaging environment for their application.

C. NGDP and BSO on Limiting Qualified Rights

1. *Introduction*

Qualified rights and freedoms secured in many liberal democracies are also adopted in the Papua New Guinea Constitution.[82] There are a number of requirements ss 38 and 39 impose on parliament when it enacts laws that restrict these rights and freedoms. One of the substantive requirement before a human right and/or freedom can be restricted in a law is that the restriction must be reasonably justifiable in a democratic society having proper regard

81 *Karingu, Enforcement of Rights Pursuant Constitution S57* [1988–89] PNGLR 277, 4 August 1989.

82 See chapter 2; and Constitution, ss 41–56.

for the rights and dignity of humanity.[83] A factor enabling the restriction of the law is to advance the NGDP and BSO.[84] What is, therefore, of relevance is the question of whether any restriction (or proposed restriction) to the legislation enacted by Parliament is in effect for the purpose of fulfilling the NGDP and/or BSO and consequently reasonably justifiable in a democratic society.[85] The Constitution provides some guidance to the courts and parliament on questions of this nature.[86] This is an area where the courts (judges) are embarking on a very subjective observation on government laws and policies with in light of their own personal views and values. It is, therefore, paramount there should be standards assisting the evaluation process. The NGDP and BSO provide this yardstick. It is imperative they are considered to maintain political legitimacy within constitutional limits.

2. *Relevance of comparative experience*

What is in operation in most cases is the balancing of civil and political rights and freedoms with social, economic and cultural rights, without any express indication this is being done. Section 39 enables a comparative approach to meaningfully consider the question of whether the restriction is reasonably justifiable. On this note it is useful to bear in mind the trend on social rights discourse. Justice Albie Sachs from the Constitutional Court of South Africa was recorded as stating 21st-century jurisprudence will see an increasing focus on socio-economic rights.[87] It is important for Papua New Guinea to take into account international experiences and provide for more just social conditions for its population.

Section 39 of the Constitution allows stakeholders in the constitutional system to have regard to international comparative legal systems.[88] Courts are given the power to consider relevant international and domestic experience to determine the appropriateness of restricting rights and freedoms. Greater

---

83 Constitution, s 38(1).

84 Section 39(3)(a).

85 Constitution, ss 38(1) and 39(3).

86 For a case where legislation was invalidated for not meeting the formal requirements of s 38 of the Constitution see *Special Reference by the Morobe Provincial Executive* [2005] PNGLR 1, 13 May 2005.

87 Albie Sachs, "Social and Economic Rights: Can They Be Made Justiciable?" (Southern Methodist University School of Law, 1999) at 18, quoted in Langford, above n 31, at v.

88 Constitution, s 39(3).

involvement of the NGDP and BSO on questions on limitations of rights were foreshadowed by commentators such as Donald Chalmers.[89] After comparing the constitutional positions in Nigeria and India to Papua New Guinea, he came to the view that the Papua New Guinea Constitution, on the question of what is "reasonably justified," offered a greater protection than that of Nigeria. But India presented an insightful experience. Chalmers thought the decision of Patanjali Sastri CJ in *State of Madras v Row* offered useful lessons for Papua New Guinea.[90]

The test of reasonableness is not a fixed or abstract application, but the result of weighing the nature of the right infringed, the purpose of the restriction, the extent of the evil to be remedied, and the prevailing political conditions at the time of the judgment.[91] Chalmers went on to describe how the NGDP can be used to balance the interests of the individual against society. This balancing exercise should be kept in mind in the following discussions.

3. *Commentary on case laws*

Two cases which considered the question of whether the restrictions were reasonably justifiable will be commented on now. They focus on the role of the Supreme Court. What is interesting about these cases is that the formal requirements of s 38 of the Constitution were met. However, the Court went on to make a subjective judgment about whether these laws were justified and found otherwise. As a result, the laws challenged were declared unconstitutional. Courts can consider whether these laws necessarily promote the NGDP and/or BSO and on that basis declare a law unconstitutional. Although no reported case has taken this approach it is argued that such an approach is constitutionally valid.

(a) Case one: *SCR No 1 of 1986; Re Vagrancy Act (Ch 268)*

The first case related to vagrancy. The government was concerned about the number of people who were migrating to the urban centres. There was escalating crime in the cities and many of the people coming in squatted on unoccupied land. Parliament responded by enacting the Vagrancy Act (Ch268). This Act made it a criminal offence to live in the city with no formal

---

89 Donald Chalmers "Human Rights and What is Reasonably Justifiable in a Democratic Society" (1975) 3 Melanesian LJ 92.

90 *State of Madras v Row* (1952) SCR 597, 1952 AIR 196.

91 Chalmers, above n 89, at 96–97.

employment. This law was challenged in the Supreme Court in *SCR No 1 of 1986; Re Vagrancy Act (Ch 268) (SCR on Vagrancy Act)* on the basis it was contrary to s 42, liberty of the person and s 52, freedom of movement.[92] The Court found the Act complied with the formal requirements of s 38 of the Constitution, including the voting requirement of absolute majority, but did not meet the substantive requirements of s 38 of the Constitution:[93]

> The exclusion orders in s 3 of the Vagrancy Act (Ch No 268) restricted the right to freedom of movement protected by s 52 of the Constitution, and the State had failed to discharge the onus under s 38(3) of the Constitution of proving that such exclusion orders were necessary for public order or public welfare or reasonably justifiable in a democratic society within the meaning of s 38(1).

The Court did not look at the NGDP and BSO, but the question of public interest in the language of s 38 arises here. For example, National Goal 2 on equality and participation should have been applied when deciding what is reasonably justifiable in a democratic society. No doubt this would require the courts to engage in a debate about how the government is to manage its problems, a role usually played by the executive and the legislature and not the judiciary. But these debates are important for the reason that social, economic and cultural rights in the international context are questioning the ideological commitment to the separation of powers. The prevailing practice of countries following the United States constitutional model is to protect negative rights (or civil and political rights and freedoms) in the Constitution.[94] Positive rights (social, economic and cultural rights) are non-justiciable, and left to the political process to secure.

The two main objections to constitutionalising positive rights are first that it may require government to provide rights to a part of the population outside of the policy platform it was elected on; and second, positive rights are expensive, such as providing housing and quality health care.[95] Different jurisdictions have provided different responses to the two objections. Some

---

[92] *SCR No 1 of 1986; Re Vagrancy Act (Ch 268)* [1988] PGSC 29, [1988-89] PNGLR 1, 13 April 1987.

[93] At 1.

[94] Gardbaum, above n 61.

[95] Langford, above n 31, at 6.

Commonwealth countries such as Canada, New Zealand and the United Kingdom, have left it to the executive to provide such rights, and empowering the courts to enforce negative rights.[96] India and Ireland have created non-justiciable directive principles in their Constitutions.[97] India has been particularly creative in applying the directive principles despite their non-justiciable nature. Constitutions adopted from the 1990s onwards such as in South Africa have made social rights directly justiciable.[98] This trend has led one commentator to conclude social rights are no longer an outlier when compared to civil and political rights in rights enforcement.[99]

At the time *SCR on Vagrancy Act* was decided in 1989, debates on enforcement of social rights may have been tilted in favour of enforcement of civil and political rights. The Court did not have the benefit of a comparative experience such as in South Africa. But had it engaged in that debate, it would have seen a situation where the Papua New Guinea legal framework could be heralded as "prophetic". The Court would have considered the social condition in the rural areas, the employment opportunities available to the people and decide whether the policies (or their lack) of the government were reasonable in the circumstances. If they were not then the law was unreasonable.

The Court could find that such legislation would contribute to a class structure between the rural and urban population of the country, with greater opportunities found only in the cities. Civil and political rights and freedoms ought to be applied consistently with the NGDP and BSO. It is both an express and implied intention of the Constitution that rights and freedoms should be applied harmoniously with the NGDP and BSO.

Grootboom provides a useful comparison. The case concerned the provision of housing to a group of people who were squatting on government land. The affected people were going to be evicted and sought first, an injunction to prevent their eviction; and second, provision of housing because of their dire

---

96 Gardbaum, above n 61.

97 Constitution of Ireland, art 45, "Directive Principles of Social Policy"; Constitution of India, Part IV, Directive Principles of State Policy, arts 36–51.

98 The Constitution of South Africa provides a number of social rights, including: art 26, labour rights; art 24, right to a healthy environment; art 26, right to housing; art 27, right to food, health care and social assistance; art 29, right to education; art 30, right to language; and art 31, right to culture.

99 David Landau "The Reality of Social Rights Enforcement" (2012) 53(1) Harv Int'l LJ 190.

circumstances. The Court made two main types of orders: the first was for temporary relief; and the second was to order the government to take reasonable steps to provide the right to housing for the applicants. As the South African Constitution made housing a right, the government was required to apply all reasonable efforts to ensure the provision of this right. Although no timeframe was provided to implement this order, the approach it took is instructive. The Court examined government laws, policies and allocation of funds to realise this right for the particular people and found them inadequate and, therefore, unreasonable in the circumstances. *Grootboom* is a positive development for courts of other countries to draw lessons from when protecting rights traditionally considered to be non-justiciable; without the criticism that the court is encroaching into other areas of government function.

(b) Case two: *Special Reference by Fly River Provincial Executive Council; Re Organic Law on Integrity of Political Parties and Candidates*

The second and more recent case, which had a lasting impact on the political development of Papua New Guinea, was *Special Reference By Fly River Provincial Executive Council; Re Organic Law on Integrity of Political Parties and Candidates (Fly River).*[100] *Fly River* could have taken greater account of the NGDP and BSO to support its conclusions.

The Papua New Guinea Parliament is notorious for instability. Constant votes of no confidence against prime ministers result in governments not serving the full five-year term. Parliament responded by enacting a constitutional law – Organic Law on the Integrity of Political Parties and Candidates (OLIPPAC). The main terms of OLIPPAC were to restrict the voting rights of the Members of Parliament in three key areas: electing a Prime Minister, constitutional amendments, and Appropriation Bills. Political parties would meet prior to Parliament sessions, and pass a party resolution on how it would vote on any of these three matters. It created an offence (misconduct) under the Leadership Code if a Member of Parliament voted against the party resolution. This law enabled Michael Somare to remain Prime Minister for a total of 10 years, a record for Papua New Guinea. In 2010, the constitutionality of the law was challenged.

[100] *Special Reference by Fly River Provincial Executive Council; Re Organic Law on Integrity of Political Parties and Candidates* [2010] PGSC 3, SC1057, 7 July 2010.

OLIPPAC complied with the formal requirements of s 38 and was not in issue. It will be recalled s 38 requires laws that restrict rights and freedoms meet a number of conditions. Further, the law can only restrict the right but not abolish it. The Supreme Court was concerned OLIPPAC had the effect of abolishing certain rights and not merely restricting them. Rights and freedoms such as freedom of association (s 47) and the right to vote and stand for public office (s 50) were under consideration as to whether they were restricted or abolished. The Supreme Court found rather than Parliament restricting those qualified rights and freedoms, it had actually abolished them and as a result gone beyond its constitutional scope. To arrive at this finding, the Court considered the Westminster Parliament as the model Papua New Guinea should aspire to.

The Court did not make specific reference to the NGDP and BSO when assessing the restrictions of OLIPPAC. Its discussions on whether political rights and freedoms were abolished or restricted were guided by common law jurisprudence and cases such as *Edwards v AG Canada*.[101] The Court could have gone further to consider the implications of OLIPPAC on the NGDP and BSO. For example, Goal 2 states: "We declare our second goal to be for all citizens to have an equal opportunity to participate in, and benefit from, the development of our country". Did the provisions of OLIPPAC in contention affect people's participation through their representatives in the political process? There was again latitude for such a question to be raised to enable a greater role for the NGDP and BSO in assessing the constitutional validity of a law.

The Court could have used this opportunity to discuss whether the challenged law adequately fulfilled the NGDP and BSO. Since it is an express requirement under ss 38 and 39 of the Constitution, the Court could do it *proprio motu*. The Court briefly referred to Goal 1 on integral human development. Politically favourable conduct was to be achieved through integral human development, and not by way of legislating into practice a particular politically desirable behaviour. The Court made this comment in passing. Obviously it had significant consequences as the Court and the legislature differed on the solution to resolve the problem of political instability. The Court should have explored in detail what it meant by reference to integral human development as the process to achieve political development.

---

101 *Edwards v AG Canada* [1930] AC 124 (PC).

D. Enforcement of Human Rights

Persons whose rights and freedoms have been infringed can approach the courts for remedies or preventive orders. These remedies are provided for under ss 57 and 58 of the Constitution. Under these provisions, both the National Court and Supreme Court have jurisdiction. These rights have been listed previously.[102]

The interaction of the NGDP and BSO with these rights are connected by the provision of s 32, "Right to Freedom" of the Constitution. This provision at the relevant part states:

> (1) Freedom based on law consists in the least amount of restriction on the activities of individuals that is consistent with the maintenance and development of Papua New Guinea and of society in accordance with this Constitution and, in particular, with the National Goals and Directive Principles and the Basic Social Obligations.

Goldring has recognised this provision as having a higher status than other human rights provisions.[103] This provision is an interpretive provision.[104] It will provide a guide to how other specific provisions on rights and freedoms may be interpreted. For example, s 46 is on freedom of expression:

> 46. Freedom of Expression.
>
> (1) Every person has the right to freedom of expression and publication, except to the extent that the exercise of that right is regulated or restricted by a law—
>
> (a) that imposes reasonable restrictions on public office-holders; or
>
> (b) that imposes restrictions on non-citizens; or
>
> (c) that complies with Section 38 (general qualifications on qualified rights).

---

[102] See chapter 2.

[103] John Goldring *The Constitution of Papua New Guinea* (The Law Book Company, Sydney, 1978) at 215.

[104] *Application by Ireeuw, Wawar, Ap, and Wakum* [1985] PGNC 7, [1985] PNGLR 430, 13 December 1985.

If a person was to make a claim to the court that their freedom of expression was breached through enforcement proceedings under s 57 of the Constitution, the question of the definition of the right to freedom of expression and publication would necessarily explore meanings consistent with the NGDP and BSO. In this way, the Constitution adopts rights and freedoms with due regard to the Papua New Guinean context.

VII. Conclusion

Adopting the proposals recommended here would enhance the court's functions to enable effective implementation of the NGDP and BSO. These proposals relate to the jurisdiction of both the National Court and the Supreme Court. In terms of the former, the proposals cover judicial review of administrative action and development of the underlying law. For the latter, the Supreme Court's power to interpret the Constitution is considered. Three areas cut across both Courts' jurisdiction. First, the interpretive function of the court using the contextual means of statutory interpretation; and second, the relationship between the justiciable human rights and freedoms and the NGDP and BSO. The third area open to both Courts is the possibility to explore comparative judicial developments of what has been described as weak-form judicial review.

CHAPTER TEN

OMBUDSMAN COMMISSION

I. Introduction

The objective of this chapter is to make proposals for the Ombudsman Commission to effectively and efficiently implement the NGDP and BSO. The Ombudsman Commission's relationship with the other branches of government was discussed in chapter 6. This chapter focuses on how the functions of the Ombudsman Commission can be used to implement the NGDP and BSO, and is organised in three main parts.

Part I provides an introduction. Part II provides a brief note on the usefulness of comparative experiences to support proposals for implementation by the Ombudsman Commission. Part III proposes how the Ombudsman Commission can implement the NGDP and BSO under its various functions. Part IV concludes by summarising the main points of the chapter.

II. Overview of Ombudsman Commission Roles

Papua New Guinea adopted an Ombudsman Commission in 1975, being inspired by the institution which began in Sweden in 1806.[1] Originally, the primary purpose of the ombudsman in Sweden was controlling the application of laws by the administration.[2] In the second half of the 19th century the ombudsman evolved into an institution by which the Swedish Parliament could exert control over the executive.[3] The extension of the functions of the ombudsman to an institution for the citizen to have redress against the arbitrariness of the bureaucracy came about in the twentieth century.[4] From

---

1 Constitutional Planning Committee *Final Report of the Constitutional Planning Committee, Part One* (Government Printer, Port Moresby, 1974) at 11/1 [4] [CPC Report].

2 Mark Bevir (ed) "Ombudsman" *Encyclopedia of Governance* (Sage Publications, Thousand Oaks, CA, 2007) vol 2 at 633–634.

3 At 633.

4 At 633.

Sweden, other Nordic countries adopted similar institutions, beginning with Finland in 1919, Denmark, 1955, and Norway in 1963.[5] Commonwealth countries followed suit in the 1960s, for example, New Zealand in 1962, Australia in 1977, and the majority of Western democracies in the 1970s and 1980s.[6]

The following features have been identified as belonging to the classical ombudsman role, emanating from the Swedish model:[7]

> ... (1) legally established, (2) functionally autonomous, (3) external to the administration, (4) operationally independent of the legislature and the executive, (5) specialist, (6) expert, (7) nonpartisan, (8) normatively universalistic, (9) client centered but not anti-administration, (10) both popularly accessible and visible.

These attributes have been incorporated into the Papua New Guinea Ombudsman system under the Constitution and the Organic Law on the Ombudsman Commission (OLOC).[8] In presenting proposals for the implementation of the NGDP and BSO through the Ombudsman Commission's functions, comparative experiences from other jurisdictions will be highlighted where relevant. In saying that, institutions that bear the name "Ombudsman" in Commonwealth countries that operate a Westminster system of government like Australia, Canada, New Zealand and the United Kingdom, are involved in investigating administrative complaints but do not possess the array of functions of the Papua New Guinea Ombudsman Commission. The Papua New Guinea Ombudsman Commission is established directly by the Constitution together with its multi-faceted functions.[9]

---

5 At 633.

6 At 633.

7 Larry B Hill "Institutionalization, the Ombudsman, and Bureaucracy" (1974) 68(3) Am Pol Sci Rev 1075 at 1077.

8 For a summary of the Ombudsman Commission's functions see David Cannings "The Ombudsman Commission: Jurisdiction, Functions and Performance" in Anthony Regan, Owen Jessep and Eric Kwa (eds) *Twenty Years of the Papua New Guinea Constitution* (Law Book Co, Pyrmont, 2001) 196 at 196–197.

9 Cannings, at 196–197.

In Australia, Canada, New Zealand and the United Kingdom, the Ombudsman are restricted to the classical role of the Swedish model: that is, the investigation of complaints against government officials for unfair or unreasonable treatment.[10] Australia and Canada do not establish their Ombudsman directly in their written constitutions, but under ordinary legislation.[11] New Zealand and United Kingdom with no written constitutions also have their Ombudsman founded by legislation. The Australian, Canadian, New Zealand and United Kingdom ombudsmen also do not have Leadership Code function as it obtains in Papua New Guinea.[12] For countries like New Zealand and the United Kingdom, the most effective means of ensuring quality leadership is through the political process. In the Pacific, Solomon Islands and Vanuatu have attempted to follow the Papua New Guinea model.[13] But in Solomon Islands, the Leadership Code Commission is separate from the Ombudsman Commission.

Another interesting addition to the multifaceted role of the Papua New Guinea Ombudsman Commission is its ability to seek the Supreme Court's binding opinion on the constitutionality of a law or proposed law. This function seems to be conferred on only one other Ombudsman-like institution, in Slovenia.[14] Of particular note for Papua New Guinea is the ability granted to the Ombudsman Commission to have a specific role to implement the NGDP and BSO. This is not a feature of Ombudsman in India and Ireland, which

---

10 For Australia there is a Commonwealth Ombudsman established by the Ombudsman Act 1976 (Cth): see Commonwealth Ombudsman "Our History" <http://www.ombudsman.gov.au>, and a number of state ombudsman, for example, in Western Australia, Victoria and New South Wales. Canada has a plethora of Ombudsmen, each province has its own, perhaps the most active is the Ontario Ombudsman established under the Ombudsman Act 1975 (Ontario). New Zealand's Ombudsman is set up by the Ombudsman Act 1975 (there is other associated legislation such as the Official Information Act 1982 which confer additional powers); United Kingdom has a number of Ombudsman, such as the Parliamentary Ombudsman (or Parliamentary Commissioner for Administration) established under the Parliamentary Commissioner Act 1967.

11 Australia has a Commonwealth Ombudsman and several state ombudsmen, while Canada has a number of provincial ombudsmen, see above n 10.

12 The Australian comparable institution to the leadership code role is perhaps its anti-corruption agency, for example, the New South Wales Independent Commission Against Corruption, a single function body.

13 Having obtained independence after Papua New Guinea: Solomon Islands in 1978 and Vanuatu in 1981.

14 Human Rights Ombudsman, established under art 159 of the Slovenian Constitution.

have directive principles enshrined in their Constitutions.[15] In circumstances like this, comparative experience on Ombudsman-like institutions will be of limited use for Papua New Guinea, especially as regards the implementation of the NGDP and BSO.

III. Implementing the NGDP and BSO in the Ombudsman Functions

A. Introduction

The proposals for the implementation of the NGDP and BSO by the Ombudsman Commission would be under the administrative complaints function, the Leadership Code function, and what is called "a watching brief" on the Constitution by dint of the Commission's recognition as an authority capable of initiating constitutional references.[16] Because the Leadership Code enforcement involves not only the Ombudsman Commission, but also the Public Prosecutor and an appropriate tribunal, the proposal for implementation will unavoidably involve discussion of the whole process; the focus here will, however, be the Ombudsman Commission.[17]

B. Administrative Complaints Functions

1. Introduction

This part presents implementation proposals for the Ombudsman Commission's administrative complaints function. Entities considered to be a state service or a governmental body are subject to the Ombudsman

---

[15] In both India and Ireland, specific ombudsmen are created to oversee the role of the financial sector and the police respectively. No function is conferred on an ombudsman-like institution to implement the state policy enshrined in their constitutions.

[16] Cannings, above n 8, at 197–198.

[17] Whether the Public Prosecutor and the Leadership Tribunal are involved depends on the category of leader being referred. In *Re Public Prosecutor's Power to Request the Chief Justice to Appoint a Leadership Tribunal* [2008] PGSC 48, SC1011, 29 August 2008 [*Public Prosecutor's Power*] the Court explained the referral process. For example, Members of Parliament are prosecuted by the Public Prosecutor in a leadership tribunal consisting of a judge and two magistrates. For a constitutional office holder (such as an Ombudsman), the tribunal is called a Constitutional office holders rights tribunal and consists of three judges. The focus is on the Public Prosecutor and the Leadership Tribunal, being the most common entities involved as a majority of the leaders prosecuted are Members of Parliament.

Commission's jurisdiction.[18] The Ombudsman Commission will investigate and establish whether there has been:[19]

- Wrongful conduct; and/or
- Defects in law or administrative practice; and/or
- Discriminatory practice.

The finding(s) against a state service or governmental body is made in a report, which the Ombudsman Commission has the discretion to either make public by presenting it to the parliament or keeping it confidential. Where a report is confidential, only the persons implicated and the head of the organisation are privy to the Commission's findings. The policies the Ombudsman Commission uses to decide whether to keep findings confidential should be publicised so the public is informed of how the Commission exercises its discretion. Reference to the NGDP and BSO in a public report draws their importance to the attention of state services and governmental bodies.

Investigating allegations of wrong conduct, defects in law or administrative practice, can only relate to matters of administration.[20] For example, criminal behaviour is outside of the scope of the Ombudsman Commission. What has become apparent is that the Ombudsman Commission has focused on the terms of the legislation to appraise the conduct of state services and governmental bodies. When a complaint is lodged, the first line of inquiry is usually whether provision(s) of the relevant legislation have been breached. It is quite possible the Ombudsman Commission can consider other avenues to ensure state services and governmental bodies implement the NGDP and BSO within the context of the provisions of the legislation alleged to have been breached. Such an approach will enable the Ombudsman Commission to ensure state services and governmental bodies fulfil their duties under ss 25 and 63 of the Constitution.

---

18 Constitution, s 219(1), and Organic Law on the Ombudsman Commission (OLOC), s 13. The definition of governmental body under the Constitution includes the three arms of government and any entity established by law or administrative act for a public purpose (Constitution, sch 1.2.2). The New Zealand Ombudsman is immune from possible jurisdictional challenges because the entities it has power to investigate are specifically listed in legislation: see New Zealand Ombudsman Act 1975, sch 1.

19 Constitution, s 219(1), and Organic Law on the Ombudsman Commission, s 13.

20 Constitution, s 219(8).

The NGDP and BSO are expressly referred to in ss 219(1)(a) and 219(3) of the Constitution, which set out the Ombudsman Commission's administrative complaints function. The first provision relates only to wrong conduct investigations; the second applies to all three types of investigation subjects. A review of Ombudsman Commission reports of since 1999 reveal a lack of use of s 219 of the Constitution to implement the NGDP and BSO.[21]

Part II, section C, presents a legal position on how Ombudsman Commission recommendations can be implemented under the administrative complaints function. The legal position stems from ss 22 and 23 of the Constitution, and the judicial review remedy of mandamus. It provides an avenue for direct enforcement of the NGDP and BSO through the recommendations. Although the Ombudsman Commission has acknowledged it has such power, it has never exercised it.[22] The Ombudsman Commission relies more on power of persuasion to support implementation of its recommendations.

2. *Ombudsman Commission reports*

The format of Ombudsman Commission reports has been standardised in the last 10 years.[23] They follow a standard outline:

- Executive Summary;
- Jurisdiction and purpose of the investigation;
- Determination of the facts of the case;
- Findings;
- Recommendations; and
- Applicable laws.

Under the section on jurisdiction and purpose of the investigation, the Ombudsman Commission outlines the legal basis of its investigations. It says why it has power to investigate and outlines the scope of its inquiry.

---

[21] Chapter 5 discussed an evaluation of the Ombudsman Commission's implementation score card. There has been one report after the report in 2011; it was not available at the time of writing.

[22] Cannings, above n 18, at 211.

[23] This observation is based on the Ombudsman Commission reports examined.

Provisions of the Constitution and the OLOC granting power to the Ombudsman Commission over the person(s) and/or entities investigated are stated. It defines for example what constitutes wrong conduct in these laws.

In the section on determination of the facts of the case, the Ombudsman Commission states the facts it has established from its investigation. Any person that is implicated is given an opportunity to respond. Where they respond, their reply will be considered and analysed as to whether it satisfactorily refutes the allegations made against them.

In the part on findings, the Ombudsman Commission states its conclusion. That is, whether the facts that have been determined constitute wrong conduct, defective administrative practice or law, or is discriminatory. A short statement is made explaining the findings with a list of reasons supporting the findings. The reasons can include just facts or an analysis of the law breached.

The other major part of the report is the recommendations. This is where the Ombudsman Commission recommends to the head of the state service or governmental body what should be done to address the problem identified in the report. Recommendations can take many different forms depending on the nature of the findings. They could include for example, that the head of the state service or governmental body take disciplinary action against a particular official found to be at fault. In other instances, the Ombudsman Commission recommends the development of more efficient policies and processes or training of officials in a particular area.

The part on applicable laws reproduce the relevant provisions of the legislation forming the basis of the Ombudsman Commission's investigations. The laws alleged to have been breached are stated here. Its utility is to ensure ease of reference in reading the report.

The implementation of the NGDP and BSO could be incorporated in the jurisdiction and purpose of the investigation, findings, recommendations and applicable laws section of the report. Proposals for their implementation are made below in some actual reports of the Ombudsman Commission where its findings and recommendations are analysed in light of the NGDP and BSO. This provides a practical means of ensuring implementation within the parameters of the present law.

3. *Wrongful conduct*

For the Ombudsman Commission to determine whether a state service or governmental body's actions and/or omissions is wrongful, it has to consider a number of factors including whether the conduct is contrary to law or is unreasonable.[24] In performing this assessment, the Ombudsman Commission can take into account the NGDP and BSO.[25] Accordingly, the NGDP and BSO should guide the implementation of law by the state services or governmental bodies. This is a similar approach to that recommended respectively for the executive and the judiciary presented in chapters 8 and 9, that is, for preference to be given to propositions that advance the NGDP and BSO over others that do not. Where there is an interpretation of the law which promotes the NGDP and/or BSO, it should be preferred by the Ombudsman Commission when it determines whether conduct is wrong or not. The state service or governmental body would be guided by Parliament as to which NGDP and/or BSO has priority and relevance to matters covered under the subject matter of the legislation if Parliament can state clearly as such in the legislation.

Chapter 7 recommended that Parliament's intention on which NGDP and/or BSO it prefers can be expressed in the preamble and/or object section of the legislation. This ensures the Ombudsman Commission addressing a grievance about the application of the law is sufficiently guided by the express terms of the legislation. A number of examples demonstrate this point.

In 2009, the Ombudsman Commission released a report entitled "Investigation Report into the Alleged Unlawful and Abuse of Human Rights by Police, Three Mile Guest House, Port Moresby, National Capital District" (Police Report).[26] This was a report arising from allegations of police unlawful entry (without a search warrant) into a private residence in Port Moresby, use of excessive force to secure a suspect's arrest, and then subjecting them to humiliating treatment. The report found the police involved had acted wrongly (ie, a finding of wrong conduct was made). Certain recommendations were

---

[24] The grounds of wrong conduct are set out in Part III of this chapter.

[25] Constitution, s 219(1)(B).

[26] The Ombudsman Commission of Papua New Guinea *Investigation Report into the Alleged Unlawful and Abuse of Human Rights by Police, Three Mile Guest House, Port Moresby, National Capital District, Final Report 2009* (Government Printer, Port Moresby, 2009) [Police Report].

made as a result, including the need for adoption of human rights courses in the Police Force Course Manual.[27]

The Police Report was a welcome initiative against the background of widespread concern about police abusing human rights. But there was scope for inclusion of the NGDP and/or BSO. First, in the standard outline of the Police Report, a section on the definition of wrongful conduct stated:[28]

> Section 219(2) of the Constitution specifies that conduct is wrong if it is—
>
> (a) contrary to law; or
>
> (b) unreasonable, unjust, oppressive or improperly discriminatory, whether or not it is in accordance with law or practice; or
>
> (c) based wholly or partly on improper motives, irrelevant grounds or irrelevant considerations; or
>
> (d) based wholly or partly on a mistake of law or of fact; or
>
> (e) conduct for which reasons should be given but were not,
>
> whether or not the act was supposed to be done in the exercise of deliberate judgement within the meaning of Section 62 (decisions in "deliberate judgement").

The statement did not cover the full definition of wrong conduct. It did not include the preceding provision, s 219(1), which states "... where the conduct is or may be wrong, taking into account, amongst other things, the National Goals and Directive Principles, the Basic Rights and the Basic Social Obligations ...". This may seem a trivial matter, but it would have expressed a commitment to the factors which the Ombudsman Commission should take into account when examining the conduct of a state service or governmental body.

Published reports by the Ombudsman Commission from 1999 up until the most recent one in 2011 show that this was the approach taken in all

---

27 At 22.

28 At 4.

the reports.[29] If the Ombudsman Commission is to make a better effort at implementing the NGDP and/or BSO, it should adopt a statement encompassing the NGDP and/or BSO. A clear indication should be given as to whether the Ombudsman Commission considered the NGDP and/or BSO in the report. Only two reports referred to the NGDP, but it was not at the commencement stages. The Commission did not determine wrongful conduct on the basis of the NGDP as it is required to do under the Constitution.[30] No reference has been made to the BSO.

Reverting to the Police Report, one of the recommendations the Ombudsman Commission made related to human rights:[31]

> Recommendation No. 5
>
> The Commission recommends to the Commissioner of Police to update and include Human Rights Courses in the Police Force Course Modules and that all members of the Force undertake refresher courses on Operational duties once in every (2) years.

This recommendation has relevance to the BSO, which was not referred to in the report by the Ombudsman Commission. Paragraph (f) of the BSO states: "to respect the rights and freedoms of others, and to co-operate fully with others in the interests of interdependence and solidarity; …". By making express reference to the BSO, evidence would be provided of the Ombudsman Commission fulfilling the aspirations of the people, and promotion of the NGDP and BSO as it is required to do under ss 25 and 63 of the Constitution.[32] This clearly was a case where the police did not respect

---

29 When a report is published, it means it is tabled in Parliament and as a result is made public: see Organic Law on the Ombudsman Commission, s 23.

30 The Ombudsman Commission of Papua New Guinea *National Forest Board Report Investigation into the Decision of the National Forest Board to Award Kamula Doso FMA to Wawoi Guavi Timber Company (A Subsidiary of Rimbunan Hijau) as an Extension to the Wawoi Guavi Timber Resource Permit* Final Report July 2002 (Government Printer, Port Moresby 2002) [*National Forest Board Report*, 2002], and The Ombudsman Commission of Papua New Guinea *Investigation into the Appointment and Conduct of Hamish Sharp in the National Maritime Safety Authority Board*, Final Report 2009 (Government Printer, Port Moresby 2002 [*NMSA Report*].

31 *Police Report*, above n 26, at 22.

32 Constitution, s 218 states as one of the purposes of the Ombudsman Commission is to fulfil the aspirations of the people of Papua New Guinea.

the rights and freedoms of others contrary to its constitutional obligation to do so.

In another report of the Ombudsman Commission, entitled "Investigation Report into the Julian Ronald Moti Affair, Final Report 2009" (Moti Report), the Ombudsman Commission investigated the breach of the Extradition Act 2005 and the Civil Aviation Act 2000. The case concerned Julian Moti, an Australian citizen wanted by the Australian Federal Police for alleged sexual offences committed in Vanuatu. Mr Moti was subsequently appointed by the Solomon Islands government as Attorney-General. Papua New Guinea Police, acting on an extradition request from Australia, detained Moti as he was transiting through Port Moresby to Honiara. While he was in police custody, a political directive was issued for Moti's release. A military plane subsequently ferried him to Solomon Islands (also upon political prompting). The Ombudsman Commission determined there were breaches of both the Extradition Act and the Civil Aviation Act by state services and governmental bodies involved in the saga. One of its findings stated:

> Finding No 10
>
> In the opinion of the Ombudsman Commission the PNGDF (Papua New Guinea Defence Force) officials' actions to facilitate the transportation of Mr Moti to Solomon Islands were in breach of the Civil Aviation Act 2000.

The PNGDF had acted at the behest of political directives to carry out the operation.[33] Again, there was scope for the use of the NGDP and/or BSO. Principle 1 of Goal 3 directs:

> (1) our leaders to be committed to these National Goals and Directive Principles, to ensure that their freedom to make decisions is not restricted by obligations to or relationship with others, and to make all of their decisions in the national interest; and

In this instance, a relationship with a foreign national (Julian Moti) resulted in the breach of national laws. This particular NGDP should have been brought to prominence in the Ombudsman Commission report. The

[33] The Ombudsman Commission of Papua New Guinea *Investigation Report into the Julian Ronald Moti Affair, Final Report 2009* (Government Printer, Port Moresby, 2009) at 47.

Moti Report had only focused on whether the government officials had complied with the Extradition Act and the Civil Aviation Act. But there was there was also scope for the Ombudsman Commission to incorporate the NGDP and BSO in its report. By referring to the NGDP and BSO, the Moti Report would have contributed to their implementation. The Ombudsman Commission would have emphasised the NGDP and BSO should guide all governmental activity.

In 2010, the Ombudsman Commission released a report entitled "Investigation into the Department of Lands and Physical Planning Rezoning, Leasing and Registering of the Land Title for Section 31 Allotment 03 Kimbe Issued to Quinquing Trading Limited" (Lands Department Report). In that Report the Ombudsman Commission investigated the allocation of a land designated for public use to private commercial purposes. One of the matters the Ombudsman Commission was concerned with was the manner in which public land was allocated to private commercial use. The Lands Department is required by the Land Act 1996 to publicly advertise any government land which it wishes to allocate for development purposes.[34] The land was exempted from advertisement and only one applicant tendered for it – Quinquing Trading Limited. The primary focus of the Report was the legality of the procedures relating to allocation of state land under the Land Act. The Ombudsman Commission found the Lands Department officials acted wrongly when they exempted Section 31 Allotment 03 Kimbe from public tender and allocated it to Quinquing Trading Limited.

Here also there was opportunity for the Ombudsman Commission to incorporate the NGDP and BSO in the Lands Department report. Directive Principle 1 of Goal 2 states:

> (1) an equal opportunity for every citizen to take part in the political, economic, social, religious and cultural life of the country … .

This idea of participation in the development of the country is also emphasised in the BSO:

> (b) to recognize that they can fully develop their capabilities and advance their true interests only by active participation in the development of the national community as a whole … .

---

[34] Land Act 1996, ss 68 and 69.

Allocating state land without public advertisement does not give the opportunity to every citizen to take part in the economic life of the country. The Lands Department Report was an important one, and should have taken the opportunity to refer to the NGDP especially Directive Principle 1 of Goal 2 and paragraph (b) of the BSO. Public reports present an important opportunity to draw the attention of state services and governmental bodies to the NGDP and BSO.

A report which has, however, demonstrated a strong commitment to implementing the NGDP and BSO was the "Investigation into the Decision of the National Forest Board to Award Kamula Doss Forest Management Area to Wawoi Guavi Timber Company (A Subsidiary of Rimbunan Hijau) As an Extension of the Wawoi Guavi Timber Resource Permit, Final Report, July 2002" (National Forest Board Report 2002).[35] It is recommended the Ombudsman Commission consistently adopt this approach.

The circumstances of the case relate to the awarding of a licence to log in an area of land described as Kamula Doss Forest Management Area, some 791,400 hectares in size.[36] The applicant, Wawoi Guavi Timber Company, did not meet the stringent requirements of the Forest Act 1991 yet a timber permit was granted to it. Part of the requirements included compliance with environmental standards and obtaining consent from the indigenous landowners. The Ombudsman Commission found the conduct of several government officials was wrongful because they did not meet the legal and policy requirements. Consequently, the Commission made several recommendations to prevent such conduct in future. In terms of the NGDP, the National Forest Board Report 2002 covered s 25 of the Constitution and goal 4 on natural resources and the environment:[37]

> Five National Goals and Directive Principles are proclaimed in the preamble to the Constitution. The preamble directs all persons and bodies, corporate and incorporated, to be guided by these declared Directives in pursuing and achieving our aims.

---

35 *National Forest Board Report*, 2002, above n 30.

36 A forest management area is a piece of land, which the government has identified for the issuance of timber permit over the area, to any company that wishes to log there; but only after a public tender process and the incumbent satisfying relevant laws and policies, especially under the Forestry Act 1991.

37 *National Forest Board Report*, 2002, above n 30, at 71.

> Directive 4 relates to natural resources and the environment. A fiduciary duty is imposed on those who are responsible for decision-making on our natural resources and environment.

This is an example the Ombudsman Commission ought to use consistently in its report to remind state services and governmental bodies of their duty to implement the NGDP and/or BSO.

If the Ombudsman Commission incorporated the NGDP and BSO directly in a public report two obvious advantages would ensue. First, it would draw the attention of state services and governmental bodies to the duty they have under ss 25 and 63 of the Constitution to implement the NGDP and BSO. The failure of Governmental bodies and state services to implement the NGDP and BSO can result in adverse findings against them. As such it is a duty that cannot be ignored.

Second, if the recommendations of the Ombudsman Commission are carried out, an opportunity for the implementation of the NGDP and BSO emerges. Later in the chapter, it will be argued there is potential for implementation of Ombudsman Commission recommendations through the administrative judicial review remedy of mandamus. This is an area of the law that is not very clear but an increasing number of cases may help clarify it.

4. *Defects in law or administrative conduct*

Determining what is "defective law" or "defective administrative conduct" is a broad inquiry. One approach taken by the Ombudsman Commission in 2009 is particularly useful for the implementation of the NGDP and BSO. The adoption of this method will ensure implementation. The Ombudsman Commission published a report entitled "Investigation Report into the Appointment and Conduct of Hamish Sharp in the National Maritime Safety Authority Board" (NMSA Report). The report inquired into whether the Minister for Transport complied with the National Maritime Safety Authority Act 2009 when he appointed members to the National Maritime Safety Authority (NMSA) Board. Section 7 of the NMSA Act required adequate board representation from the four regions of the country. The Ombudsman Commission found the NMSA Board did not have any policy in place to implement s 7(1)(d) of the Act and, therefore, the appointment practice (or process) was defective.

The Commission's relevant finding was:[38]

> Finding No 3
>
> In the opinion of the Ombudsman Commission, the National Maritime Safety Authority's administrative practice is defective in that it does not have a policy in place to guide appointments under section 7(1)(d) of the NMSA Act.

There is a stronger case for investigating a state service or governmental body for defective administrative practice for failure to put in place policies for the implementation of the NGDP and/or BSO. A proposal for what such an investigation would involve is presented below. This would be a possible legal avenue for the Ombudsman Commission to explore means of implementing the NGDP and BSO on a broad scale.

5. *Discriminatory practice*

The function of the Ombudsman Commission as an anti-discrimination body would also by inference incorporate National Goal two on equality and participation and the BSO, paragraph (f) to observe human rights. Section 55 of the Constitution is the main anti-discrimination provision.[39] National Goal 2 on equality and participation is reinforced by s 55 and often referred to when human rights claims in court are made for breaching s 55.[40] Ombudsman Commission reports dealing with discrimination should refer to the NGDP and BSO as a matter of course.

In cases where the Ombudsman Commission investigates discrimination, active reference must be made to the NGDP and BSO, so that an impression is made on the government of the basic purpose of its existence which is to fulfil the NGDP and BSO aspirations. Furthermore, the BSO calls for the respect of human rights and freedoms.

---

38 *NMSA Report*, above n 30, at 24.

39 There are two Acts which also prevent discrimination, which the Ombudsman Commission administers: Discriminatory Practices Act 1963 and the HIV/AIDS Management and Prevention Act 2003.

40 See for example *Re Application under Section 57 of the Constitution; Application by Individual and Community Rights Advocacy Forum Inc (ICRAF); Re Miriam Willingal* [1997] PGNC 7 N1506, 10 February 1997 where the Court held the custom of "head pay", which allows the giving of an unmarried woman as part of compensation, was declared unconstitutional for being inconsistent with human rights provisions of the Constitution, including s 55. Reference was also made to the NGDP in the Court's decision.

In the 2009 Police Report discussed above, the residence the police raided was alleged to have been a brothel.[41] Persons apprehended were accused of being involved in prostitution. The Ombudsman Commission found the suspects' treatment was humiliating:

> Finding No 4
>
> In the opinion of the Ombudsman Commission the Police actions were humiliating to the victims.

The evidence the Ombudsman Commission relied on to substantiate its findings was:[42]

- The victims were required to blow, chew condoms and hold them above their heads as they marched to Boroko Police Station;
- The victims were subjected to bystanders' comments like: "Oh look at them what do they look for and they are the ones mostly affected by the AIDS virus";
- The bystanders shouted and made humiliating remarks such as: "You are the carriers of HIV and all these are spreading to other people and you shouldn't do that."; and
- The parading of the victims through the streets was humiliating and unnecessary and cannot be excused as necessary policing activity.

The suspects were discriminated against because of the nature of the offence they were alleged to have committed. The following NGDP and BSO were applicable to the facts established by the Ombudsman Commission:

- Everyone [is] to be involved in our endeavours to achieve integral human development of the whole person for every person and to seek fulfilment through his or her contribution to the common good (Directive Principle 1 of Goal 1); and
- To respect the rights and freedoms of others, and to co-operate fully with others in the interests of interdependence and solidarity (paragraph (f) of BSO).

---

41 Prostitution is illegal in Papua New Guinea, see Summary Offences Act 1977, ss 55– 57.

42 *Police Report*, above no 26, at 17.

The suspects were treated contrary to the Goal on integral human development and the obligation to respect their rights and freedoms were not observed.

It is proposed that where the Ombudsman Commission investigates acts of discriminatory practice, it should make reference to relevant NGDP and/or BSO applicable to the circumstances of the case.

6. *A proposal for investigation into government policy-making under defective laws and/or administrative practice jurisdiction of the Ombudsman Commission*

Investigating defects in law or administrative practice can provide an opportunity to implement the NGDP and BSO meaningfully. It enables the Ombudsman Commission to comment on broader policy and legal issues from the angle of the NGDP and BSO.

There may be policies or legislation that do not adequately provide for the NGDP and BSO or that are even inconsistent with them. Another provision in addition to s 219(1) of the Constitution that amplifies the Ombudsman Commission's administrative complaints function in relation to the NGDP and BSO is s 219(3):

> (3) The Commission shall not inquire into the justifiability of a policy of the National Government or a Minister or a provincial government or a member of a provincial executive, except insofar as the policy may be contrary to law or to the National Goals and Directive Principles, the Basic Rights or the Basic Social Obligations, or of any act of the Parliament.

The only likely limitation would be that it should relate to a matter of administration, consistent with s 219(8) of the Constitution. Consequently, a liberal definition of what constitutes "administrative conduct" should replace the present interpretation to strengthen the role of the Ombudsman Commission to address general societal concerns. The current authority on the point is *SCR No 1 of 1978; Re Ombudsman Commission Investigations of the Public Solicitor* where the Court observed:[43]

---

[43] *SCR No 1 of 1978; Re Ombudsman Commission Investigations of the Public Solicitor* [1978] PGSC 7, [1978] PNGLR 345, 6 October 1978.

> The powers of the Ombudsman Commission, save and except with regard to discriminatory practices and under Div. III.2 (leadership code), are limited to the investigation of administrative conduct. "Conduct" in s. 219 of the Constitution means any action (or alleged action) or inaction (or alleged inaction) relating to a matter of administration. It is government officials or public servants or members of the State Services who perform most of the administrative functions at which ombudsman legislation of this type is primarily directed. If one looks at the mischief aimed at by the ombudsman legislation in Papua New Guinea, the object was to protect the public from maladministration by government officials and hardly to protect the public (which already has recourse to other remedies) from professional misconduct or the mal-performance of legal aid services.

This interpretation is helpful but may be restrictive as s 219(3) specifically refers to government policy. A useful definition of what constitutes administrative conduct broad enough to incorporate the NGDP and BSO was made in the Canadian case of *Re British Columbia Development Corporation v Friedmann*, where Dickson J held:[44]

> There is nothing in the words administration or administrative which excludes the propriety of business decisions of governmental organisations. On the contrary, the words are fully broad enough to encompass all conduct engaged in by a governmental authority in furtherance of government policy-business or otherwise. In my view, the phrase "a matter of administration" encompasses everything done by governmental authorities in the implementation of government policy. I would exclude only the activities of the legislature and the courts from the Ombudsman's scrutiny.

It is submitted that where a governmental body does not have an adequate policy to demonstrate how it can implement the NGDP and/ or BSO, this amounts to defective administrative practice (or conduct).[45]

---

[44] *Re British Columbia Development Corporation v Friedmann* (1984) 14 DLR (4th) 129 (SCC) at 139–140.

[45] "Administrative practice" and "administrative conduct" are used interchangeably.

Defective administrative practice occurs because a governmental body has not implemented its constitutional duty under ss 25 and 63. Such an approach is based on the current practice of the Ombudsman Commission discussed above in the NMSA Report. The Ombudsman Commission found as defective administrative practice a lack of policy to implement s 7 of the NMSA Act. By analogy, it is recommended the Ombudsman Commission adopt a similar approach to see whether state services and governmental bodies have policies in place to implement the NGDP and BSO. The Ombudsman Commission is ideally placed to investigate state services and governmental bodies' policies and decision-making processes to understand at least from an administrative point of view why the NGDP and BSO are not being implemented. Based on this inquiry the Ombudsman Commission can recommend measures to overcome the deficiency.

There are many state services and governmental bodies.[46] The Ombudsman Commission could identify two or three of these entities and use them as a pilot study to conduct investigations. The main outcomes of these findings can be used by other governmental bodies to develop their policies to implement the NGDP and BSO.

An investigation of this nature would cover the aspects presented below. What is significant about s 219(3) in the implementation framework is that it presents an opportunity the courts would not have, because often, they only intervene when there is an actual dispute. Under this function, general societal concerns about the direction of the country can be reviewed and commented on by the Ombudsman Commission in light of the failure to implement the NGDP and BSO.

(a) Enabling legislation

The first part of the Ombudsman Commission's investigation would define the objectives and functions of the state service or governmental body. The Commission would be able to define the functions from a close study of the legislation and the provisions in the law that establish the state service and governmental body. Defining the specific function of a state service or governmental body helps formulate the findings of the report

---

46 This observation is based on definition of governmental bodies and state services in the Constitution: see sch 1.2(1) and s 188, respectively.

and point to the Ombudsman Commission which NGDP and/or BSO is most appropriate for the state service or governmental body to implement; or whether a more generic policy is more suitable to allow discretion to the state service or governmental body. Obviously enabling legislation that has made express reference to the NGDP and/or BSO in line with the recommendations in chapter 7 would enable a clearer direction for the Commission's inquiry.

(b) Relevant NGDP and/or BSO

After the Ombudsman Commission has considered the functions of the state service or governmental body from the latter's operating legislation, the relevant NGDP and/or BSO applicable will usually become clear. For example, the National Housing Corporation (NHC) under its operating legislation has as its first function the improvement of housing conditions.[47] The relevant goals and principles relevant to the National Housing Corporation would be Goal 1 on integral human development:

> … every person to be dynamically involved in the process of freeing himself or herself from every form of domination or oppression so that each man or woman will have the opportunity to develop as a whole person in relationship with others.

Living in oppressive housing conditions is not a fulfilment of this Goal. In fact having good accommodation is interrelated with achieving many other developmental aspirations, for instance good health. This would mean that the NHC in its policies and decision-making process should make reference to these goals and principles.

(c) Current Practice/Policy

After identifying which NGDP and/or BSO is relevant to the state service or governmental body, the Ombudsman Commission would look at the existing policies and practices to see how a particular state service or governmental body have incorporated the NGDP and/or BSO in them. The Ombudsman Commission would determine whether there are adequate provisions in the policy to implement the NGDP and/or BSO.

---

47 National Housing Corporation Act 1990, s 28(1)(a).

(d) Recommendations

The final part of the report would contain recommendations. After studying the enabling legislation and existing policy practices, the Ombudsman Commission would recommend which NGDP and/or BSO is particularly relevant for the state service or governmental body and avenues in which they can be implemented. Alternatively, the Ombudsman Commission may recommend a more general policy to engage the NGDP and/or BSO as and when the state service or governmental body sees fit. This may result in the state service or governmental body having to amend its current policies.

After the recommendations are made, it falls on the state service or governmental body to implement them. Failure to implement the recommendations without good reason(s) can result in the Ombudsman Commission taking up enforcement proceedings. The nature of such enforcement proceedings is discussed in the next part of the chapter.

C. Legal Consideration of Ombudsman Commission Reports/Recommendations

The position on the status of the Ombudsman Commission reports is unclear. In s 219(6), the Constitution states:

> Except as provided by or under Division III.2 (leadership code), the Commission's powers of enforcement are limited to publicity for its proceedings, reports and recommendations, to the making of reports and recommendations to the Parliament and other appropriate authorities as provided by an Organic Law, and to the giving of advice.

The Constitution limits the enforcement of recommendation to publicity, but goes further to provide for the enactment of an Organic Law to give effect to this. The Organic Law that gives effect to this provision is the Organic Law on the Ombudsman Commission. Section 22(3) states:

> If the Commission so requests, the responsible Minister, Permanent Head or statutory head as the case may be, shall, within such period as specified by the Commission, notify the Commission as to the steps (if any) that he proposes to take to give effect to its recommendations.

This is how the Ombudsman Commission has interpreted the legal effect of s 22(3) in its reports:[48]

> Accordingly, there is a duty placed on each recipient of a recommendation to notify the Commission; and if it is proposed not to implement any recommendation, there is a further duty to give cogent and convincing reasons why recommendations cannot or should not be implemented. These duties arise due to a combined effect of the Constitution and the Organic Law on the Ombudsman Commission.
>
> A failure to comply with these duties may result in the Ombudsman Commission commencing enforcement proceedings in the National Court, pursuant to s 23 of the Constitution.

A decision of the National Court may provide an avenue to support the legal duty to provide reasons for not complying with the Ombudsman Commission's recommendations.[49] In *Niggints v Tokam*, a terminated government employee had his dismissal reviewed by the Public Service Commission.[50] The Public Service Commission recommended Niggints' reinstatement to his previous position. The recommendation was not attended to and he sought judicial review of his former employer's decision. The Court held the Commission's recommendation should not be ignored:[51]

> The departmental head is, in my view, required by common-sense and the need for public administrative accountability to give serious consideration to the Commission's recommendation and the reason for it. Having considered the recommendation, if it is decided not to accept it, then the reason for not so accepting the recommendation should be provided to the aggrieved officer, because the officer has a right to seek judicial review as the applicant has done in this case … .

---

48 The Ombudsman Commission of Papua New Guinea *Investigation into the Purchase of The Conservatory, Cairns by the Public Officers Superannuation Fund Board and associated transactions and arrangements, Final Report November 1999* (Government Printer, Port Moresby, 1999) at 354.

49 Cannings, above no 8, at 208.

50 *Niggints v Tokam* [1993] PNGLR 66.

51 Per Amet J.

The recommendation of the Ombudsman Commission in the report is made under law after according natural justice to those adversely commented on. In fact, the recommendations are authorised by a constitutional law. Interpreting these two provisions (Constitution s 219(6) and OLOC s 22(3)) in a way they apply concurrently, the Ombudsman Commission would not be able to directly implement its recommendations, but could compel the head of the state service or governmental body to whom the recommendations are addressed, to demonstrate what steps he or she intends to take to implement them. "Cogent and convincing" reasons should be provided in the event of non-implementation of the recommendations.

Section 22 of the Constitution empowers courts to create procedures to enforce constitutional duties, where there are no mechanisms to enforce them.[52] The duty in this instance is created by an Organic Law and sanctioned by the Constitution. Further, s 23 of the Constitution provides various alternative remedies for breach of constitutional duties.[53] In any case, it is a duty stemming from statute. What would be the appropriate process to enforce duties arising from Ombudsman Commission recommendation(s)? United Kingdom decisions have recognised administrative judicial review procedures with the remedy of mandamus to enforce statutory duties.[54] Ombudsman Commission's recommendations confer a public duty, directed to public authorities. That is to say, the basis of the Ombudsman Commission's recommendations are designed rectify conduct of public entities falling short of constitutional expectations, which should be considered a public duty. Kapi Dep CJ remarks in *Special Reference Pursuant to Constitution Section 10; Calling of the Parliament; Reference by the Ombudsman Commission* (*Calling of Parliament*) allows scope for the enforcement of constitutional duties.[55] Kapi Dep CJ held the remedy of

52 Chapter 7 also discusses ss 22 and 23 of the Constitution.

53 Organic Laws are considered as part of constitutional laws, see Constitution, sch 1.2.2. The Organic Law on the Ombudsman Commission would therefore be regarded as constitutional law.

54 See *R v Commissioner of Police of the Metropolis, ex parte Blackburn (No 1)* [1968] 2 QB 118 (CA), [1968] 1 All ER 763; *R v Police Commissioner, ex parte Blackburn (No 3)* [1973] QB 241 (CA); *R v Greater London Council, ex parte Blackburn* [1976] 3 All ER 184 (CA).

55 *Special Reference Pursuant to Constitution Section 10; Calling of the Parliament; Reference by the Ombudsman Commission* [1999] PGSC 21, SC628, 25 June 1999 [*Calling of Parliament*]. This case was referred to in chapter 7.

mandamus in an administrative judicial review, can be used to implement constitutional (and public) duties.[56] The reasoning was based on an analogy from the United Kingdom where statutory duties can be implemented by mandamus.[57]

The Ombudsman Commission would institute proceedings against the head of the state service or governmental body as the case may be. The court would be asked to compel the head of the state service or governmental body to provide an explanation for non-implementation of the recommendation(s). If an order is successfully obtained against the head of the entity, he or she must provide adequate reasons for not implementing the recommendations.

D. Leadership Code Function

1. Introduction

Not all government leaders are subject to the Leadership Code; only those that have been expressly identified in s 26 of the Constitution are. They are Members of Parliament, Ministers and judges amongst others. The duties and responsibilities of leadership are only expected of leaders covered under s 26; failure to meet the standards of the Leadership Code is considered misconduct.

This chapter will focus on the Ombudsman Commission, but there are also other bodies involved in the implementation of the NGDP and BSO in the Leadership Code process.[58] They are the Public Prosecutor and the Tribunal.[59] Each one of them makes its decision independently of the other. The following is a brief description of what each body does.

The Ombudsman Commission investigates the allegations for misconduct in office based on s 27 of the Constitution and the OLDRL. If there is a case against the leader, the Ombudsman Commission asks the leader to

---

56 Constitution, s 218.

57 See *Calling of Parliament*, above n 55, where English cases were discussed to draw useful analogy.

58 See *Public Prosecutor's Power*, above no 17, for a discussion of the extent of the involvement of each of these bodies, such as the Public Prosecutor and the appropriate tribunal.

59 The name of the tribunal and its constitution depends on the category of leader referred: see *Public Prosecutor's Power*, above n 16.

respond by way of what is called a "right to be heard".[60] If the Ombudsman Commission is not satisfied with the leader's explanation, believing there is a prima facie case against the leader, it refers the allegations to the Public Prosecutor to independently review the case, accompanied by a statement of reasons.[61] The statement of reasons sets out the nature of the allegations. If the Public Prosecutor is also satisfied there is a case against the leader (based on the statement of reasons), the Public Prosecutor requests the Chief Justice to empanel a tribunal to inquire into the allegations. The Public Prosecutor then prosecutes the leader before the Tribunal. It can be seen the Ombudsman Commission has the initial role to set the scene (or terms of reference) for the implementation of the NGDP and BSO under the Leadership Code function despite there being other independent entities involved, too.[62]

2. *Methodology*

If the Ombudsman Commission's investigation against a leader reveals a prima face case of misconduct in office, the allegations are prepared against the leader. The leader is then formally (and confidentially) informed of his or her alleged infringement of the Leadership Code. The allegations are eventually inquired into by the Tribunal.

It is, therefore, important to understand the way the allegations are formulated to determine the scope of implementation of the NGDP and BSO. Essentially, the facts of the case are considered against the standards of the

---

60 A right to be heard is a natural justice requirement where allegations against a leader is put to the leader, for a response within a specific time period. Depending on the response, the Ombudsman Commission then decides to refer the leader for prosecution for misconduct in office.

61 The statement of reasons is referred to in s 27(1) of the Organic Law on the Duties and Responsibilities of Leadership. A statement of reasons was described by Kapi J in *Re The Leadership Tribunal; Bonga v Sheehan* [1997] PGNC 20 N1512, 4 March 1997 as two-fold. For the Public Prosecutor, it provides the basis to consider whether he or she should proceed with prosecution. Second, when it is placed before the tribunal by the Public Prosecutor (required by law) it is not evidence, but simply indicates the nature and direction the inquiry may take.

62 But the Ombudsman Commission has a reserve power to initiate prosecution, if the Public Prosecutor has not commenced prosecution within a reasonable time of the referral: see Constitution, s 29(2). The Supreme Court held in *Public Prosecutor's Power* a reasonable time was considered to be one to four months, except where the special circumstances of a case require longer period, above n 16, at [23].

general duties expected of leaders under s 27 of the Constitution. These duties are stated in broad terms:

- Not to have a conflict of interest;
- Not to demean the office;
- Not to allow their official or personal integrity to be called into question; and
- Not to endanger or diminish respect for confidence in the integrity of government in Papua New Guinea.

In *Application of John Mua Nilkare*, a decision of the Supreme Court, Kapi Dep CJ made an important observation about the ambit of s 27 of the Constitution on what kind of behaviour constitutes misconduct in office:[63]

> The other three types of conduct (s 27(1)(b) to (d)) are expressed in very wide and general terms. It is incapable of precise definition. In fact any kind of definition is likely to fall short of what this provision was intended to cover. These provisions cast a very wide net to catch all kinds of conduct by leaders. One thing is clear; it is the public perception of the leader, which is the dominant theme. Section 27(2) speaks about "doubt in the public mind". When a leader demeans his office or his integrity is called into question this will diminish the respect for and confidence of government.

As s 27 has wide scope of application, it is submitted that a leader can commit misconduct for breaching the NGDP and BSO. The NGDP and BSO were expected by the CPC to be the basis upon which the performance of a leader is judged.[64] The public perception of a leader is determined by the leader's efforts to realise the NGDP and BSO. If there are any doubts to including the NGDP and BSO in determining misconduct, ss 25(4) and 63(4) of the Constitution conclusively settle the issue by making them justiciable. In *SCR No 2 of 1992; Re The Leadership Code* the court said:[65]

---

63 *Application of John Mua Nilkare*, SC 536 at [27] per Kapi DCJ.

64 CPC Report, above n 1, at 2/1 [6].

65 *SCR No 2 of 1992; Re The Leadership Code* [1992] PGSC 16, [1992] PNGLR 336, 31 July 1992 per Kidu CJ, Amet, Los and Andrew JJ.

Subsection 25(4) enables the Tribunal, for the purposes of the Leadership Code, to take the National Goals and Directive Principles fully into account in all cases as appropriate.

In *In the Matter of a Reference by the Public Prosecutor and the Hon Melchior Pep, Member of Parliament* (*Melchior Pep*), the tribunal stated that a leader was bound by the NGDP by virtue of s 25 of the Constitution.[66] This observation would equally apply to the BSO because s 63 of the Constitution is similar to s 25. The justiciability of the NGDP and BSO under the Leadership Code should as a result support the incorporation of the NGDP and BSO in the misconduct assessment performed by the Ombudsman Commission.

Essentially, a leader's conduct is assessed against the general duties under s 27 of the Constitution and then against the specific duties in the OLDRL. In addition to the specific offences under the OLDRL, misconduct also occurs where breach of specific rules and guidelines (for example financial procedures), are breached.

The CPC was of the view that if Papua New Guinea was to have a good opportunity to implement its NGDP and BSO, the ultimate responsibility firmly rested with the country's leaders.[67] It is, therefore, not surprising that the Constitution expressly made the NGDP and BSO justiciable under the Leadership Code function.[68] This is a clear indication to the Ombudsman Commission by the Constitution of the importance of the NGDP and BSO to its functions under the Leadership Code.

3. *Formulation of the misconduct allegations*

A review undertaken of the allegations inquired into by the Tribunal revealed that the Ombudsman Commission do not commonly charge (for want of a better word) leaders for breaching the NGDP and BSO under their leadership duties and responsibilities.[69] That is, the practice by the Ombudsman Commission to use the NGDP and BSO as directly justiciable in framing misconduct allegations. If the Ombudsman Commission framed

66 *Re Reference by the Public Prosecutor and the Hon Melchior Pep, Member of Parliament*, Unreported decision of the Leadership Tribunal, 14 October 1992, [*Melchior Pep*] at 1.

67 CPC Report, above n 1, at 3/2 [13].

68 Constitution, ss 25(4) and 63(4).

69 Many of the Tribunal decisions are not publicly available, and were obtained from the records of the Ombudsman Commission office in Port Moresby.

allegations to cover breaches of the NGDP and BSO more commonly, then there would be a greater opportunity to measure the conduct of leaders against them when it comes to the tribunal stage because the terms of reference would have been set earlier in the process.

Re reference by the Public Prosecutor and the Hon Edward Ramu Diro (*Diro*) was an important case in which the Ombudsman Commission could have formulated its charges to take greater account of the NGDP and BSO.[70] It concerned a former Member of Parliament and Minister, Edward Diro. There were 76 misconduct counts levelled against the leader and considered by the Tribunal in 1991; he was found guilty of all except five counts. Two counts which could have directly incorporated the NGDP were counts 44 and 45. The allegation covered Diro's receipt of $US139,400 from a foreign military general, which he did not declare to the Ombudsman Commission. This was a matter that directly relates to Goal 3, national sovereignty and self-reliance. The leader's actions compromised the sovereignty of the country. Whilst the Tribunal found the allegation to be true, the non-reference to the NGDP suggests a lack of awareness by the Ombudsman Commission of the importance the CPC placed on leaders to implement the NGDP and BSO. The allegations could have been couched in terms including the NGDP and BSO. Alternatively, the Tribunal could have also have alluded to the NGDP and BSO on its own initiative in deciding the moral culpability of the leader. The Tribunal did not do so.

An example of a case investigated by the Ombudsman Commission and prosecuted in the Leadership Tribunal that did take the duty under ss 25(4) and 63(4) into account was *Re Peter Yama, Member of Parliament*.[71] The relevant misconduct charge against the leader, incorporating the NGDP, is quoted in full from the Tribunal's reported decision:[72]

> ALLEGATION 16: THAT in 1995, the Leader failed to carry out the obligations imposed by Section 27 (1) of the Constitution;
>
> By conducting himself in his public life and in his associations with other persons in such a way that he:

---

[70] *Re reference by the Public Prosecutor and the Hon Edward Ramu Diro*, unreported decision of the Leadership Tribunal, Recommendations on Penalty, 27 September 1991.

[71] *Re Peter Yama, Member of Parliament* [2004] PGLT 2; N2746, 1 December 2004 [*Peter Yama*].

[72] Peter Yama.

(a) placed himself in a position in which he had a conflict of interests; and

(b) demeaned his office as the member for Sumkar Open and Minister for Transport and Works; and

(c) allowed his official integrity and his personal integrity to be called into question; and

(d) endangered and diminished respect for and confidence in the integrity of government in Papua New Guinea

AND FURTHERMORE the Leader failed to carry out the obligations imposed by Section 27(2) of the Constitution;

BY using his office for personal gain and entering into transactions that might be expected to give rise to doubt in the public mind as to whether he was carrying out the duty imposed by Section 27(1) of the Constitution;

IN THAT having been politically responsible for K21.8 million of public money intended for allocation among the 109 members of the National Parliament under Vote No 259-3601-5-202 for those members to in turn apply to specific transport projects in each of their electorates approved for funding under the Rural Transport Development Program, he—

(i) *distributed that public money contrary to the principles of fair and equitable distribution required by the National Goals and Directive Principles*; and [emphasis added]

(ii) failed to allocate any funds under the Rural Transport Program to a considerable number of electorates; and

(iii) allocated the grossly disproportionate amount of K1,557,640.00 of that public money to projects in his own electorate; and

(iv) having allocated a grossly disproportionate amount of funds to projects in his electorate, failed to apply those funds to his nominated projects and applied those funds to other unauthorised purposes; and

(v) converted a substantial part of the funds intended for his electorate, being public money, to his personal use and the use of his associates; and

(vi) failed to provide to the administering authority, the Department of Transport, a full and prompt acquittal of how the funds were disbursed, despite being the Minister with political responsibility for the Rural Transport Development Program.

THEREBY being guilty of misconduct in office under s. 27 (5) (b) of the Constitution.

This allegation of a breach of the general duty under s 27 of the Constitution is followed by a detailed explanation of the circumstances constituting the breach. The provisions of s 27 can be interpreted in light of the NGDP and BSO and furthermore, the specific NGDP and/or BSO offended are spelt out after highlighting the general duty breached.

Peter Yama was accused of breaching the NGDP in one of the series of allegations. The Tribunal decision was subjected to a number of judicial reviews and appeals, but at no point was the question of the justiciability of the NGDP challenged.[73] The reason is because this is allowed for under ss 25(4) and 63(3) of the Constitution. As was highlighted previously in this chapter, this method of using the NGDP and/or BSO is not common in the Ombudsman Commission. The Commission should use this approach more consistently when a leader's conduct breaches the NGDP and BSO. What is important is that the reference to the NGDP and/or BSO operates in tandem with s 27 of the Constitution and the OLDRL.

Yama was eventually found guilty of misconduct in office by the Leadership Tribunal. The Tribunal then proceeded to determine the penalty. As a result of allegation 16, the Tribunal observed:[74]

---

[73] See for example *Ombudsman Commission v Yama* [2004] PGSC 30; SC747, 2 June 2004.

[74] Per Manuhu, senior magistrate at page 44 of the unedited decision on recommendation on penalty handed down on 1 December 2004. The edited version in the reported decision of the tribunal by the same member of the tribunal was to the following effect:

> The K21.8 million under the Rural Transport Development Program Fund of 1995, as the title implies were intended to improve the road infrastructure network of rural areas of the country where each of the 109 Members of Parliament may have identified in their respective electorates.

> I am reminded that you have failed to distribute fairly and equitably K21.8 million in public funds. The fact that you got for yourself K1,557,640 which was six times more than your approved share is indeed a cause for concern to all Papua New Guineans. As a leader you are bound by the National Goals and Directive Principles by virtue of s 25 of the Constitution.

If the Ombudsman Commission adopts the approach in *Peter Yama* consistently in the formulation of allegations, it would become a standard consideration by the tribunal. It will form the basis upon which the tribunal focuses its determinations on the misconduct charges. This will ensure the leaders of the country are made increasingly sensitive to the NGDP and BSO and in turn influence the organisations they lead. In this way the NGDP and BSO can guide the government.

In a later case of *Re Reference by the Public Prosecutor under s 27(2) of the Organic Law on the Duties and Responsibilities of Leadership and in the Matter of the Honourable Charlie Benjamin, Member of Parliament and Member for Manus Open*, (*Charlie Benjamin*), with similar facts to the Peter Yama decision, the leader also misappropriated public funds, but no reference was made to breach of NGDP in the allegations referred to the tribunal.[75] The comparable allegation to *Peter Yama's* matter was stated this way:

> Allegation 9:
>
> That from October 1998 to March 2002 the Leader intentionally applied money forming part of a fund under the control of Papua New Guinea to purposes to which it could not lawfully be applied;

By the conduct of the leader, six electorates were deprived of the use of those public funds which were rightfully theirs in every sense of it.

In my view his actions are not only unconstitutional but undemocratic. The political ministry he held belongs to the people of Papua New Guinea and as such all Papua New Guineans, regardless of their cultural background, language, tribe, or region, have equal constitutional rights to be treated equally and fairly, more so in this case, to receive their share of the national wealth. Furthermore, the actions of the leader do not promote the constitutional spirit of a united Papua New Guinea.

75 *Re Reference by the Public Prosecutor under s 27(2) of the Organic Law on the Duties and Responsibilities of Leadership and in the Matter of the Honourable Charlie Benjamin, Member of Parliament and Member for Manus Open*, unreported decision of the Leadership Tribunal, 18 July 2006.

> In that having received K1,070,000 (NZ$500,000) in the form of fifteen (15) cheques from the National Government, under the Rural Action Program, being funds intended for the development of the Manus Open electorate in respect of the years 1998, 1999, 2000, 2001 and 2002, he-Applied a significant part of that public money to his personal use; and
>
> (a) Made approximately 198 unverifiable and/or improper debit transactions totalling about K667,507.48 (NZ$330,000) by writing out cheques to pay cash; and
>
> (b) Failed to properly acquit that money;
>
> Contrary to—
>
> (i) The requirements of the Organic Law on Provincial Governments and Local-Level Governments; and
>
> (ii) The requirements of the Public Finances (Management) Act; and
>
> (iii) The implied conditions subject to which he was given control of that public money;
>
> Thereby being guilty of misconduct in office under Section 13 (a) of the Organic Law on the Duties and Responsibilities of Leadership

What the leader did was contrary to National Goal 2 on equitable distribution of state resources. The allegations focused on breach of the Organic Law on Provincial Governments and Local-Level Governments, the Public Finance (Management) Act and the conditions of the grant of the funds. The Commission could have included the NGDP in the list of laws breached, so the tribunal would have deliberated on the allegation.

A tribunal decision which took into account the NGDP despite the lack of reference in the allegations to the NGDP and/or BSO by the Ombudsman Commission was *Melchior Pep.*[76] The Tribunal considered a number of allegations, one of which included the leader writing to the Prime Minister demanding financial support in exchange for supporting him in Parliament

[76] *Melchior Pep*, above n 66.

against potential votes of no confidence. After finding the leader guilty, the Tribunal proceeded to determine the penalty. In its decision on penalty the Tribunal stated the following with regards to the NGDP:[77]

> The Leadership Code under our Constitution places an onerous duty on our leaders. The public expects leaders to be committed to the National Goals and Directive Principles enshrined in our Constitution. Our leaders must ensure that their decisions are not restricted by obligations to or relationship with others and most importantly to make all of their decisions in the interests of the people and the country as a whole.

Again the Tribunal has not been consistent in making such references to the NGDP and/or BSO. It should be. Although the Tribunal can refer to the NGDP and/or BSO on its own initiative, if allegations are framed on the basis of the NGDP and BSO, it would be required to make a finding on the allegation.

In a case similar to *Diro*, concerning the serving military commander of the Papua New Guinea military, Jerry Singirok received money from a private international firm in the hope of the firm securing a military contract with the national government. Such conduct compromised the sovereignty of the country, which leaders are expressly required to observe under Goal 3 of the NGDP.[78] The breach of this Goal should have been raised in the allegation against the leader for the Tribunal to consider.

4. *Section 27(4) constitutional direction*

The constitutional mechanisms available to the Ombudsman Commission in its Leadership Code function also include the power to prevent the commission of misconduct by the leader. This is provided for in s 27(4) of the Constitution:

> (4) The Ombudsman Commission or other authority prescribed for the purpose under Section 28 (further provisions) may, subject to this Division and to any Organic Law made for the purposes

---

77 At 1.

78 *In the Matter of a Reference by the Public Prosecutor Pursuant to the Organic Law on the Duties and Responsibilities of Leadership and in the Matter of Major General Jerry Singirok*, unreported decision of the Leadership Tribunal on Penalty, 21 March 2000.

> of this Division, give directions, either generally or in a particular case, to ensure the attainment of the objects of this section.

The extent of this power is similar to a court injunction.[79] Any person to which the direction is addressed is bound by its terms. Persons that can be covered under the direction do not only include the leader and public institutions but can extend to private entities. For example, commercial banks can be directed to freeze accounts where leaders have deposited funds which are the subject of investigations. What is important is the subject of the direction relates to investigation of a leader. For example, in *Peter Yama*, on allegation 16, if the Ombudsman Commission had evidence before it that the leader had the intention of unfairly distributing money , it would have issued a direction under s 27(4) to prevent inequitable distribution. The Ombudsman Commission does not only have the power to investigate an event after it occurs, but can also ensure leaders perform their duties and responsibilities.

The power under s 27(4) has been a matter of great debate in Papua New Guinea. It resulted in Parliament successfully passing constitutional amendments to curtail it in 2010, amongst a number of other amendments to the Ombudsman Commission powers and functions. The Ombudsman Commission subsequently challenged these amendments in court under s 19 of the Constitution as a constitutional reference.[80] The Supreme Court declared all the amendments unconstitutional. Of note was the Supreme Court's ruling on s 27(4). The amendments to s 27(4) were interpreted by the Court to give the government wide power to lift a direction if it interfered with government policy. The Court held the amendment to s 27(4) was unconstitutional. The basis of the finding of unconstitutionality of amendments to s 27(4) was breach of s 217(6) of the Constitution. Section 217(6) protects the Ombudsman Commission from direction or control by any person in the discharge of its functions. Section 27(4), therefore, continues to operate in its original form. It is a significant tool of the Ombudsman Commission in its supervision and enforcement of the Leadership Code.

---

79 See for example *Ombudsman Commission v Yer* [2009] PGSC 45, SC1041, 3 August 2009, where the direction issued by the Ombudsman Commission was overturned by the court through a judicial review.

80 *SC Ref No. 1 of 2010, Special Reference Pursuant to Constitution, Section 19(2), In the Matter of: Constitutional (Amendment) Law 2008, Reference by the Ombudsman Commission of Papua New Guinea*, SC 1302, 19 December 2013.

E. Ability to Raise Constitutionality of Laws, Bills, etc

1. *Introduction*

Another important avenue the Ombudsman Commission has to ensure the implementation of the NGDP and BSO is the power to institute constitutional reviews under s 19 of the Constitution.[81] The Ombudsman Commission is ideally placed to assume the role of initiating cases for the court to review the constitutionality of laws or Bills on the basis of whether adequate provision(s) have been made in the legislation or Bill to implement the NGDP and/or BSO. This is supported by the Ombudsman Commission's general purpose under the Constitution to realise the aspirations of the people and its constitutional independence. The legal case for review of legislation or Bills for failure to implement the NGDP and BSO under s 19 was made in chapter 7. Other authorities are also conferred standing to invoke this constitutional review jurisdiction. But it is constitutionally desirable for the Ombudsman Commission to take up this role vis-à-vis the NGDP and BSO.[82]

A general overview constitutional review follows. The section then outlines some arguments to support this role for the Ombudsman Commission. Constitutional review should take place as early as possible perhaps through preventative injunctive relief to avoid inconvenience to legal relations arising as a result of the new law taking effect.

2. *Constitutional review/advisory opinion generally*

This section provides an overview of the nature of constitutional review and the legal nature of the Papua New Guinea model.[83] Constitutional review in Papua New Guinea can take place absent an actual dispute.

(a) Different procedures of constitutional review

Constitutional review in Papua New Guinea can be invoked in a number of ways.[84] Three common avenues are ss 18(1), 18(2), and 19(1) of the Constitution. Under s 18(1) any person can raise a constitutional issue by

---

81 Section 19 of the Constitution was discussed in chapter 7.

82 These authorities identified under s 19(3) of the Constitution.

83 The term constitutional review is used as opposed to judicial review because the latter is used to describe administrative judicial reviews.

84 See Peter Bayne *Constitutional Review Jurisdiction in Papua New Guinea* (Law Reform Commission of Papua New Guinea, Waigani, 1981) which discusses the various options.

filing proceedings directly in the Supreme Court. The Supreme Court will hear the matter as the court of first instance and there is no further appeal. For example, if the government makes a decision inconsistent with the Constitution, a person who is directly affected can ask the Supreme Court to review the decision and make declarations as to its constitutional validity.[85]

The second example, s 18(2), is where a court other than the Supreme Court (such as the National Court) or tribunal hears a matter and a constitutional issue(s) arises during the proceedings. The proceedings will be suspended and the matter sent to the Supreme Court to resolve the referred issue(s). After the issue is resolved in the Supreme Court it is remitted to the court or tribunal to complete the hearing.[86] The third option is reserved for specific authorities which can raise constitutional issues before the Supreme Court under s 19(1). Whereas it is important in the first two examples for the litigant to demonstrate an interest in the issue and to have standing, in this third example, an entity's appearance before the court is by reference to the law and no interest in the issue has to be demonstrated.[87] The focus on constitutional reviews is under the third option: s 19(1).

(b) Advisory opinions under s 19(1)

The procedure created under s 19(1) combines both the judicial (constitutional) review function of courts and the advisory opinion role as in other jurisdictions. Like the United States' model, this jurisdiction confers power on the court to invalidate legislation; but unlike the United States which has a diffuse constitutional review system where any court can hear constitutional disputes, in Papua New Guinea, the Supreme Court alone has power to hear constitutional disputes unless the Constitution expressly confers jurisdiction on another court such as the National Court.[88] Further, there does not have to be an actual controversy.[89]

---

85 See for example *Ombudsman Commission v National Parliament* [2003] PGSC 19, SC721, 21 November 2003.

86 For example see *Re Powers, functions, duties and responsibilities of the Commissioner of Police* [2014] PGSC 19, SC1388, 2 October 2014.

87 See *Special Reference by Fly River Provincial Executive Council; Re Organic Law on Integrity of Political Parties and Candidates* [2010] PGSC 3, SC1057, 7 July 2010 at [13].

88 Constitution, ss 18(1) and 57.

89 The "case and controversy" characterises the United States position under art III, s 2, cl 1 of its Constitution; see also *Muskrat v United States* 219 US 346 (1911) and *Alabama State Federation of Labor v McAdory* 325 US 450 (1945).

The Papua New Guinea Supreme Court can issue its opinion on specific constitutional questions referred to it.[90] Following the example of countries like Canada and also the International Court of Justice, the Papua New Guinea Supreme Court can issue its opinion on any question referred to it by any of the specified authorities on questions of constitutional interpretation and application.[91] But the opinion is binding like a court declaration, meaning it must be complied with.[92] Such an express binding legal status is not conferred on the Canadian Supreme Court or the International Court of Justice under its advisory jurisdiction.

(c) Primacy of the Constitution

The constitutional review of legislation or Bills to ensure consistency with the Constitution, is an example of the operation of the principle of the primacy of the Constitution, as opposed to Parliamentary supremacy.[93] In the common law tradition, the leading jurisdiction operating under the former is the United States and of the latter is the United Kingdom. *Marbury v Madison* is the often cited authority to support the primacy of the Constitution in the United States.[94] Papua New Guinea has recognised the implications of *Marbury v Madison* in constitutional review.[95] In the United

---

90 Constitution, s 19.

91 For Canada, a reference to the Supreme Court is not directly established under its Constitution but by legislation (Supreme Court Act) after the decision in *Attorney General (Ont) v Attorney General (Can)* [1912] AC 571 (PC). For the United Nations see ch IV of the Statute of International Court of Justice, arts 65–68. For a useful article comparing the Canadian and American position see James L Huffman and Mardilyn Saathoff "Advisory Opinions and Canadian Constitutional Development: The Supreme Court's Reference Jurisdiction" (1989–1990) 74 Minn L Rev 1251.

92 Constitution, s 19(2), which states "An opinion given under Subsection (1) has the same binding effect as any other decision of the Supreme Court." See also *Re Re-Election of the Governor General* [2010] PGSC 32, SC1085, 10 December 2010.

93 Primacy of the Constitution.

94 *Marbury v Madison* 5 US 137 (1803), 1 Cr 137.

95 *Calling of Parliament*, above n 55, per Los J:

> It is an agonizing thought that the Judiciary would even think of sanctioning the Legislature. But greater and older countries like the USA had agonized over such thoughts before us. I refer in particular to the historical case of *Marbury v Madison* [1 Cranch 2 L Ed 60 (1803)]. The question asked in that historical case was whether it was the Judiciary's task to interpret the law or should it be Legislature or the Executive. The decision of course went in favour of the Judiciary, the least dangerous branch of the governmental structure where the Executive held the sword of the community while the Legislature commanded the purse and held power to prescribe rules by which the duties and rights of every citizen were regulated.

Kingdom, parliamentary supremacy reigns and is defended by noted legal and constitutional commentators such as Dicey.[96] Papua New Guinea, having adopted a written Constitution, has specifically entrenched procedures for constitutional review.[97] It is interesting to note that Australia, with which Papua New Guinea had a close relationship before independence, despite recognising the supremacy of the Constitution, does not expressly provide for constitutional review in its Constitution. [98]

(d) Distribution of power

Another important role that constitutional review plays is to act as a check and balance on the exercise of power. The Papua New Guinea Constitution has opted to distribute powers amongst various institutions to make sure government operates effectively and also to prevent abuse of power.[99] Different institutions play a role to ensure constitutional compliance. In terms of s 19(1), various authorities (in addition to the Ombudsman Commission) are conferred standing to seek the Supreme Court's binding opinion on a constitutional question as well as on the validity of a law or proposed law.[100] The Supreme Court has the power to invalidate legislation or Bills as unconstitutional at the behest of one of the authorities listed under s 19(3). The legislation or Bill ceases to exist on declaration by the Supreme Court.

(e) Mixed model judicial review

Specific courts can be granted exclusive constitutional review jurisdiction. This is known as the centralised model of judicial review. An example is South Africa, with its Constitutional Court. Decentralised models operate in the United States where any court can hear constitutional disputes. There is no specific constitutional court in Papua New Guinea. The Supreme Court has been given this special role, and is often described as the guardian of the Constitution.[101] However, Papua New Guinea appears to have a mixed model

[96] AV Dicey *An Introduction to the Study of the Law of the Constitution* (1885).

[97] Many commentators use the term judicial review, but this book adopts the judicial review terminology for judicial review of administrative actions.

[98] Mathew Stubbs "A Brief History of the Judicial Review of Legislation under the Australian Constitution" (2012) 40 FL Rev 227.

[99] Independent constitutional institutions were discussed in chapter 2.

[100] Constitution, s 19(1).

[101] *Haiveta, Leader of the Opposition v Wingti, Prime Minister, Attorney-General, and National Parliament* [1994] PGSC 6, [1994] PNGLR 197, 25 August 1994 per Amet CJ.

of judicial review. Although the Supreme Court deals with most constitutional disputes, the National Court also hears a number of constitutional issues such as human rights matters.[102] It has elements of both a centralised model and decentralised version.

(f) Judicial review ex-ante and judicial review ex-post

Commentators have categorised the legal ability to review Bills and legislation for constitutional compatibility as either "judicial review ex-ante"[103] or "judicial review ex-post".[104] The former is abstract in nature, while the latter looks at the constitutionality of measures after they have been taken. Section 19 allows for the filing of hypothetical questions,[105] without there being any actual "case and controversy".[106] Bills can be reviewed by the Supreme Court as the Constitution refers to "a law or proposed law".[107] This presents the basis for an early review of legislation or Bills against the requirements of ss 25(3) and 63(3) of the Constitution before the legislation takes effect or in the case of a Bill, becomes law. If a Bill is found unconstitutional it would not become law.

In the United States and Australia, there are no specific procedures to ask the court to decide the constitutionality of a law per se, whether in an actual controversy or in hypothetical circumstances. For example, a party cannot institute proceedings challenging the constitutionality of a law without the involvement of a person whose interests have been affected by the law. In such a scenario, it is even less possible to challenge a Bill, as it has not taken effect. The seminal case of *Marbury v Madison*, which declared the Judiciary Act 1789 unconstitutional, arose out of a dispute between two persons. A claim was made under ordinary legislation, and although the Supreme Court recognised the merit of the claim under the Act, refused the claim on the basis the Act was inconsistent with the Constitution. It therefore could not grant the relief sought by the plaintiff.

---

102 Juliane Kokott and Martin Kaspar, "Ensuring Constitutional Efficacy" in *The Oxford Handbook of Comparative Constitutional Law*, Michel Rosenfeld and Andras Sajo (eds) (Oxford, Oxford University Press, 2012) 792 at 806.

103 At 806.

104 At 807.

105 *SCR No 5 of 1982; Hugo Berghuser and ors v Joseph Aoae* [1982] PNGLR 379 at 383.

106 *Muskrat v United States*, above n 90.

107 Constitution s 19(1). See also *Reference by the Ombudsman Commission; Re Section 19 of the Constitution* [2010] PGSC 43, SC1027, 17 May 2010 at [36].

Many of the important constitutional cases in the United States follow *Marbury*.[108] African-Americans affected by the segregation laws sought invalidation of the laws on the grounds of inconsistency with the fourteenth amendment of the United States Constitution. The United States Supreme Court ruled in favour of the plaintiffs on the basis the principle of separate but equal, upheld in *Plessy v Ferguson,* was no longer constitutional.[109] The segregation laws could not be challenged unless a person (or persons) claimed their rights were affected.

Many laws in Papua New Guinea have been found to be unconstitutional on the basis of a special reference to the Supreme Court by the recognised authorities. The Ombudsman Commission has been a frequent referrer using the procedure under s 19 of the Constitution. The Ombudsman Commission should take up this role for reviewing of legislation or Bills on the basis of the NGDP and BSO.

3. *Special references by the Ombudsman Commission to the Supreme Court for compliance with the NGDP and/or BSO*

A number of reasons suggest the Ombudsman Commission would be the ideal candidate, of the authorities listed under s 19(3), to assume the role of filing special references to the Supreme Court under s 19(1) for the constitutional review of legislation or Bills on the issue of whether Parliament has discharged its duty under ss 25(3) and 63(3) of the Constitution. The reasons are listed now.

(a) CPC position

The view a body that has a close connection to implementing the NGDP and BSO should have authority to file special references to the Supreme Court is made clearly in the CPC Report on its recommendations on s 19.[110] The CPC recommended the establishment of a body that would review laws and recommend how they should be reformed to be consistent with the NGDP and/or BSO. Further, such a body would have authority to seek advisory opinion of the Supreme Court. The Constitution did not establish such a body. Since the Ombudsman Commission has a great deal of scope to implement the NGDP and BSO in both its administrative complaints and

---

108 *Brown v Board of Education of Topeka* 347 US 483 (1954).

109 *Plessy v Ferguson* 163 US 537 (1896).

110 CPC Report, above n 1, at 8/16 [154].

Leadership Code functions, it would be the ideal alternative to take up this role. This complements the other proposals for the administrative complaints function and the leadership code function for the implementation of the NGDP and BSO.

(b) Consistency with objectives and functions of the Ombudsman Commission

Section 218 of the Constitution sets out the purposes of the Ombudsman Commission. One of these purposes is to ensure governmental bodies fulfil the aspirations of the people, which the NGDP and BSO express. Parliament is a governmental body.

This means the Ombudsman Commission is required to ensure it fulfils the aspirations of the people. Legislation or Bills that do not implement the NGDP and/or BSO arguably do not fulfil the aspirations of the people. It is submitted that challenging such legislation or Bills is an activity mandated by the Constitution for the Ombudsman Commission.

(c) Independence of the Ombudsman Commission

The independence of the Ombudsman Commission distinguishes it from the other authorities listed under s 19(3) of the Constitution.[111] There may be controversial legislation that Parliament has passed without adequate legislative scrutiny due to executive dominance. Other authorities, not as independent as the Ombudsman Commission, may be discouraged from taking up the case. The Ombudsman Commission can take up such a case without fear or favour.

An example of where the Ombudsman Commission has filed a constitutional reference under s 19(1) of the Constitution on a matter which was politically sensitive as it had implications on the stability of government was *Calling of Parliament*.[112] In this reference the Ombudsman Commission was concerned about the long adjournments of Parliament. The Government, using its numerical strength over the opposition, adjourned Parliament for long periods of time. This was perhaps to avoid potential votes of no confidence being brought. The constitutionality of Parliament's long adjournment was

---

[111] Constitution, s 217(6) states the Ombudsman Commission is not subject to direction or control by any person in the performance of its constitutional functions.

[112] *Calling of Parliament*, above n 55.

challenged by the Ombudsman Commission under s 19(1). The Court ruled long adjournments were unconstitutional and Parliament could be legally compelled to sit more regularly in accordance with the Constitution. Other authorities listed under s 19(3) may not have the independence to take up cases of this nature.

(d) Past record

The Ombudsman Commission has frequently sought the Supreme Court's binding opinion under s 19. This is due to the high constitutional ideals conferred on the Ombudsman Commission to realise,[113] and its independence.[114] A study of a number of constitutional references decided by the Supreme Court reveals that of the authorities granted standing under s 19 of the Constitution, the Ombudsman Commission has been a frequent referrer to the Supreme Court.[115]

One of the first cases filed by the Ombudsman Commission was in 1982 where it challenged the constitutionality of the amendments to the Electoral Commission Act for breach of s 50 of the Constitution.[116] In 1993 the Ombudsman Commission challenged the validity of the Internal Security Act 1993 for offending the right to presumption of innocence under s 37 of the Constitution.[117] Another piece of legislation it challenged was the amendments to the Organic Law on Provincial and Local Level Governments 1995 in 2010.[118] Also in 2010 the Ombudsman Commission sought constitutional review of amendments to the Forestry Act 1991. These cases are examples which show the strong position the Ombudsman Commission is in to take up the role of review of legislation or Bills in relation to the NGDP and BSO.

---

113 Constitution, s 218.

114 Constitution, s 217(5).

115 From the cases surveyed this role proposed for the Ombudsman Commission is not unique as it has previously on two occasions initiated a constitutional reference on the basis of the NGDP and/or BSO. These were the cases of *Reference by the Ombudsman Commission of Papua New Guinea* [2010] PGSC 10, SC1058, 4 June 2010, and *Reference by the Ombudsman Commission of Papua New Guinea* [2010] PGSC 40, SC1088, 17 December 2010.

116 *SCR No 2 of 1982 (No 1); Re the Organic Law on National Elections (Amendment) Act 1981* [1982] PGSC 19, [1982] PNGLR 214, 5 April 1982.

117 *Internal Security Act; Reference by the Ombudsman Commission, Re* [1994] PGSC 9, [1994] PNGLR 341, 4 May 1994.

118 *Reference by the Ombudsman Commission; Re Section 19 of the Constitution* [2010] PGSC 43, SC1027, 17 May 2010.

(e) Comparative experience

There is no useful comparative experience to draw on to support the Ombudsman Commission for the type of constitutional review proposed here. Other Ombudsman Commissions, or Ombudsman-like institutions considered, reveal that the ability to question the constitutionality of Acts and Bills generally has not been conferred on an Ombudsman. Australia, with a written Constitution, established its Ombudsman by ordinary legislation. Outside the Pacific, Constitutions modelled after the Westminster system, such as in Canada and India also do not possess this function. New Zealand and the United Kingdom, with unwritten Constitutions, cannot provide a useful experience for Papua New Guinea, at least on this specific question on the Ombudsman Commission assuming standing to file constitutional references. The only other country that confers such standing to an Ombudsman is Slovenia, but its Constitution was adopted in 1991, much later than Papua New Guinea and may not have built up a body of case law to enable sufficient comparison.[119] This would mean that Papua New Guinea Ombudsman Commission stands in a unique position to advance constitutional compliance.

IV. Conclusion

The Ombudsman Commission was established as an important institution to ensure control of the exercise of government power in Papua New Guinea. Its purposes are clearly established in the Constitution, one of which is to fulfil the aspirations of the people. The NGDP and BSO are a constitutional recognition of these aspirations.

As a result, the Ombudsman Commission has an important role to implement the NGDP and BSO. Mechanisms to put this into place are two-fold: the administrative complaints function, and the Leadership Code function. To enable it to do its functions properly, the Commission has been conferred a great deal of independence. There is ample opportunity provided within the legal structures of these functions to implement the NGDP and BSO. It falls on the Ombudsman Commission to take these opportunities seriously to implement the NGDP and BSO. The third role presented in this chapter to fulfil the NGDP and BSO is for the Ombudsman Commission to use its authority to institute constitutional references to initiate cases on the basis Parliament may not have adequately taken the NGDP and BSO into account.

---

119 Slovenian Constitution, art 159.

CHAPTER ELEVEN

CONCLUSION

I. Introduction

This Chapter concludes this book by providing a summary of the implementation proposals for the legislature, the executive, the judiciary and the ombudsman. There are three parts: Part I is this short introduction; Part II presents a summary of the implementation proposals; and Part III is the conclusion.

II. Implementation Proposals

A. Overview

There are four areas of government within which the implementation proposals are made: the legislature, the executive, the judiciary, and the ombudsman. A constant feature of this exercise is to suggest implementation within the existing constitutional framework and implementation by one branch has an implication for the other, which in chapter 6 is described as the interconnectedness approach. Implementation must be explored within the existing framework before looking at legislative reforms. Sections 25(3) and 63(3) of the Constitution are interpreted as creating an indirectly justiciable duty on each of the entities addressed.

1. Legislature

The proposals for the implementation of the NGDP and BSO by the legislature fall under two broad categories: direct and indirect means of implementing the NGDP and BSO.

Firstly, for direct implementation, it is suggested a constitutional norm exists where Parliament is required to demonstrate it has considered the implementation of the NGDP and/or BSO in any legislation that goes before it. A failure to comply would result in the Bill or legislation being invalidated by the Supreme Court for being unconstitutional. The importance of this proposal ties in with what is being presented for the other arms of government.

The second proposal presents an indirect mechanism of implementing the NGDP and BSO. Indirect implementation relates to the political process. It is called indirect because failure to implement does not result in any legal process to enforce implementation. Several proposals are offered:

(a) The use of preambles and object provisions in legislation to refer to the NGDP and BSO. When Parliament points out the particular NGDP and/or BSO in the legislation, it assists those interpreting and applying the law, to be guided by Parliament's intentions as to which NGDP and/or BSO is being implemented. It provides clarity and demonstrates which NGDP and BSO has priority with respect to the matter at hand.

(b) Before the passing of the annual budget, the National Executive Council consults the Budget and Estimates Committee on ways the NGDP and BSO can be adequately resourced. Such report is then made available to the government, which has the task of preparing the budget for the year.

(c) When Parliament scrutinises decisions of the executive, it should do so on the basis of the NGDP and BSO. This provides a point of reference to assess the decisions of the executive.

2. *Executive*

A single proposal is made for the executive. The NEC should adopt a Cabinet (or NEC) Manual to guide its operations. The Manual would make clear reference to the NGDP and BSO. Decisions would have to be made that implements the NGDP and/or BSO by virtue of the Manual. In time, a legal expectation will be created for NEC decisions to be referenced to the NGDP and BSO.

3. *Judiciary*

There are a number of ways the judicial function can be used to implement the NGDP and BSO. The following conclusions have been reached.

First, the role of preambles in constitutional interpretation. Two main roles are identified: the "in case of doubt" approach, and contextual role. It was found the latter presented a better chance of implementing the NGDP and BSO. As the NGDP and BSO are contained in the preamble to the Constitution, it should be considered in all cases to provide the context of the Constitution when matters go before the court. The "in case of doubt" approach would only see reference to the NGDP and BSO when there is an ambiguity in the provisions of the Constitution.

Second, judicial review of administrative actions. Judicial review process should engage the NGDP and BSO more often. This is encouraged by the Constitution under ss 22, 23 and 59. For example, remedies such as mandamus can be used to enable an outcome that would be consistent with the NGDP and BSO.

Third, the use of the NGDP and BSO in the development of the underlying law. This process is assisted now with the Underlying Law Act 2000. The NGDP and BSO can contribute directly to developing new principles of law, directing a movement away from relying solely on the common law.

Fourth, the use of weak-form judicial review. By this method, the court will point out the inconsistency of a law or government decision with the NGDP and/or BSO for either parliament or the executive arm of government to correct it. It is weak in the sense the court's view does not invalidate the law or government decision.

Fifth, the interaction of the NGDP and BSO with human rights and freedoms. Rights and freedoms are to be protected by the Constitution in a way that harmonises with the NGDP and BSO. This is provided for by ss 38 and 39 of the Constitution.

4. *Ombudsman*

The Ombudsman Commission has two main functions: administrative complaints, and supervision and enforcement of the Leadership Code. The third function relates to its ability to raise questions on the constitutionality of decisions of Parliament, such as Bills and legislation.

Under the first two functions, there is an express requirement for the Ombudsman Commission to take into account the NGDP and BSO. A review of the reports of the Ombudsman Commission and the Leadership Tribunal decisions suggests the Ombudsman Commission has not actively engaged its express constitutional mandate to implement the NGDP and BSO. Because of the extensive reach of its jurisdiction to almost all activities of the government machinery, it would provide an effective means of implementing the NGDP and BSO. This is especially true for this study, which only focuses on four areas. The Ombudsman Commission would be able to extend the implementation further than the judiciary, the executive and the legislature.

The third function proposes the Ombudsman Commission is an ideal institution to challenge Bills and legislation in court that do not comply with the constitutional norm of Parliament consulting the NGDP and/or BSO for all legislation that goes before Parliament. One of its objectives is to fulfil the aspirations of the people, and it can do this through the ability to enforce the constitutional norm of consultation with the NGDP and/or BSO.

III. The Proposal

This work proposes practical and efficient means to implement the NGDP and BSO within the present constitutional arrangement, where each implementing entity influences the other in the context of their constitutional function. Implementation of the NGDP and/or BSO would make a positive contribution to Papua New Guinea's political, social, cultural and economic advancement.

APPENDIX ONE

NATIONAL GOALS AND DIRECTIVE PRINCIPLES

National Goals and Directive Principles.

WE HEREBY PROCLAIM the following aims as our National Goals, and direct all persons and bodies, corporate and unincorporate, to be guided by these our declared Directives in pursuing and achieving our aims:—

1. Integral human development.

   We declare our first goal to be for every person to be dynamically involved in the process of freeing himself or herself from every form of domination or oppression so that each man or woman will have the opportunity to develop as a whole person in relationship with others.

   WE ACCORDINGLY CALL FOR—

   (1) everyone to be involved in our endeavours to achieve integral human development of the whole person for every person and to seek fulfilment through his or her contribution to the common good; and

   (2) education to be based on mutual respect and dialogue, and to promote awareness of our human potential and motivation to achieve our National Goals through self-reliant effort; and

   (3) all forms of beneficial creativity, including sciences and cultures, to be actively encouraged; and

   (4) improvement in the level of nutrition and the standard of public health to enable our people to attain self fulfilment; and

   (5) the family unit to be recognized as the fundamental basis of our society, and for every step to be taken to promote the moral, cultural, economic and social standing of the Melanesian family; and

(6) development to take place primarily through the use of Papua New Guinean forms of social and political organization.

2. Equality and participation.

We declare our second goal to be for all citizens to have an equal opportunity to participate in, and benefit from, the development of our country.

WE ACCORDINGLY CALL FOR—

(1) an equal opportunity for every citizen to take part in the political, economic, social, religious and cultural life of the country; and

(2) the creation of political structures that will enable effective, meaningful participation by our people in that life, and in view of the rich cultural and ethnic diversity of our people for those structures to provide for substantial decentralization of all forms of government activity; and

(3) every effort to be made to achieve an equitable distribution of incomes and other benefits of development among individuals and throughout the various parts of the country; and

(4) equalization of services in all parts of the country, and for every citizen to have equal access to legal processes and all services, governmental and otherwise, that are required for the fulfilment of his or her real needs and aspirations; and

(5) equal participation by women citizens in all political, economic, social and religious activities; and

(6) the maximization of the number of citizens participating in every aspect of development; and

(7) active steps to be taken to facilitate the organization and legal recognition of all groups engaging in development activities; and

(8) means to be provided to ensure that any citizen can exercise his personal creativity and enterprise in pursuit of fulfilment that is consistent with the common good, and for no citizen to be deprived of this opportunity because of the predominant position of another; and

(9) every citizen to be able to participate, either directly or through a representative, in the consideration of any matter affecting his interests or the interests of his community; and

(10) all persons and governmental bodies of Papua New Guinea to ensure that, as far as possible, political and official bodies are so composed as to be broadly representative of citizens from the various areas of the country; and

(11) all persons and governmental bodies to endeavour to achieve universal literacy in Pisin, Hiri Motu or English, and in "tok ples" or "ita eda tano gado"; and

(12) recognition of the principles that a complete relationship in marriage rests on equality of rights and duties of the partners, and that responsible parenthood is based on that equality.

3. National sovereignty and self-reliance.

We declare our third goal to be for Papua New Guinea to be politically and economically independent, and our economy basically self-reliant.

WE ACCORDINGLY CALL FOR—

(1) our leaders to be committed to these National Goals and Directive Principles, to ensure that their freedom to make decisions is not restricted by obligations to or relationship with others, and to make all of their decisions in the national interest; and

(2) all governmental bodies to base their planning for political, economic and social development on these Goals and Principles; and

(3) internal interdependence and solidarity among citizens, and between provinces, to be actively promoted; and

(4) citizens and governmental bodies to have control of the bulk of economic enterprise and production; and

(5) strict control of foreign investment capital and wise assessment of foreign ideas and values so that these will be subordinate to the goal of national sovereignty and self-reliance, and in particular for the entry of foreign capital to be geared to internal social and economic policies and to the integrity of the Nation and the People; and

(6) the State to take effective measures to control and actively participate in the national economy, and in particular to control major enterprises engaged in the exploitation of natural resources; and

(7) economic development to take place primarily by the use of skills and resources available in the country either from citizens or the State and not in dependence on imported skills and resources; and

(8) the constant recognition of our sovereignty, which must not be undermined by dependence on foreign assistance of any sort, and in particular for no investment, military or foreign-aid agreement or understanding to be entered into that imperils our self-reliance and self-respect, or our commitment to these National Goals and Directive Principles, or that may lead to substantial dependence upon or influence by any country, investor, lender or donor.

4. Natural resources and environment.

We declare our fourth goal to be for Papua New Guinea's natural resources and environment to be conserved and used for the collective benefit of us all, and be replenished for the benefit of future generations.

WE ACCORDINGLY CALL FOR—

(1) wise use to be made of our natural resources and the environment in and on the land or seabed, in the sea, under the land, and in the air, in the interests of our development and in trust for future generations; and

(2) the conservation and replenishment, for the benefit of ourselves and posterity, of the environment and its sacred, scenic, and historical qualities; and

(3) all necessary steps to be taken to give adequate protection to our valued birds, animals, fish, insects, plants and trees.

5. Papua New Guinean ways.

We declare our fifth goal to be to achieve development primarily through the use of Papua New Guinean forms of social, political and economic organization.

WE ACCORDINGLY CALL FOR—

(1) a fundamental re-orientation of our attitudes and the institutions of government, commerce, education and religion towards Papua New Guinean forms of participation, consultation, and consensus, and a continuous renewal of the responsiveness of these institutions to the needs and attitudes of the People; and

(2) particular emphasis in our economic development to be placed on small-scale artisan, service and business activity; and

(3) recognition that the cultural, commercial and ethnic diversity of our people is a positive strength, and for the fostering of a respect for, and appreciation of, traditional ways of life and culture, including language, in all their richness and variety, as well as for a willingness to apply these ways dynamically and creatively for the tasks of development; and

(4) traditional villages and communities to remain as viable units of Papua New Guinean society, and for active steps to be taken to improve their cultural, social, economic and ethical quality.

APPENDIX TWO

BASIC SOCIAL OBLIGATIONS

Basic Social Obligations.

WE HEREBY DECLARE that all persons in our country have the following basic obligations to themselves and their descendants, to each other, and to the Nation:—

(a) to respect, and to act in the spirit of, this Constitution; and

(b) to recognize that they can fully develop their capabilities and advance their true interests only by active participation in the development of the national community as a whole; and

(c) to exercise the rights guaranteed or conferred by this Constitution, and to use the opportunities made available to them under it to participate fully in the government of the Nation; and

(d) to protect Papua New Guinea and to safeguard the national wealth, resources and environment in the interests not only of the present generation but also of future generations; and

(e) to work according to their talents in socially useful employment, and if necessary to create for themselves legitimate opportunities for such employment; and

(f) to respect the rights and freedoms of others, and to co-operate fully with others in the interests of interdependence and solidarity; and

(g) to contribute, as required by law, according to their means to the revenues required for the advancement of the Nation and the purposes of Papua New Guinea; and

(h) in the case of parents, to support, assist and educate their children (whether born in or out of wedlock), and in particular to give them a true understanding of their basic rights and obligations and of the National Goals and Directive Principles; and

(i) in the case of the children, to respect their parents.

IN ADDITION, WE HEREBY DECLARE that all citizens have an obligation to themselves and their descendants, to each other and to the Nation to use profits from economic activities in the advancement of our country and our people, and that the law may impose a similar obligation on non-citizens carrying on economic activities in or from our country.

APPENDIX THREE

LEGISLATION REFERRING TO THE NGDP AND BSO

Legislation	Provision incorporating the NGDP and/or BSO	Particular reference to NGDP and/or BSO
Bougainville Constitution	NGDP and BSO referred to in s 180, "Qualifications on the Qualified Rights."	NGDP and BSO generally referred to, with no particular mention of any specific NGDP or BSO.
Classification of Publication (Censorship) Act 1989	Section 1 on compliance with constitutional requirements refers to both NGDP and BSO.	NGDP and BSO generally referred to.
Community Services Trust Act 2002	Section 1 on compliance with constitutional requirements refers to both NGDP and BSO.	Section refers to Goal 1, integral human development, Goal 3 equality and participation, Goal 3 national sovereignty and self-reliance, Goal 5, Papua New Guinea Ways and BSO generally.
Compensation (Prohibition of Foreign Legal Proceedings) Act 1995	NGDP only referred to in the preamble of the Act and NGDP and BSO both referred to in s 1 on compliance with constitutional requirements	Goal 3 on national sovereignty and self-reliance referred to in the preamble and makes reference to National Goal 3 on national sovereignty and self-reliance and National Goal 5 on Papua New Guinea Ways in s 1. Also refers to BSO on maximising wealth of Papua New Guineans in s 1.

Legislation	Provision incorporating the NGDP and/or BSO	Particular reference to NGDP and/or BSO
Compulsory Third Party Motor Vehicle Insurance Industry Act 2002	Section 1 on compliance with constitutional requirements refers to both NGDP and BSO.	Makes reference to National Goal 3 on national sovereignty and self-reliance and National Goal 5 on Papua New Guinea Ways. Also refers to BSO on maximising wealth of Papua New Guineans.
Conservation Areas Act 1978	NGDP referred to in the long title of the legislation and in s 1 on compliance with constitutional requirements. Reference to BSO only in s 1.	National Goal 4 on natural resources and environment referred to. BSO referred to generally.
Electricity Commission Privatisation Act 2002	Section 1 on compliance with constitutional requirements refers to both NGDP and BSO.	National Goal 3 on national sovereignty and self-reliance and National Goal 5 on Papua New Guinea Ways referred to and BSO on protecting Papua New Guineans and the interest of future generations (BSO para (d)).
Employment of Non-citizens Act 2007	Section 3 (not s 1 as in most legislation) on compliance with constitutional requirements refers to both NGDP and BSO.	NGDP and BSO referred to generally.
Environment Act 2000	NGDP referred to in the long title of the legislation only. No reference to the BSO.	National Goal 4 on natural resources and environment referred to.

Legislation	Provision incorporating the NGDP and/or BSO	Particular reference to NGDP and/or BSO
Environmental Contaminants Act 1978	NGDP referred to in the long title of the legislation and in s 1 on compliance with constitutional requirements. No reference to BSO.	National Goal 4 on natural resources and environment referred to. Act also refers to s 25 of the Constitution in the long title.
Environmental Planning Act 1978	NGDP referred to in the long title of the legislation and in s 1 on compliance with constitutional requirements. No reference to BSO.	National Goal 4 on natural resources and environment referred to. Act also refers to s 25 of the Constitution in the long title.
Essential Services Act 2002	Section 1 on compliance with constitutional requirements refers to both NGDP and BSO.	National Goal 3 on national sovereignty and self-reliance and National Goal 5 on Papua New Guinea Ways referred to and BSO on protecting Papua New Guineans and the interest of future generations (BSO para (d)).
Fisheries Management Act 1998	NGDP only referred to in the long title of the Act.	National Goal 4 on natural resources and environment referred to by implication and not expressly.
Forestry Act 1991	NGDP referred to in the long title of the legislation. No reference to the BSO.	National Goal 4 on natural resources and environment referred to by implication and not expressly.
Gaming Control Act 2007	Section 1 on compliance with constitutional requirements refers to both NGDP and BSO.	Refers to NGDP and BSO generally and also makes specific reference to National Goal 3 on national sovereignty and self-reliance and National Goal 4 on natural resources and environment.

Legislation	Provision incorporating the NGDP and/or BSO	Particular reference to NGDP and/or BSO
Harbours Board Act 1963	Section 1 on compliance with constitutional requirements refers to both NGDP and BSO.	National Goal 3 on national sovereignty and self-reliance and National Goal 5 on Papua New Guinea Ways referred to and BSO on protecting Papua New Guineans and the interest of future generations (BSO para (d)).
Higher Education Act 1983	NGDP referred to in the objectives of the legislation under s 4. No reference to BSO.	National Goal on integral human development referred to.
Independent Consumer and Competition Commission Act 2002	Section 1 on compliance with constitutional requirements refers to both NGDP and BSO.	National Goal 3 on national sovereignty and self-reliance and National Goal 5 on Papua New Guinea Ways referred to and BSO on protecting Papua New Guineans and the interest of future generations (BSO para (d)).
Informal Sector Development and Control Act 2004	Section 1 on compliance with constitutional requirements refers to both NGDP and BSO.	NGDP and BSO generally referred to, with no particular mention of any specific NGDP or BSO.
Mineral Resource Act 2005	Section 1 on compliance with constitutional requirements refers to both NGDP. No reference to BSO.	Refers to National Goal 3 on national sovereignty and self-reliance and National Goal 5 on Papua New Guinea Ways.

Legislation	Provision incorporating the NGDP and/or BSO	Particular reference to NGDP and/or BSO
Mining (Ok Tedi Mine Continuation (Ninth Supplement) Agreement Act 2001	NGDP and BSO referred to in the preamble and in s 1 on compliance with constitutional requirements.	The Preamble refers to National Goal 3 on national sovereignty and self-reliance and National Goal 4 on natural resources and environment. Under the Preamble the BSO on wealth maximisation also referred to. Same goals and BSO referred to in s 1 of the Act.
Mining (Ok Tedi Restated Eighth Supplement) Agreement Act 2001	Section 1 on compliance with constitutional requirements refers to both NGDP and BSO.	Refers to National Goal 3 on national sovereignty and self-reliance and National Goal 4 on natural resources and environment. BSO on wealth maximisation also referred to.
Mining (Safety) Regulation Act 1977	Section 1 on compliance with constitutional requirements refers to both NGDP and BSO.	Refers to National Goal 3 on national sovereignty and self-reliance and BSO referred to generally.
Motor Vehicles Insurance (PNG) Trust (Administrative Arrangements) Act 1996	NGDP and BSO referred to in the preamble of the Act.	Preamble refers to National Goal 3 on national sovereignty and self-reliance and the BSO on wealth maximisation.
Mutual Assistance in Criminal Matters Act 2005	Section 1 on compliance with constitutional requirements refers to both NGDP and BSO.	NGDP and BSO generally referred to.

Legislation	Provision incorporating the NGDP and/or BSO	Particular reference to NGDP and/or BSO
National Agricultural Research Institute Act 1996	NGDP generally mentioned in the long title of the Act. No reference to the BSO.	NGDP generally referred to.
National Capital District Commission Act 2001	Section 1 on compliance with constitutional requirements refers to both NGDP and BSO.	As s 1(3) of the Act elaborately uses NGDP and BSO it is quoted here: (3) The Parliament, in enacting this law, considers it is reasonably justifiable, taking into account— (a) the National Goals and Directive Principles (including, in particular, the goals that citizens of Papua New Guinea should, among other things, have equal opportunity to participate in, and benefit from the political life of the country, and in the creation of political structures that will enable effective, meaningful participation by the people of Papua New Guinea in political, social and economic life, and for every citizen to be able to participate, either directly or through a representative, in the consideration of any matter affecting his interests or the interests of his community and to ensure that, as far as possible, political and official bodies are so composed as to be broadly representative of citizens); and

Legislation	Provision incorporating the NGDP and/or BSO	Particular reference to NGDP and/or BSO
		(b) the Basic Rights and Basic Social Obligations (including, in particular, the right of all persons whatever their race, tribe, place of origin, political opinion, colour, creed or sex, to take part in political activities), for providing for composition of the National Capital District Commission for the purpose recited in this section, in a democratic society that has a proper regard for the rights and dignity of mankind.
National Parks Act 1982	NGDP referred to in the long title of the legislation. No reference to BSO.	National Goal 4 on natural resources and environment referred to.
National Development Bank Act 2007	Section 1 on compliance with constitutional requirements refers to both NGDP and BSO.	Refers to NGDP and BSO generally and also makes specific reference to National Goal 3 on national sovereignty and self-reliance and National Goal 4 on natural resources and environment.
Oil and Gas Act 1998	Section 1 on compliance with constitutional requirements refers to both NGDP and BSO.	Refers to NGDP and BSO generally and also makes specific reference to National Goal 3 on national sovereignty and self-reliance and national goal 4 on natural resources and environment.
Organic Law on the Integrity of Political Parties and Candidates	Section 1 on compliance with constitutional requirements refers to both NGDP and BSO.	No particular NGDP and BSO referred to.

Legislation	Provision incorporating the NGDP and/or BSO	Particular reference to NGDP and/or BSO
Proceeds of Crime Act 2005	Section 1 on compliance with constitutional requirements refers to both NGDP and BSO.	No particular NGDP and BSO referred to.
Provincial Health Authorities Act 2007	NGDP referred to in the long title of the legislation and in s 1 on compliance with constitutional requirements. No reference to BSO.	General reference to integral human development without reference to NGDP specifically in the long title. But National Goal 1 on integral human development specifically referred to in s 1 on constitutional compliance.
Regulatory Statutory Authorities (Appointment to Certain Offices) Act 2004.	Section 1 on compliance with constitutional requirements refers to both NGDP and BSO.	Section 1 of the Act refers to National Goal 3 on national sovereignty and self-reliance and natural resources and environment and to the BSO generally.
Salaries and Remuneration Commission Act 1983	Referred to in s 14 of the Act, "Guidelines in Fixing Salaries etc." There is no reference to the BSO.	NGDP referred to generally in s 14(1) that in fixing the salaries, allowances, pensions and other benefits, Parliament shall give consideration to the NGDP generally, amongst other considerations.
Telecommunications Act 1988	Section 1 on compliance with constitutional requirements refers to both NGDP and BSO.	Refers to National Goal 3 on national sovereignty and self-reliance, National Goal 5 on Papua New Guinea Ways and BSO on protecting the wealth of Papua New Guineans.

Legislation	Provision incorporating the NGDP and/or BSO	Particular reference to NGDP and/or BSO
Telecommunications Industry Act 2002	Section 1 on compliance with constitutional requirements refers to both NGDP and BSO.	Refers to National Goal 3 on national sovereignty and self-reliance, National Goal 5 on Papua New Guinea Ways and BSO on protecting the wealth of Papua New Guineans.
Underlying Law Act 2000	Section 4 of the Act, "Application of Sources of Underlying Law	Refers to the NGDP and BSO generally as sources of the underlying law and as tests to guide the development of the underlying law.
Water Resources Act 1982	The long titles refers to the NGDP only and not the BSO.	National Goal 4 on natural resources and environment referred to.

BIBLIOGRAPHY

A. Cases

1. Papua New Guinea

(a) National Court

Aimo v Anisi [2012] PGNC 182, N4870, 28 November 2012.

Application by Ireeuw, Wawar, Ap, and Wakum [1985] PGNC 7, [1985] PNGLR 430, 13 December 1985.

Bari v Governing Council, St Paul's Teachers College, Vunakanau; Chairman, National Education Board Appeal Committee; Minister for Education; Ministry for Education and The State [1994] PGNC 158, [1995] PNGLR 364, 6 April 1994.

Central Pomio Logging Corporation Pty Ltd v The Independent State of Papua New Guinea [1990] PNGLR 195.

Inakambi Singorom v John Kalaut [1985] PNGLR 238.

Magiten v Beggie [2005] PGNC 75 N2880, 21 April 2005.

Medaing v Ramu Nico Management (MCC) Ltd [2011] PGNC 95 N4340, 26 July 2011.

Niggints v Tokam [1993] PNGLR 66.

Otto Benal Magiten v Bernadette Beggie (No 2) (2005) N2908.

Peter v South Pacific Brewery Ltd [1976] PNGLR 537.

Public Curator of Papua New Guinea v Public Trustee of New Zealand [1976] PGNC 48, [1976] PNGLR 427, 28 September 1976.

Re Application under Section 57 of the Constitution; Application by Individual and Community Rights Advocacy Forum Inc (ICRAF); Re Miriam Willingal [1997] PGNC 7 N1506, 10 February 1997.

Re The Leadership Tribunal; Bonga v Sheehan [1997] PGNC 20 N1512, 4 March 1997.

Special Reference by the Morobe Provincial Executive [2005] PNGLR 1, 13 May 2005.

Tienstein v Koim [2011] PGNC 127; N4420, 14 October 2011.

(b) Supreme Court

Application of Gabriel Dusava (1998) SC581.

Application of John Mua Nilkare (1996) SC536.

Board of Inquiry appointed under Public Service (Interim Arrangements) Act 1973 Re Alleged Disciplinary Offences in Office by Mr Phillip Bouraga [1982] PGSC 11, [1982] PNGLR 178, 23 March 1982.

Dusava v Justice Doherty [1999] PGSC 43, [1999] PNGLR 419, 1 October 1999.

Enga Provincial Sales Tax, Re [1988] PGSC 12, [1988–89] PNGLR 225, 2 December 1988.

Haiveta, Leader of the Opposition v Wingti, Prime Minister, Attorney-General, and National Parliament [1994] PGSC 6, [1994] PNGLR 197, 25 August 1994.

Internal Security Act; Reference by the Ombudsman Commission, Re [1994] PGSC 9, [1994] PNGLR 341, 4 May 1994.

In the Matter of Constitutional Validity of Constitutional Amendment (Provincial Governments and Local-Level Governments) [1995] PGSC 12; [1995] PNGLR 481, 20 September 1995.

James Eki Mopio v The Speaker of the National Parliament [1977] PNGLR 420.

Karingu, Enforcement of Rights Pursuant Constitution S57 [1988-89] PNGLR 277, 4 August 1989.

Kekedo v Burns Philip (PNG) Ltd [1988-89] PNGLR 122, 13 April 1989.

Lupari v Somare [2008] PGSC 33, SC951, 10 November 2008.

Madaha Resana v PNG (1991) PNGLR 174.

Mairi v Tololo, Secretary for Education [1976] PGSC 9, [1976] PNGLR 125, 15 April 1976.

Marat v Hanjung Power Ltd [2014] PGSC 33; SC1357, 4 July 2014.

Mileng v Tololo [1976] PGSC 12, [1976] PNGLR 447, 6 October 1976.

Medaing v Ramu Nico Management (MCC) Ltd [2011] PGSC 40, SC1144, 22 December 2011.

Mineral Resources Development Company Ltd v Ombudsman Commission of Papua New Guinea [2008] PGSC 17, SC931, 20 August 2008.

Mopio v Speaker of Parliament [1977] PNGLR 420.

New Britain Oil Palm Ltd v Sukuramu [2008] PGSC 29, SC946, 30 October 2008.

Nilkare v Ombudsman Commission [1996] PGSC 2, SC498, 3 May 1996.

Nilkare v Ombudsman Commission of Papua New Guinea [1996] PGSC 26, [1999] PNGLR 333, 3 May 1996.

Nilkare v Ombudsman Commission of Papua New Guinea [1996] PGSC 27, [1996] PNGLR 413, 7 June 1996.

Ombudsman Commission of PNG v Denis Donohoe [1985] PGSC 14, [1985] PNGLR 348, 3 December 1985.

Ombudsman Commission v National Parliament [2003] PGSC 19, SC721, 21 November 2003.

Ombudsman Commission v Yer [2009] PGSC 45, SC1041, 3 August 2009.

Ombudsman Commission v Yama [2004] PGSC 30, SC747, 2 June 2004.

Peipul v The Leadership Tribunal [2002] PGSC 1, SC706, 24 May 2002.

Peter v South Pacific Brewery Ltd [1976] PGSC 28, SC109, [1976] PNGLR 345, 29 November 1976.

Placer Holdings v PNG [1982] PNGLR 16.

PLAR No 1 of 1980; Request by Principal Legal Adviser on a Point of Law arising in a case where a Person tried upon Indictment has been Acquitted [1980] PGSC 15, [1980] PNGLR 326, 10 October 1980.

Premdas v The State [1979] PGSC 20, [1979] PNGLR 329, 1 September 1979.

Public Prosecutor v Rooney (No 2) [1979] PGSC 23, [1979] PNGLR 448, 11 September 1979.

Ragi and State Services & Statutory Authorities Superannuation Fund Board v Maingu [1994] PGSC 3, SC459, 29 June 1994.

Rakatani v The State [1979] PNGLR 556.

Raz v Matane [1985] PNGLR 325.

Re Constitutional Validity of Constitutional Amendment (Provincial Governments and Local-Level Governments) [1995] PGSC 12, [1995] PNGLR 481, 20 September 1995.

Re Fly River Provincial Executive [2007] PGSC 42, SC917, 31 August 2007.

Re Organic Law on National Elections; Kuberi Epi v Tony Farapo (1983) (unreported) SC247.

Re Powers, functions, duties and responsibilities of the Commissioner of Police [2014] PGSC 19, SC1388, 2 October 2014.

Re Public Prosecutor's Power to Request the Chief Justice to Appoint a Leadership Tribunal [2008] PGSC 48, SC1011, 29 August 2008.

Re Re-Election of the Governor General [2010] PGSC 32, SC1085, 10 December 2010.

Re Re-election of the Governor General [2010] PGSC 38, SC1089, 22 December 2010.

Re Reference by the Attorney General and Principal Legal Adviser to the National Executive [2010] PGSC 48, SC1078, 26 October 2010.

Re Reference by Mondiai [2010] PGSC 39, SC1087, 17 December 2010.

Re Reference to Constitution section 19(1) by East Sepik Provincial Executive [2011] PGSC 41, SC1154, 12 December 2011.

Re Reference Pursuant to Constitution section 19(1) by Allan Marat [2012] PGSC 1, SC1149, 23 January 2012.

Reference by the Executive Council of the Enga Provincial Government [1990] PGSC 10, [1990] PNGLR 532, 28 December 1990.

Reference by the Ombudsman Commission; Re Section 19 of the Constitution [2010] PGSC 43, SC1027, 17 May 2010.

Reference by the Ombudsman Commission of Papua New Guinea [2010] PGSC 10, SC1058, 4 June 2010.

Reference by the Ombudsman Commission of Papua New Guinea [2010] PGSC 40, SC1088, 17 December 2010.

SCR No 1 of 1977; Re Rights of Person Arrested or Detained [1977] PGSC 15, [1977] PNGLR 362, 26 October 1977.

SCR No 1 of 1978; Re Ombudsman Commission Investigations of the Public Solicitor [1978] PGSC 7, [1978] PNGLR 345, 6 October 1978.

SCR No 1 of 1978; Re Tribunal established under the Organic Law on the Duties and Responsibilities of Leadership S 27 and Leo Robert Morgan [1978] PNGLR 460.

SCR No 1A of 1981; Re Motor Traffic Act [1982] PNGLR 122.

SC Ref No 1 of 2010; Special Reference Pursuant to Constitution, Section 19(2), Re Constitutional (Amendment) Law 2008, Reference by the Ombudsman Commission of Papua New Guinea, SC 1302, 19 December 2013.

SCR No 1 of 1984; Re Minimum Penalties Legislation [1984] PGSC 13, [1984] PNGLR 314, 2 November 1984.

SCR No 1 of 1986; Re Vagrancy Act (Ch 268) [1988] PGSC 29, [1988-89] PNGLR 1, 13 April 1987.

SCR No 1 of 1997; Reference by the Principal Legal Advisor under Section 19 of the Constitution [1997] PGSC 8, SC526, 14 July 1997.

SCR No 2 of 1976; Re Motion of No Confidence [1976] PGSC 17, [1976] PNGLR 228, 2 June 1976.

SCR No 2 of 1978; Re Corrective Institutions Act 1957 [1978] PGSC 9, [1978] PNGLR 404, 25 October 1978.

SCR No 2 of 1981; Re Electoral Boundaries [1981] PGSC 22, [1981] PNGLR 518, 10 December 1981.

SCR No 2 of 1982 (No 1); Re the Organic Law on National Elections (Amendment) Act 1981 [1982] PGSC 19, [1982] PNGLR 214, 5 April 1982.

SCR No 2 of 1984; Re New Ireland Provincial Constitution [1984] PGSC 14, [1984] PNGLR 81, 27 April 1984.

SCR No 2 of 1987; Reference by Robert Henry Seeto Member for West Coast Namatanai in the New Ireland Provincial Assembly and Former Premier [1987] PGSC 16, [1987] PNGLR 31, 1 April 1987.

SCR No 2 of 1989; Re Village Courts Act (Ch 44) [1988] PGSC 30, [1988-89] PNGLR 491, 28 November 1989.

SCR No 2 of 1992; Re The Leadership Code [1992] PGSC 16, [1992] PNGLR 336, 31 July 1992.

SCR No 3 of 1976; Re Calling of a General Election [1976] PGSC 18, [1976] PNGLR 242, 21 June 1976.

SCR No 3 of 1986; Ref by Simbu Provincial Executive [1987] PGSC 17, [1987] PNGLR 151, 10 April 1987.

SC Reference No 3 of 1999; Re Calling of the Parliament [1999] PGSC 55, [1999] PNGLR 285, 25 June 1999.

SCR No 4 of 1990; Reference by the Acting Principal Legal Adviser [1994] PGSC 17, [1994] PNGLR 141, 11 January 1991.

SCR No 4 of 1980; Re Petition by MT Somare [1981] PNGLR 265.

SCR No 5 of 1982; Hugo Berghuser v Joseph Aoae [1982] PNGLR 379.

SCR No 5 of 1992; Re Organic Law on National Elections (Amendment No 1) Law 1991 [1992] PGSC 17, [1992] PNGLR 114, 5 June 1992.

Special Reference by Fly River Provincial Executive Council; Re Organic Law on Integrity of Political Parties and Candidates [2010] PGSC 3, SC1057, 7 July 2010.

Special Reference by Morobe Provincial Executive; re Election of Governor General (2010) SC 1085, 10 December 2010.

Special Reference by Simbu Provincial Executive [1988] PGSC 31, [1988-89] PNGLR 213, 30 November 1988.

Special Reference Pursuant to Constitution Section 10; Calling of the Parliament; Reference by the Ombudsman Commission [1999] PGSC 21, SC628, 25 June 1999.

Special Reference Pursuant to Constitution Section 19; Reference by Frances Damem, Attorney General [2002] PGSC 7, SC689, 26 July 2002.

Special Reference Pursuant to Constitution Section 19; Re Sitting Days of Parliament and Regulatory Powers of Parliament [2002] PGSC 2, SC722, 31 December 2002.

Special Reference Pursuant to Constitution Section 19; Section 365 of the Income Tax Act [1995] PGSC 3, SC482, 29 June 1995.

Special Reference Pursuant to Constitution Section 19; Special Reference by Morobe Provincial Government [2002] PGSC 9, SC693, 27 September 2002.

Special Reference Pursuant to Constitution Section 19; Special Reference by the Morobe Provincial Executive [2005] PGSC 32, SC785, 13 May 2005.

Supreme Court Reference by the Western Highlands Provincial Executive [1995] PGSC 6, SC486, 20 September 1995.

The State v Alan Woita (No 2) [1978] PNGLR 113.

The State v Independent Leadership Tribunal; Ex Parte Sasakila [1976] PNGLR 491, 5 November 1976.

The State v NTN Pty Ltd and NBN Ltd [1992] PGSC 11, [1992] PNGLR 1, 7 April 1987.

The State v Wonom [1975] PGSC 43; [1975] PNGLR 311, 6 October 1975.

Supreme Court Reference by the Western Highlands Provincial Executive [1995] PGSC 6, SC486, 20 September 1995.

Sukuramu v New Britain Palm Oil Ltd [2007] PGNC 21, N3124, 16 February 2007.

Yer, Secretary, Department of Finance v Yama [2009] PGSC 28, SC996, 30 October 2009.

b) Leadership Tribunal Decisions*

No	Case	Date
1.	*In the matter of Michael Pondros, Member of Parliament* [1983] PGLT 1, N425.	21 June 1983.
2.	*Chan, In the matter of* [1988] PGLT 1, [1988-89] PNGLR 260, 1 July 1988.	1 July 1988.
3.	*Uru, Re* [1988] PGLT 3, [1988-89] PNGLR 226.	20 July 1989.
4.	*Sigulogo, Re* [1988] PGLT 2, [1988-89] PNGLR 384.	2 October 1989.
5.	Edward Ramu Diro, Member of Parliament (MP) and Minister for Foreign Affairs and later Minister for Forestry.	27 September 1991.
6.	Melchior Pep, MP.	14 October 1992.
7.	Peter Garong, MP.	29 October 1992.

No	Case	Date
8.	Philip Laki, MP.	18 March 1994.
9.	Andrew Posai, MP and Minister for Home Affairs.	6 July 1995.
10.	Timothy Bonga, Chairman of Lae City Authority (allegations relate to matters arising during term as an MP).	30 April 1996.
11.	John Mua Nilkare, MP.	2 July 1996.
12.	Jeffrey Balakau, MP	13 December 1996.
13.	Gabriel Dusava, MP (Allegations relate to another leadership position held, not as MP).	10 October 1997.
14.	Jerry Singirok, Commander of PNG military.	21 March 2000.
15.	Jim Kas, MP.	27 September 2000.
16.	Anderson Agiru, MP.	18 January 2002.
17.	Mao Zeming, MP.	27 May 2003.
18.	*In the matter of Michael Nali, Member of Parliament (No 1)* [2003] PGLT 2, N2398.	29 April 2003.
19.	*In the matter of Andrew Kumbakor* [2003] PGLT 5, N2363.	8 May 2003.
20.	*In the matter of Michael Nali, Member of Parliament (No 2)* [2003] PGLT 3, N2388.	6 June 2003.
21.	*In the matter of Michael Nali, Member of Parliament (No 3)* [2003] PGLT 4, N2399.	10 July 2003.
22.	*In the matter of Bernard Hagoria, Member of Parliament* [2003] PGLT 1, N2525.	27 August 2003.
23.	Bernard Hargoria, MP.	3 September 2003.
24.	Mark Wani, Auditor General.	14 January 2004.
25.	Michael Nali, MP.	29 April 2004.
26.	*In the matter of Peter Yama, Member of Parliament* [2004] PGLT 2.	1 December 2004.

No	Case	Date
27.	*In the matter of Raho Hitolo, Member of the Ombudsman Commission* [2004] PGLT 1, N2745.	3 December 2004.
28.	*In the matter of Peter Ipatas, Member of Parliament* [2006] PGLT 1, N3078.	4 August 2006.
29.	*In the Matter of Puka Temu, Member of Parliament* [2006] PGLT 2, N3099.	24 August 2006.
30.	*In re Gallus Yumbui* [2006] PGLT 3, N3993.	31 October 2006.
31.	Gabriel Kapris, MP.	13 November 2006.
32.	Andrew Baing, MP.	20 December 2006.
33.	Charlie Benjamin	15 January 2007.
34.	*In re Gallus Yumbui* [2007] PGLT 2, N4052.	2 March 2007.
35.	*In the matter of Melchior Pep, Member for Dei Open Electorate Western Highlands Province* [2007] PGLT 1, N3134.	8 May 2007.
36.	*In the Matter of Hon Sir Moi Avei MP* [2007] PGLT 3, N4632 (LT).	4 April 2007.
37.	Moi Avei, MP.	19 April 2007.
38.	*In the Matter of Hon Sir Moi Avei* [2007] PGLT 4, N4633 (LT).	11 May 2007.
39.	Michael Somare, MP and Prime Minister.	24 March 2011.

* The tribunal decisions are not consistently reported. Decisions that are reported are indicated. The Ombudsman Commission keeps records of most Tribunal decisions.

2. *Australia*

Amalgamated Society of Engineers v Adelaide Co Ltd (1920) 28 CLR 129.

Australian Communist Party v Commonwealth [1951] HCA; (1951) 83 CLR 1.

Bowtell v Goldsbrough, Mort & Co Ltd (1906) 3 CLR 444.

Victorian Stevedoring and General Contracting Co Pty Ltd v Dignan (1931) 46 CLR 73 [*Dignan's Case*].

Wacando v Commonwealth [1981] HCA 60; (1981) 148 CLR 1.

Walton Stores (Interstate) Ltd v Maher (1988) 164 CLR 387.

3. Canada

Attorney General (Ont) v Attorney General (Can) [1912] AC 571 (PC).

Doucet-Boudreau v Nova Scotia (Department of Education) (2001) 203 DLR (4th) 128.

Edwards v Attorney General of Canada [1930] AC 124 (PC).

Re British Columbia Development Corporation v Friedmann (1984) 14 DLR (4th) 129 (SCC).

Re Provincial Judges Reference [1997] SCR 3.

Reference re a Resolution to amend the Constitution [1981] 1 SCR 753.

4. France

French Constitutional Council, decision no 71-44DC, 16 July 1971, JO 7114, 18 July 1971, Recueil 29.

5. India

Bandhua Mukti Morcha v India [1981] 2 SCR 516.

Bandhua Mukti Morcha v Union of India (1984) 3 SCC 161, [1984] AIR 802.

Kesavananda v State of Kerala (1973) 4 SCC 255, (1973) AIR 146.

Minerva Mills v Union of India [1980] AIR 1789 (SC).

State of Madras v Champakam Dorairajan [1951] AIR 226 (SC).

State of Madras v Row (1952) SCR 597, 1952 AIR 196.

6. New Zealand

Attorney-General v Whangarei City Council [1987] 2 NZLR 150 (CA), BCL [1587].

Awatere Huata v Prebble [2005] 1 NZLR 289 (SC).

Brooker v Police [2007] NZSC 30; [2007] 3 NZLR 91.

Flickinger v Crown Colony of Hong Kong [1991] 1 NZLR 439 (CA).

Hopkinson v Police [2004] 3 NZLR 704 (HC).

Lawson v Housing New Zealand [1997] 2 NZLR 474 (HC).

Moonen v Film and Literature Board of Review [1999] NZCA 329, [2000] 2 NZLR 9.

Moonen v Film and Literature Board Review [2002] 2 NZLR 754 (CA).

Simpson v Attorney-General [1994] 3 NZLR 667 (CA) [*Baigent's case*].

Taylor v Attorney-General [2015] NZHC 1706.

Te Waka Hi Ika O Te Arawa v Graham CA556/96, 27 November 1996.

7. *Solomon Islands*

Folotalu v Attorney-General [2001] SBHC 149, HC-CC 234 of 2001, 19 October 2001.

Guadalcanal Provincial Assembly v Speaker of National Parliament [1997] SBHC 5, HC-CC 309 of 1996, 26 February 1997.

Minister for Provincial Government v Guadalcanal Provincial Assembly [1997] SBCA 1, CA-CAC 003 of 1997, 11 July 1997.

8. *South Africa*

Government of the Republic of South Africa v Grootboom (CCT11/00) [2000] ZACC 19, [2001] 1 SA 46 (CC), [2000] 11 BCLR 1169, 4 October 2000.

Minister of Health and Others v Treatment Action Campaign and Others (No 2) (CCT8/02) [2002] ZACC 15, [2002] 5 SA 721 (CC), [2002] 10 BCLR 103, 5 July 2002.

Soobramoney v Minister of Health (Kwazulu-Natal) (CCT32/97) [1997] ZACC 17, [1998] 1 SA (CC) 765 (CC), 1997 (12) BCLR 1696, 27 November 1997.

9. *United Kingdom*

Attorney-General for Ontario v Attorney-General for Canada [1912] AC 571 (PC).

Attorney-General v Prince Ernest Augustus of Hanover [1957] AC 436 (HL).

Attorney-General v Wilts United Dairies Ltd (1921) 37 TLR 884 (HL).

Associated Provincial Picture Houses Ltd v Wednesbury Corporation [1948] 1 KB 223 (CA).

Central London Property Trust Ltd v High Trees House Ltd [1947] KB 130 (HC).

Davis v Johnson [1978] UKHL 1, [1979] AC 264.

Edwards v Attorney-General Canada [1930] AC 124 (PC).

Eton College v Minister of Agriculture, Fisheries and Food [1964] 1 Ch 274.

Grey v Pearson (1857) 6 HL Cas 61.

In re M [1993] UKHL 5, [1994] 1 AC 377.

Minister of Home Affairs v Fisher [1980] AC 319 (PC).

The Norwhale [1975] QB 589, [1975] 2 All ER 501.

Pepper (Inspector of Taxes) v Hart [1992] UKHL 3, [1993] AC 593.

Powell v Kempton Park Racecourse Co Ltd [1897] 2 QB 242.

R (Animal Defenders International) v Secretary of State for Culture, Media and Sport [2008] UKHL 15, [2008] 1 AC 1312.

R v Commissioner of Police of the Metropolis, ex parte Blackburn (No 1) [1968] 2 QB 118 (CA), [1968] 1 All ER 763.

R v Greater London Council, ex parte Blackburn [1976] 3 All ER 184 (CA).

R v Minister of Agriculture ex parte Padfield [1968] AC 997 (HL).

R v Pierce (1814) 3 M & S 62, [1814] 105 ER 534.

R v Metropolitan Police Commissioner, ex parte Blackburn (No 3) [1973] QB 241 (CA).

R v Secretary of State for Foreign and Commonwealth Affairs, ex parte World Development Movement Ltd [1994] EWHC 1 (Admin), [1995] 1 All ER 611.

R v Secretary of State for the Home Department, Ex parte Anderson [1984] 1 QB 778.

R v Secretary of State for the Home Dept, ex p Simms [2000] 2 AC 115 (HL).

10. United States of America

Alabama State Federation of Labor v McAdory 325 US 450 (1945).

Brown v Board of Education of Topeka 347 US 483 (1954).

Swann v Charlotte-Mecklenburg Board of Education [1971] USSC 121, 402 US 1 (1971).

Marbury v Madison 5 US 137 (1803), 1 Cr 137.

Muskrat v United States 219 US 346 (1911).

Plessy v Ferguson 163 US 537 (1896).

B. Legislation

1. Papua New Guinea

(a) Constitution

(b) Organic Laws

Organic Law on Certain Constitutional Office-holders.

Organic Law on Immediate and Transitional Constitutional Provisions.

Organic Law on National and Local-level Government Elections.

Organic Law on Peace-Building in Bougainville-Autonomous Bougainville Government and Bougainville Referendum 2002.

Organic Law on Provincial Boundaries.

Organic Law on Provincial Governments and Local-level Governments.

Organic Law on Residence.

Organic Law on the Advisory Committee on the Power of Mercy.

Organic Law on the boundaries of the National Capital District.

Organic Law on the calling of Meetings of the Parliament.

Organic Law on the Duties and Responsibilities of Leadership.

Organic Law on the Guarantee of the Rights and Independence of Constitutional Office-holders.

Organic Law on the Integrity of Political Parties and Candidates.

Organic Law on the Integrity of Political Parties and Candidates 2003.

Organic Law on the Internment Tribunal.

Organic Law on the Judicial and Legal Services Commission.

Organic Law on the Nomination of the Governor-General.

Organic Law on the Number of Ministers.

Organic Law on the Ombudsman Commission.

Organic Law on the Relief of Members of Disciplined Forces from the Responsibility for the Consequences of Carrying out a Lawful Order.

Organic Law on the Terms and Conditions of Employment of Judges.

Organic Law on the Terms and Conditions of Employment of the Governor-General.

(c) Ordinary Legislation

Business Groups Incorporation Act c144.

Classification of Publication (Censorship) Act 1989.

Community Services Trust Act 2002.

Compensation (Prohibition of Foreign Legal Proceedings) Act 1995.

Compulsory Third Party Motor Vehicle Insurance Industry Act 2002.

Conservation Areas Act 1978.

Constitution of the Autonomous Region of Bougainville 2004.

Constitution of the Independent State of Papua New Guinea.

Constitutional Development Commission Act 1997.

Constitutional Documents (Manner of Proof) Act 1976.

Constitutional and Law Reform Commission Act 2004.

Customs Recognition Act 1963.

Discriminatory Practices Act 1963.

District Court see District Court Act 1963.

Education Act 1983.

Electricity Commission Privatisation Act 2002.

Employment of Non-citizens Act 2007.

Environment Act 2000.

Environmental Contaminants Act 1978.

Environmental Planning Act 1978.

Essential Services Act 2002.

Fairness of Transaction Act 1993.

Fisheries Management Act 1998.

Forestry Act 1991.

Gaming Control Act 2007.

Harbours Board Act 1963.

Higher Education Act 1983.

HIV/AIDS Management and Prevention Act 2003.

Independent Consumer and Competition Commission Act 2002.

Informal Sector Development and Control Act 2004.

Investment Promotion Act 1992.

Interpretation Act c2.

Land Act 1996.

Land Dispute Settlement Act 1975.

Marriage Act 1963.

Mineral Resource Act 2005.

Mining Act 1992.

Mining (Ok Tedi Mine Continuation (Ninth Supplement) Agreement Act 2001.

Mining (Ok Tedi Restated Eighth Supplement) Agreement Act 2001.

Mining (Safety) Regulation Act 1977.

Motor Vehicles Insurance (PNG) Trust (Administrative Arrangements) Act 1996.

Motu Koita Assembly Act 2007.

Mutual Assistance in Criminal Matters Act 2005.

National Agricultural Research Institute Act 1996.

National Capital District Commission Act 2001.

National Development Bank Act 2007.

National Economic and Fiscal Commission Act 2007.

National Housing Corporation Act 1990.

National Museum and Art Gallery Act 1992.

National Parks Act 1982.

Oil and Gas Act 1992.

Prime Minister and National Executive Council Act 2002.

Proceeds of Crime Act 2005.

Provincial Health Authorities Act 2007.

Regulatory Statutory Authorities (Appointment to Certain Offices) Act 2004.

Salaries and Remuneration Commission Act 1983.

Telecommunications Act 1988.

Telecommunications Industry Act 2002.

Summary Offences Act 1977.

Underlying Law Act 2000.

Village Courts Act 1989.

Water Resources Act 1982.

(d) Court Rules

National Court Judicial Review (Amendment) Rules 2005.

National Court Rules 1983.

Rules of the National Court of Justice (Underlying Law Amendment) 2011.

Supreme Court Rules 1984.

2. *Australia*

Acts Interpretation Amendment Act 1984 (Australia, Cth).

Constitution of the Commonwealth of Australia.

3. *Canada*

Constitution Act 1867.

Constitution Act 1982.

Ombudsman Act 1975 (Ontario).

4. *Colombia*

Constitution of Columbia.

5. *India*

Constitution of India

6. *Ireland*

Constitution of Ireland.

7. *New Zealand*

Ombudsman Act 1975.

New Zealand Bill of Rights Act 1990.

Treaty of Waitangi.

8. *Samoa*

Constitution of Samoa.

9. *Slovenia*

Constitution of Slovenia

10. *Solomon Islands*

Constitution of Solomon Islands.

11. *South Africa*

Constitution of the Republic of South Africa.

12. *Uganda*

Constitution of Uganda.

13. *United Kingdom*

Constitutional Reform Act 2005.

Government of Wales Act 2006.

Human Rights Act 1998.

Northern Ireland Act 1998.

Parliamentary Commissioner Act 1967.

Scotland Act 1998.

14. *Vanuatu*

Constitution of Vanuatu.

15. *United States of America*

Constitution of the United States of America.

Massachusetts Constitution of 1780.

C. Treaties

Declaration on the Rights of Indigenous Peoples (Adopted on 13 September 2007 by the United Nations General Assembly).

International Covenant on Civil and Political Rights 999 UNTS 171 (opened for signature on 16 December 1966, entered into force 23 March 1976).

International Covenant on Economic, Social and Cultural Rights 993 UNTS 3 (opened for signature on 19 December 1966, entered into force 3 January 1976).

Universal Declaration on Human Rights (Adopted and proclaimed on 10 December 1948 by the United Nations General Assembly).

D. Books and Chapters in Books

HA Amankwah "Chapter 11: Human Rights in the Superior Courts" in Rudy James and Ian Fraser (eds) *Legal Issues in a Developing Society* (Faculty of Law, University of Papua New Guinea, Port Moresby, 1992).

Chester James Antieau Adjudicating Constitutional Issues (Oceana Publications Inc, London, 1985).

Dennis Austin (ed) Liberal Democracy in Non-Western States (Professors World Peace Academy, St Paul, 1995).

Graham Austin *The Indian Constitution: Cornerstone of a Nation* (Oxford University Press, Oxford, 1999).

JA Ballard (ed) *Policy-Making in a New State: Papua New Guinea 1972–1977* (University of Queensland Press, Brisbane,1981).

Ahron Barak *Purposive Interpretation in Law* (transl S Bashi, Princeton University Press, 2005), relevant excerpts reprinted in Tony Blackshield and George William Australian Constitutional Law and Theory (5th ed, The Federation Press, Sydney, 2010).

Mark Bevir (ed) "Ombudsman" *Encyclopedia of Governance* (vol 2, Sage Publications, Thousand Oaks, CA, 2007).

Tony Blackshield and George William Australian *Constitutional Law and Theory* (5th ed, The Federation Press, Sydney, 2010).

Gary D Bouma, Rod Ling and Douglas Pratt *Religious Diversity in Southeast Asia and the Pacific, National Case Studies* (Springer Dordrecht Heidelberg, London and New York, 2010).

Durga Dus Basu *Comparative Constitutional Law* (Prentice Hall of India, New Delhi, 1984).

FAR Bennion *Statutory Interpretation: A Code* (2nd ed, Butterworths, London, 1992)

Peter Biskup, B Jinks and H Nelson *A Short History* of New Guinea (Angus and Robertson, Melbourne, 1968).

Brian Brunton and Duncan Colquhoun-Kerr *The Annotated Constitution of Papua New Guinea* (University of Papua New Guinea Press, Port Moresby, 1984).

Takele Soboka Bulto "The Indirect Approach to Promote Justiciability of Socio-Economic Rights of the African Charter on Human and Peoples' Rights" in RH Murray (ed) *Human Rights Litigation and the Domestication of International Human Rights Standards in Sub-Saharan Africa* (jointly published by The Kenyan Section of the International Commission of Jurists, Nairobi and The Swedish Section of the International Commission of Jurists, Stockholm, 2009).

David Cannings "The Ombudsman Commission: Jurisdiction, Functions and Performance" in Anthony Regan, Owen Jessep and Eric Kwa (eds) *Twenty Years of the Papua New Guinea Constitution* (Law Book Co, Pyrmont, 2001).

Rachel Cleland *Papua New Guinea, Pathways to Independence: Official and Family Life 1951–1975* (Artlook Books, Perth, 1983).

Joel Colon-Rios *Weak constitutionalism: democratic legitimacy and the question of constituent power* (Routledge, New York, 2012).

DJ Colquhoun-Kerr "Sources of Political Legitimacy in Conflict and Naturalised Foreigners: Some Comments on the General Constitutional Commission's Final Report, 1983" in De Vere, Colquhoun-Kerr and Kaburise (eds) *Essays on the Constitution of Papua New Guinea* (Government Printer, Port Moresby, 1985).

Owen Cox *Papua New Guinea's Law and Legal System* (Pacific Adventist University, Boroko, 2004).

APW Deklin "The Legal Control of the Executive in Papua New Guinea" in *Pacific Constitutions: Proceedings of the Canberra Law Workshop VI* Peter Sack (ed) (Law Department Research School of Social Science, ANU, 1982).

Tony Deklin "In Search of a Home-Grown Constitution: The Constitutional Development in Papua New Guinea Between 1962 and 1975" in Sione Latukefu (ed) *Papua New Guinea: A Century of Colonial Impact 1884–1984* (The National Research Institute and the University of Papua New Guinea in association with the PNG Centennial Committee, Port Moresby, 1989).

Sean Dorney *Papua New Guinea: People, Politics and History Since 1975* (rev ed, ABC Books, Sydney, 2000).

AV Dicey *An Introduction to the Study of the Law of the Constitution* (1885).

Ronald Dworkin *Taking Rights Seriously* (Harvard University Press, Cambridge, 1977).

Ronald Dworkin *Law's Empire* (Harvard University Press, Cambridge, 1986).

Cecile Fabre *Social Rights Under the Constitution* (Oxford University Press, Oxford, 2000).

Peter Fitzpatrick "Popular Participation and the Constitution" in Ross de Vere, Duncan Colquhoun-Kerr and John Kaburise (eds) *Essays on the Constitution of Papua New Guinea* (Tenth Independence Anniversary Advisory Committee, Port Moresby, 1985).

John Goldring *The Constitution of Papua New Guinea* (The Law Book Company, Sydney, 1978).

Jeffrey Goldsworthy (ed) *Interpreting Constitutions, A Comparative Study* (Oxford University Press, Oxford, 2007).

Peter Hanks *Australian Constitutional Law, Materials and Commentary* (Butterworths, Sydney, 1990).

Andrew Heywood *Politics* (Macmillan Press Ltd, London, 1997).

HLA Hart *The Concept of Law* (Clarendon Press, Oxford, 1994).

Graham Hassall and Cheryl Saunders *Asia-Pacific Constitutional Systems* (Cambridge University Press, Cambridge, 2002).

Duncan Ivison, Paul Patton and Will Sanders (eds) *Political Theory and the Rights of Indigenous People* (Cambridge University Press, Cambridge, 2000).

Gary J Jacobsohn *The Supreme Court and the Decline of Constitutional Aspiration* (Rowman & Littlefield Publishers, Totowa, 1986).

Ernest A Jelf "Justiciable Disputes" *Transactions of the Grotius Society Vol 7, Problems of Peace and War, Papers Read before the Society in the Year 1921* (1921) 59–71 (published by Cambridge University Press on behalf of the British Institute of International and Comparative Law) <http.labs.jstor.org>.

Owen Jessep and John Luluaki *Principles of Family Law in Papua New Guinea* (2nd ed, UPNG Press, Port Moresby, 1994).

Philip A Joseph *Constitutional & Administrative Law in New Zealand* (3rd ed, Thomson Brookers, Wellington, 2007).

Peter King, Wendy Lee and Vincent Warakai *From Rhetoric to Reality, Papua New Guinea's Eight Point Plan and National Goals After a Decade* (University of Papua New Guinea Press, Port Moresby, 1985).

Juliane Kokott and Martin Kaspar "Ensuring Constitutional Efficacy" in Michel Rosenfeld and Andras Sajo (eds) *The Oxford Handbook of Comparative Constitutional Law* (Oxford, Oxford University Press, 2012) 792.

Eric Kwa *Constitutional Law of Papua New Guinea* (Law Book Co, Sydney, 2001).

Malcolm Langford (ed) *Social Rights Jurisprudence, Emerging Trends in International and Comparative Law* (Cambridge University Press, Cambridge, 2009).

Ian Maddocks and Edward P Wolfers *Living History and Evolving Democracy* Living (University of Papua New Guinea Press, Port Moresby, 2010).

Alexei M Marcoux "Social Contract" in David S Clark (ed) *Encyclopaedia of Law and Society: American and Global Perspectives* (Thousand Oaks, Sage Publications, 2007) vol 3.

Geoffrey Marshal *Constitutional Theory* (Clarendon Press, Oxford, 1971).

Ron May (ed) *Micronationalist Movements in Papua New Guinea* (Department of Political and Social Change, Research School of Pacific Studies, The Australian National University, Canberra, 1982).

Ron May *From Promise to Crisis: A Political Economy of Papua New Guinea – State and Society in Papua New Guinea* (ANU Press, Canberra, 2004).

Baron de Montesquieu *The Spirit of the Laws* (transl Thomas Nugent, Hafner Press, 1949) at 150; cited in Blackshield and Williams *Australian Constitutional Law and Theory* (5th ed, The Federation Press, Sydney, 2010).

Bernard Narokobi *The Melanesian Way, Total Cosmic Vision of Life* (Institute of Papua New Guinea Studies, Port Moresby, 1980).

Bernard Narokobi *Life and Leadership in Melanesia* (Institute of Pacific Studies, University of the South Pacific, Suva and University of Papua New Guinea, Port Moresby, 1983).

Bernard Narokobi *Law and Custom in Melanesia* (Institute of Pacific Studies of the University of South Pacific and Melanesian Institute for Pastoral and Socio-Economic Service, Goroka, 1996).

Bernard Narokobi "The Constitutional Planning Committee, nationalism and vision" in Anthony Regan, Owen Jessep and Eric Kwa (eds) *Twenty Years of the Papua New Guinea Constitution* (Lawbook Co, Sydney, 2001).

Bernard Narokobi *Foundations for Nationhood* (UPNG Press, Port Moresby, 2010).

Bernard Narokobi "Walking the Footpath of the Constitutional Planning Committee's Five National Goals and Directive Principles" in Ian Maddocks and Edward P Wolfers *Living History and Evolving Democracy Living* (University of Papua New Guinea Press, Port Moresby, 2010).

Michael A Ntumy "Separation of Powers" in Anthony J Regan, Owen Jessep and Eric L Kwa (eds) *Twenty Years of the Papua New Guinea Constitution* (Lawbook Co, Sydney, 2001).

Michael A Ntumy *Administrative Law of Papua New Guinea, Cases Texts and Materials* (2nd ed, CBS Publishers, New Delhi, 2003).

Dennis C Pearce and Robert S Geddes *Statutory Interpretation in Australia* (6th ed, LexisNexis Butterworths, Chatswood, 2006).

DC Pearce and RS Geddes *Statutory Interpretation in Australia* (7th ed, LexisNexis Butterworths Australia, Chatswood, 2011).

Owen Hood Philips and Paul Jackson *Constitutional and Administrative Law* (7th ed, Sweet and Maxwell, London, 1987).

John Quick and Robert Garran *The Annotated Constitution of the Australian Commonwealth* (Legal Books, Sydney, 1976).

John Rawls *A Theory of Justice* (Harvard University Press, Massachusetts, 1971).

Anthony J Regan, Owen Jessep and Eric L Kwa (eds) *Twenty Years of the Papua New Guinea Constitution* (Lawbook Co, Sydney, 2001).

Anthony Regan "Constitutionalism, Legitimacy and the Judiciary" in RW James and I Fraser (eds) *Legal Issues in a Developing Society* (Faculty of Law, University of Papua New Guinea, Port Moresby, 1992).

Michael Rosenfeld *The Identity of the Constitutional Subject* (Routledge, London, 2010).

Jean-Jacques Rousseau *The Social Contract* (1712-1778).

Peter Sack (ed) *Pacific Constitutions* (Australian National University, Canberra, 1982).

Massimo La Torre *Constitutionalism and Legal Reasoning – A New Paradigm for the Concept of Law* (Springer, Dordrecht, 2007).

Meg Taylor "The Constitution and the Environment" in Anthony J Regan, Owen Jessep and Eric L Kwa (eds) *Twenty Years of the Papua New Guinea Constitution* (Lawbook Co, Sydney, 2001).

Michael J Trebilock and Ronald J Daniels *Rule of Law Reform and Development, Charting the Fragile Path of Progress* (Edward Elgar, Northhampton, 2008).

David Robertson *The Judge as Political Theorist* (Princeton University Press, Princeton, 2010).

Kenneth Wheare *The Constitutional Structure of the Commonwealth* (Clarendon Press, Oxford, 1960).

Leslie Zines *The High Court and the Constitution* (5th ed, The Federation Press, Annandale, 2008).

E. Journal Articles

Carolyn Archer and Gaze Bert "Section 7 of the Bill of Rights Act" (2004) NZLJ 320.

Jack M Balkin "Framework Originalism and the Living Constitution" (2009) 103 Northwest U L Rev 549.

Jeffrey Barnes "Statutory Interpretation, Law Reform and Sampford's Theory of the Disorder of Law" (Pt 2) (1995) 22 FL Rev 77.

Peter Bayne "Judicial Method and the Interpretation of Papua New Guinea's Constitution" (1980) 11 FL Rev 121.

Andrew Blick "The Cabinet Manual and the Codification of Conventions" (2014) 67 Parl Aff 191.

Takele Soboka Bulto "The Utility of Cross-Cutting Rights in Enhancing Justiciability of Socio-Economic Rights in the African Charter on Human and Peoples' Rights" (2010) 29(2) U Tas LR 142.

Andrew Butler "Judicial Indications of Inconsistency – A New Weapon in the Bill of Rights Armoury?" (2000) NZ L Rev43.

Petra Butler "15 Years of the NZ Bill of Rights: Time to Celebrate, Time to Reflect, Time to Work Harder?" [2006] HRR 1.

Gerard Carney "Separation of Powers in the Westminster System" (1994) 8(2) Legis Stud 59.

Donald Chalmers "Human Rights and What is Reasonably Justifiable in a Democratic Society" (1975) 3 Melanesian LJ 92.

Laurence Claus "Montesquieu's Mistakes and the True Meaning of Separation" (2005) 25(3) OJLS 419.

Jennifer Corrin Care "Negotiating the Constitutional Conundrum: Balancing Cultural Identity with Principles of Gender Equality in Post-Colonial Pacific State" (2006) 5 Indigenous LJ 51.

Jennifer Corrin Care and Jean G Zorn "Legislating Pluralism, Statutory Developments in Melanesian Customary Law" (2001) 33 J Legal Pluralism 49.

Benedict Coxon "Human Rights at Common Law: Two Interpretive Principles" (2014) 35(1) Statute Law Review 35.

Michael J Dennis and David Stewart "Justiciability of Economic, Social and Cultural rights: Should there be an international complaints mechanism to adjudicate the rights to food, water, housing and health?" (2004) 98(3) AJIL 462.

Bertus De Villiers "Directive Principles of State Policy and Fundamental Rights: The Indian Experience" (1992) 8 S Afr J Hum Rts 29.

Grant Duncan "New Zealand's Cabinet Manual: How Does It Shape Constitutional Conventions?" (2014) Parl Aff 1.

Richard H Fallon Jr "Judicially Manageable Standards and Constitutional Meaning" (2006) 119 Harv L Rev 1274.

Stephen Gardbaum "The New Commonwealth Model of Constitutionalism" (2001) 49 Am Comp L 707.

Claudia Geiringer and Matthew SR Palmer "Human Rights and Social Policy in New Zealand" (2007) Soc Pol J NZ 12.

JK Gawi, YP Ghai and A Paliwala "National Goals and Law Reforms: A Report on the Goroka Seminar" (1976) 4 Melanesian LJ 259.

Yash Ghai "Establishing a Liberal Political Order through a Constitution: The Papua New Guinea Experience" (1997) 28 Dev & Change 303.

John Goldring "Responsibility of the Executive Government – To Whom and for What" (1981) 9 Melanesian LJ 116.

BV Harris, "Judicial Review, Justiciability and the Prerogative of Mercy" (2003) 62 The Cambridge Law Journal 631.

Graham Hassall "The Parliamentary Committee System in Papua New Guinea, 1975–1997" (2011) 17 CLJP-RJP 29.

Milton Handler, Brian Leiter and Carole E Handler "A Reconsideration of the Relevance and Materiality of the Preamble in Constitutional Interpretation" (1990–1991) 12 Cardozo L Rev 117.

Fraser Harland "Constitutional Convention and Cabinet Manuals" (2011) 34(2) Canadian Parl Rev 25.

Bruce Hicks "Advice to the Ministers of democratic reform: Senate reform, constitutional amendments, fixed election dates, and a Cabinet Manual" Constit Forum (Fall, 2012) 23.

Janet L Hiebert "Rights-Vetting in New Zealand and Canada: Similar Idea, Different Outcomes" (2005) 3 NZJPL 63.

Larry B Hill "Institutionalization, the Ombudsman, and Bureaucracy" (1974) 68(3) Am Pol Sci Rev 1075.

Roderick M Hills Jr "The Pragmatist View of Constitutional Implementation and Constitutional Meaning" (2006) 119 Harv L Rev 173.

Peter W Hogg and Allison A Bushel "The Charter Dialogue between Courts and Legislature (Or Perhaps The Charter Of Rights Isn't Such A Bad Thing After All)" (1997) 35 Osgoode Hall LJ 75.

James L Huffman and Mardilyn Saathoff "Advisory Opinions and Canadian Constitutional Development: The Supreme Court's Reference Jurisdiction" (1989-1990) 74 Minn L Rev 1251.

Salamo Injia "Presentation by the Chief Justice to the Underlying Law Conference, Alotau, December 2010 (2012) 8 The Underlying Law Journal Developments in the Underlying Law of Papua New Guinea 3.

Catherine J Iorns Magallanes "The 'Just Do It' Approach to Using Parliamentary Materials in Statutory Interpretation" (2009) 15 Canta LR 205.

Owen Jessep "The Underlying Law of Papua New Guinea" (2012) 4 The Underlying Law Journal Developments in the Underlying Law of Papua New Guinea 25.

Solomon Kantha "Papua New Guinea" (2011) The Contemporary Pacific 23.

David Landau "The Reality of Social Rights Enforcement" (2012) 53(1) Harv Int'l LJ 190.

Sanford Levinson "Do Constitutions Have a point? 'Reflections on Parchment Barriers' and Preambles" 28(1) Soc Phil & Pol'y 150.

Nicholas A MacDonald and James W Bowden "The Manual of Official Procedure of the Government of Canada: An Exposé" (2011) 20(1) Constit Forum 33.

Patrick Macklem and Craig Scott "Constitutional Ropes of Sand or Justiciable Guarantees? Social Rights in a New South African Constitution" (1992) 141 U Pa L Rev 1.

Anthony Mason "The Role of a Constitutional Court in a Federation: A Comparison of the Australian and the United States Experience" (1986) 16 FL Rev 1.

Janet McLean "Legislative Invalidation, Human Rights Protection and s 4 of the New Zealand Bill of Rights Act" (2001) 4 NZ L Rev 421.

Janet McLean "The New Zealand Bill of Rights Act 1990 and the Constitutional Propriety" (2013) 11 NZJPIL 19.

Elizabeth McLeay "What is the Constitutional Status of the New Zealand Cabinet Office Manual?" (1999) PLR 10.

Frank J Michelman "The Constitution, Social rights and Liberal Political Justification" (2003)1(1) ICON 13.

Lanse Minkler "Economic Rights and Political Decision Making" (2009) 31(2) Hum Rts Q 368.

Vergil Narokobi "The Papua New Guinea 'Two Prime Minister's Saga': Parliament Testing the Supremacy of the Constitution" (2013) 24(2) PLR 92.

Vergil Narokobi "The Justiciability of the National Goals and Directive Principles and Basic Social Obligations in the Context of the Underlying Law Act 2000" (2015) The Underlying Law Journal Developments in the Underlying Law of Papua New Guinea (forthcoming).

Cathy Nijman "Ascertaining the Meaning of Legislation – A Question of Context" (2011) 38(3) VUWLR 629.

Liav Orgad "The Preamble in Constitutional Interpretation" (2010) 8 Int'l J Const L 714.

John Philips and Louis Proksch "*Walton Stores (Interstate) Ltd v Maher*: Implications for the Law of Contract" (1989) 19(1) UWA L Rev 171.

AJ Regan and EP Wolfers "Aids to Interpretation of the Constitution – Some Preliminary Thoughts" (1986) 14 Melanesian LJ 153.

Kent Roach "The Uses and Audiences of Preamble in Legislation" (2001) 47(1) McGill LJ 129.

Lori Sterling and Sean Hanley "Judicial Independence Revisited" (2006) SCLR (2d) 34.

Freda Talao "Country Reports: Papua New Guinea: Country Report on Human Rights" (2009) 40 VUWLR 1.

Craig Scott "The Interdependence and Permeability of Human Rights Norms: Towards a Partial Fusion of the International Covenants on Human Rights" (1989) 27 Osgoode Hall LJ 769.

Dawinder S Sidhu "Judicial Review as Soft Power: How the Courts Can Help Us Win the Post-9/11 Conflict" (2011) 1(1) Am U Nat'l Sec L Brief 69.

Jonathan A Siegel "A Theory of Justiciability" 86 Tex L Rev 73.

D Srivastava and D Roebuck, "The Reception of the Common Law and Equity in Papua New Guinea: The Problem of the Cut-Off Date" (1985) 34 ICLQ 850.

Mathew Stubbs "A Brief History of the Judicial Review of Legislation under the Australian Constitution" (2012) 40 FL Rev 227.

Mark Tushnet "Forward: The New Constitutional Order and the Chastening of Constitutional Aspiration" (1999–2000) 113 Harv L Rev 29.

Mark Tushnet "New Forms of Judicial Review and the Persistence of Rights – and Democracy-Based Worries" (2003) 38 Wake Forest L Rev 813.

Anne Twomey "The Preamble and Indigenous Recognition" (2011) 15(2) A Ind LR 4.

Jeffrey Usman "Non-justiciable Directive Principles: A Constitutional Design Defect" (2007) 15 Mich St J Int'l L 643.

Anne Winckel "The Contextual Role of a Preamble in Statutory Interpretation" (1999) 23(1) MULR 184.

Edward P Wolfers "Finding the Law in the Pacific Islands: Observations with Special Reference to Papua New Guinea and Solomon Islands" (1982) 10 Int'l J Legal Info 93.

F. Parliamentary and Government Materials

Australian Government Department of the Prime Minister and Cabinet *Cabinet Handbook* (7th ed, 2014).

Cabinet Office *Cabinet Manual 2008* (NZ).

Cabinet Office *The Cabinet Manual* (1st ed, October 2011) (UK).

Constitutional Planning Committee *Final Report of the Constitutional Planning Committee, Part One* (Government Printer, Port Moresby, 1974).

Constitutional Planning Committee *Second Interim Report of the Constitutional Planning Committee* (Port Moresby, 1973).

Department of the Prime Minister and Cabinet "Constitutional Convention: Transcript of Proceedings" (1998) <www.aph.gov.au>.

Government Paper "Proposals on Constitutional Principles and Explanatory Notes" (Port Moresby, August 1974).

House of Assembly Debates from 23 September 1974 to 27 September 1974.

House of Commons *Political and Constitutional Reform Committee Constitutional Implications of the Cabinet Manual, Sixth Report of Session 2010-11, Volume 1* (29 March 2011).

National Constituent Assembly Debates, Volume 1, No 1 from 23 May 1975 to 26 August 1975.

National Parliament of Papua New Guinea Manual of Practice and Procedure (1st ed, prepared by the Clerk of Parliament, Port Moresby, 2009).

National Development Strategy (summary ed, Government Printer, Port Moresby, 1976).

National Strategic Plan Taskforce *Papua New Guinea Vision 2050* (Government Printer, Port Moresby, 2009).

Papua New Guinea Department of Treasury *Budget Manual* (10 September 2014).

G. Reports

Law Reform Commission of Papua New Guinea *Role of Customary Law in the Legal System* (Law Reform Commission, Waigani, 1977) vol 7.

Law Reform Commission of Papua New Guinea *Occasional Paper No 16: Constitutional Review Jurisdiction in Papua New Guinea* (September 1981).

New Zealand Law Commission *A New Interpretation Act to Avoid "Prolixity and Tautology"* (NZLC R17, 1990).

The Ombudsman Commission of Papua New Guinea *Investigation into the Purchase of The Conservatory, Cairns by the Public Officers Superannuation Fund Board and associated transactions and arrangements, Final Report November 1999* (Government Printer, Port Moresby, 1999).

The Ombudsman Commission of Papua New Guinea *National Forest Board Report Investigation into the Decision of the National Forest Board to Award Kamula Doso FMA to Wawoi Guavi Timber Company (A Subsidiary of Rimbunan Hijau) as an Extension to the Wawoi Guavi Timber Resource Permit Final Report July 2002* (Government Printer, Port Moresby 2002.

The Ombudsman Commission of Papua New Guinea *Investigation Report into the Alleged Unlawful and Abuse of Human Rights by Police, Three Mile Guest House, Port Moresby, National Capital District, Final Report 2009* (Government Printer, Port Moresby, 2009).

The Ombudsman Commission of Papua New Guinea *Investigation into the Appointment and Conduct of Hamish Sharp in the National Maritime Safety Authority Board, Final Report 2009* (Government Printer, Port Moresby 2002.

The Ombudsman Commission of Papua New Guinea *Investigation Report into the Julian Ronald Moti Affair, Final Report 2009* (Government Printer, Port Moresby, 2009).

Papua New Guinea Law Reform Commission *Report No 7 "The Role of Customary Law in the Legal System"* (Government Printer, Port Moresby, 1977).

President's Committee on Administrative Management *Administrative Management in the Government of the United States* (United States Government Printing Office, 1937).

UNESCO *Adult and Youth Literacy, 1990-2015, Analysis of data of 41 Countries* (Unesco Institute for Statistics, Montreal, 2012) <www.uis.unesco.org>.

Transparency International *Corruption Perception Index 2013* (2 September 2014) <www.transparency.org>.

H. Dissertations

Sam Sirox Kari "The Origin and setting of the National Goals and Directive Principles in the Setting and Writing of the Constitution" (PhD Thesis, Queensland University of Technology, 2005).

Jonathan Ritchie "Making Their Own Law: Popular Participation in the Development of Papua New Guinea's Constitution" (PhD Thesis, University of Melbourne, 2003).

I. Internet resources

Brookers Online Library.

HeinOnline <http://heinonline.org>.

Lexis Nexis NZ.

National Parliament of Papua New Guinea <www.parliament.gov.pg>.

Pacific Legal Information Institute <www.paclii.org>.

Prime Minister's Office of Papua New Guinea <www.officeofprimeminister.com>.

Social Science Research Network <www.ssrn.com>.

Stanford Encyclopaedia of Philosophy <http://plato.stanford.edu>.

J. Other

Peter Bayne *Constitutional Review Jurisdiction in Papua New Guinea* (Law Reform Commission of Papua New Guinea, Waigani, 1981).

Francis Bennion "Hansard – Help or Hindrance? A Draftsman's View of *Pepper v Hart*" (paper delivered to the conference of the Commonwealth Association of Legislative Counsel, Cyprus, May 1993).

Rowan Callick "High-cost bid secures tender for drug distribution in PNG" *The Australian* (online ed, Surry Hills, NSW, 14 March 2014).

Ian Darling, "The Role of the Ombudsman in Canada and the USA" (presentation to 1 e Congresso Internacional de Ouvidores e Ombudsman. 13e Congresso Brasileriro de Ouvidores e Ombudsman 6e Seminario Nacional Ouvidores & Ouividorias Bello Horizonte, Brazil, 29 July 2010) <www.tarion.com>.

Bal Kama "Can PNG democracy survive without the Opposition?" (3 September 2014) Dev Policy Blog <http://devpolicy.org>.

Rebecca Kitteridge "The Cabinet Manual: Evolution with Time" (paper presented to the 8th Annual Public Law Forum, Wellington, 20–21 March 2006).

Tobias Kulang "We need complete review of Constitution" *The National* (online ed, PNG, 16 July 2013).

Judy McGregor "Balancing responsibilities with rights: freedom of expression and hate speech in New Zealand" (paper presented to Ministry of Justice Symposium on the Bill of Rights Act, Wellington, February 2006).

Martyn Namarong "The Regime, the Drug Company and the 'murder' of #PNG Citizens!" (14 January 2014) Namarong Blog Spot <http://namorong.blogspot.com.au>.

Vergil Narokobi "The Justiciability of the National Goals and Directive Principles and Basic Social Obligations in the Context of the Underlying Law Act 2000" (unpublished paper presented to Underlying Law Conference in Port Moresby, Papua New Guinea, 18 October 2013).